MANIPULATION, BODY LANGUAGE, DARK PSYCHOLOGY

HOW TO ANALYZE AND READ PEOPLE WITH THE BEST 7 TECHNIQUES. LEARN EVERYTHING YOU NEED TO KNOW ABOUT PERSUASION, NPL, BODY LANGUAGE, AND MIND CONTROL.

ADAM JOHNSON

Table Of Contents
The art of reading people

How to analyze people

Dark psychology secrets

Manipulation techniques

THE ART OF READING PEOPLE

ADAM JOHNSON

Manipulation

Introduction

The first step in trying to read people is to realize that people around you are a source of abundant knowledge. Written on their faces, in their clenched fists or squinted eye, is the story of their life, which they are as a person, and even explanations for their behavior. Of course, studying people is an inexact science, and the human mind is so complex that one cause can't be attributed to have resulted in a certain action or expression, which is why it's better to take the study of human behavior with a pinch of salt. Over the years, scientists and behavioral psychologists have found different standards to judge people on their behavior – they are accurate because these 'tells' that people have are true across a vast majority of the population, so we can accurately determine that human beings, in general, tend to have certain physical 'tells' that are caused by certain stimuli.

To 'read' people is to quickly look at their different features, expressions, adorations, and anything else that is connected to them, to determine accurately what kind of a person they are. People are only a representation of the environment they exist in, and everything that can be physically seen and judged is likely to be an explanation for someone's inner character. In a lot of ways, the focal point of 'reading' people is not to determine who they are entirely and write a thesis on it, but rather just at that moment to determine the signaling that person is doing. By signaling what we mean is that in different kinds of clothing, makeup, or expressions, we can determine what people are trying to communicate with other people around them subtly.

Of course, nobody would wear an expensive ring unless they wanted to virtue signal everyone about their beauty, riches, taste, and whatnot, so by reading these things, you can at least determine how people want to be perceived in different situations and settings. It might not tell you who they are entire as a person of course, but you will be able to see people for what they want to be seen as, and that reveals a lot of information about people; you can see all the needs people are trying to fulfill, all the insecurities they are trying to cover up, and all their desires and motivations.

Now, the most important aspect of understanding how to read people is to learn to read you. All knowledge and understanding that we have come from experience, so if you haven't experienced something, you might get it, but it will be hard for you to understand it. It's only when you can study yourself and how you function that you will be able to understand similar things in other people. So, the first step in trying to understand others and analyze them is to analyze you.

Knowledge of the self can never be complete; the whole purpose of the brain is to hide from you so that you can function without getting crippled by self-doubt, past trauma, or things about yourself you may not particularly like.

Talk About the Ethics Of Communication

The analysis of people is not a passive skill. It's not some kind of a special burst of attention that could be activated at will, after which it automatically tells you things about people around you, Sherlock Holmes way. The analysis of people implies normal observation, not supernatural zoom-in slow motion injections of private knowledge. The more attentive you are to people around you, the better you'll be able to analyze them, but this attention doesn't mean perfect vision and superhuman insight, this attention is more of what Bill Murray's character does by the end of The Groundhog Day – this attention means caring about people around you, noticing what they do, and what happens to them.

And this is a very important point we have to start from: mindfulness and kindness towards people. After you practice the techniques described in this book, you will learn to know more about those you will interact with. You'll know what makes these people happy, and you'll know what makes them sad. Basically, you will know how these individuals react to different stimuli, what makes them tick.

You may be inclined to use this knowledge, this special understanding of people, to manipulate somebody, to exploit someone's weak spots, to overpower their insufficient will with yours, or cause harm to them. After you read this book, you'll know that human conscience, the knowledge of rights and wrongs, is merely a social instinct telling you whether you'll be accepted and loved by your own kind for every consecutive word you speak and action you take. Like many instincts, this one could be dampened or even overridden with reason and rationalization. Many people do harm to others consciously with no morals to stop them, just because they know this will go unpunished, or is somehow sanctioned or allowed, or even generally approved of amongst their peers.

So in fact it's not your conscience that must stop you from using this book's methods for a wrong cause, but your honor, your knowledge of yourself as a decent, trustworthy, and caring person. Let's just finish by saying we're all adult people, and deep inside we all know right from wrong, merely by knowing how we wouldn't like to be treated ourselves; so the caution line is there, and it's visible at all times.

In this book, we will, as Sherlock Holmes would, put cold reason in the first place, and brush emotions aside. We will talk about the dangers of compassion as something undesired, distorting your worldview. We will praise logic a lot, and it may seem we talk about matters of the heart as if they are something lowly and primitive. This is not so.

Analysis of people is a research, it demands objectivity, it relies on logic and reason, so naturally, it is a task best done with a cool head on one's shoulders. Still, while applying the knowledge, always remember to consult with your heart first. May your deeds be as pleasant to those around you as they are pleasant to you.

We're all social beings after all, and cold analytical people are little fun. Just so those you interact with feel comfortable, never allow the methods we describe in this book overrule your normal human communication. Even more so, some of the techniques we describe will work better if your subject feels love from your side, or at least is unaware of your cold analytical activities, if they're going on in the background. Your correspondent being relaxed and feeling warmth from your side is always beneficial to you.

Communication comes in two different categories, verbal and non-verbal. Understanding both can help you understand people better, as a whole. We need to look at them separately and discuss the details to promote a solid base of knowledge around communication. Let's start with verbal communication.

Not only do good communication skills make it easier for you to understand other people it also makes it easier for them to understand you. While some people are very effective communicators others truly need to work on it. Taking a look in the mirror and participating in some communication activities can help you understand how well you are communicating with the people around you. You may be surprised to find that you have some work to do.

As it sounds, verbal communication is communication with words. This piece seems obvious; however, did you know that there are four different types of verbal communication? Most people don't look at it this closely, however, it can help us understand what people are really trying to say to us. Each type of verbal communication can give us insight into ourselves, as well as, others.

The first type is intrapersonal communication. This is the conversations we have with ourselves internally. While we figure out a difficult problem or are working out our grocery list, we all spend time in our own heads talking. Intrapersonal communication is very different between people. Some of us are very good at building ourselves up while others tear themselves apart with their thoughts.

It is not uncommon for criminals and those that fall into the Dark Triad to have terrible intrapersonal communication skills. They may literally feel as if they have a tiny devil inside their brain that always wins over the even smaller angel. Intrapersonal communication should not be confused with schizophrenia, that condition is quite different.

The next type of verbal communication is interpersonal communication. This is the conversation that you have with just one other person. Sometimes, people handle one on one conversations very well because it is more personal. In addition to being more personal, it also tends to leave you a bit more vulnerable. This is because the sole focus of the conversation is between the two of you. If someone is trying to manipulate you, it is likely they are going to try and get you off on your own. Working against someone one-on-one is always going to be easier than trying to persuade or manipulate a crowd. On your own, you need to keep your defenses up. People that are trying to manipulate you will spend the time to look at your verbal and nonverbal communication skills. This helps them to pinpoint what they need to do to get you to bend to their will.

Then there is small-group verbal communication. Obviously, there will be more than two people involved here, however, a small group for verbal communication is not exactly defined. It is a number of people that can all be actively involved in the conversation. Think of things like team meetings at work or press conferences. Everyone is taking their turn to give their opinions and thoughts.

Small group communication is where most people thrive. It's not nearly as intense as a one-on-one conversation and it is not as intimidating as speaking in front of a large crowd. You will still need to pay attention to your verbal and nonverbal skills when dealing with a small group to make sure that you are promoting clear and concise understanding of what it is that you are saying.

Manipulators that are very charismatic thrive in this type of conversation. They are good at getting the attention of the group. In turn, they are good at getting that group to see things from their point of view. It is more of a game to them than anything else. Gaining control is all they are looking for and some do it very successfully.

The last type of verbal communication is public communication. When dealing with public communication there is, typically, only one speaker. They will be addressing a larger crowd. Election speeches are a very good example of this. You need to remember that many people will conduct themselves differently in public than they do in private. Looking for drastic changes can clue you in to the darker tendencies of verbal communication.

Conquering the art of good communication is hard. There are a variety of factors that equal good communication and the words you pick are only part of it. Most people need to work on their communication skills but be aware that those that are scheming against you will focus on it.

The way a criminal communicates verbally can make or break their plans. Being careful with what they say they are able to more easily persuade and manipulate those that are around them. When you have improved communication skills it can make it easier to pick up on the trick's others are using around you.

So, what does it take to communicate effectively in a verbal manor? You need to be friendly and kind in the things that you say. In addition, thinking before you speak plays a major role. Those that prattle on without thinking tend to be looked down on and people tend to stop listening as they simply never stop talking. If you have this bad habit you will find that people look at their cell phones more while you are talking, talk with others around them, or simply go into a trance state until you stop talking.

Your word choice also is a component that needs to be considered. Thinking about the crowd that is in front of you or the person that you are speaking with individually can help you communicate with them effectively. Knowing what their common languages and the words they typically use can give you clues as to how you need to handle them. When you take these types of things into consideration people are more apt to open to you and tell you what is really going on. It gives you some common ground with them and makes you more relatable.

Effective verbal communication also takes confidence. When you are solid in the things you are saying it shows. Be well prepared with your thoughts and people will be able to understand you. Giving others time to speak their piece is also very important in verbal communication. When someone feels like you don't give them time to talk they start to tune you out. It's very rude when there is only one person talking and other people have things to say. Obviously, if you are giving a speech the people that are there are not going to be doing much talking. So, you will need to take your surroundings in the consideration to figure out how much you should actually be saying and how much you should be listening.

Sometimes, it is very hard to say exactly what you mean. Being concise in what you are saying is important. If there is a lot of fluff in your thoughts it can be confusing to the person listening. This could lead to questions that do not relate to what you are talking about at all. In addition, telling a story in a streamed line is important. If you jump from one point to another it causes a lot of confusion and a lack of

Interest. Here again, spending the time to think about what you want to say before you say it will be advantageous.

Verbal communication can be really difficult for some people. They may not be comfortable speaking in public or exactly the opposite and become increasingly awkward when put into a one on one situation. There are different strategies that can help you become better at verbal communication, regardless of what type makes you uncomfortable.

There are a variety of different activities that you can try to make yourself a better and more comfortable verbal communicator. With a few minutes a day you can find the tact and confidence to say what you really mean. This can be a major benefit in life and lead to less misunderstandings and drama.

You can get yourself a word of the day calendar, thesaurus, or use an app for a similar type of thing. By broadening your vocabulary, you will have the words you need regardless of the crowd you are in. Be mindful of things like common language. If you want people to listen, they need to be able to understand what you are saying. So, using the words that the people around you use will ensure they are on the same page as you.

Expressing our wants and needs can be difficult especially for kids and teenagers. This is partially due to all of the electronic devices we are stuck in nowadays. Sending a message makes it easy to feel confident and say what you mean but when that same thing needs to be said out loud it can be difficult.

Parents can help their children with communication by making time without electronics. In addition, encouraging talking without distraction and taking a genuine interest in what they are saying and feeling without overreacting can promote better verbal communication.

Also, making sure that you communicate your feelings, needs, wants, and Thoughts with your kids will encourage them to do the same with you. This goes to more people than just your children. Being open and honest with those that are around you will help them be open and honest with you.

Of course, you want to be careful and not put too much trust in people. Keeping some things to yourself is advantageous and ensuring that you aren't taken advantage of.

We all know that practice makes perfect. If you are trying to become more comfortable with public speaking, you need to practice. You can start by going through your speech out loud but by yourself. Then when you feel confident with what you have get a group of trusted friends and family members together. Present your speech to them. You can gain constructive criticism from those that care about you and it can truly help to calm the nerves. You can practice this way many times to build your level of confidence.

As you become more confident it will be easier to address larger crowds. Working on things like your pitch, tone, and pace can also make you a more confident speaker. When you truly believe the words, you are saying and can say them with conviction you will be more confident. Practicing will certainly help here. Confidence is not only seen in these aspects. It also goes with your nonverbal communication.

These are only a couple of the many verbal communication skill improving activities that are out there. If you truly want to learn to communicate better there are a ton of sources out there to help you. With a bit of work and dedication you will be much more prepared to vocalize your wants, needs, and ideas. This can give you some advantages throughout your life that a lack of communication skills could hinder. Including things like promotions at work or getting hired for certain jobs.

Heading to a job interview well-prepared and well-articulated is definitely going to help you land it. If you are lacking in communication skills, you can basically say goodbye to that wonderful job you're working for.

Explains Human Characters

O n the most basic levels of cognition, or, poetically speaking, deep inside – we are all wild animals, primates obeying certain primal urges and drives. Our basic behavior is instinctive – you know that feeling when you travel to work early in the morning "riding on autopilot" and only really wake up on arriving there? Or, how you become bored of Tetris because you start playing it without really thinking? This learned behavior all belongs to our primal core, our monkey carrying around our reason, the computer, which could be preoccupied with something totally different while the primate is riding a subway playing a primate-oriented mobile game.

Reason is defined very directly. Reason is the part of us that speaks. It's the part of us that either talks or converses within us. Reason defines where our attention and active imagination are currently directed, so while the primate is playing its mobile game, the computer may be actively analyzing someone of opposite sex sitting across.

Sometimes the monkey and the computer argue. Think of how a person trying to quit smoking feels. Their reason demands certain things, while their primal being may respond with an entire tantrum to get its point across, and who knows who will win in the end!

The trick is, the "you", the thinking part of you, associates itself with the talking part, the reason. And the reason is always happy to explain things away. Which is why, even if your choice and the actions that followed it were instinctive, done on autopilot, in response to some primal urge, your reason will still claim responsibility for them, and rationalize anything you chose and done in the past, then explain to you why such choices were made, based on logic. It will be done in retrospective, in hindsight, yet fed to you as something that truly and certainly happened before you acted, not after.

It's really important to differentiate between the things one does automatically, acting on a whim, without thinking slowly and attentively prior to it – and the things done consciously, after a true consideration, which would involve the revision of all possible outcomes, weighing them against each other, etc.

In his book Thinking, Fast and Slow, Daniel Kahneman discusses two modes of thinking – fast and slow thinking, as you might have guessed. This is exactly it. Our monkey thinks fast, it basically always knows what it wants and how do get it. It only turns to the computer it carries around when it doesn't know what to do, when it needs something difficult dealt with, things calculated, slowly and carefully – the way the computer does it.

So this is what you absolutely have to remember when approaching another person from the analytical standpoint: you're dealing with a dualistic being, the reason of which may work in two modes: either doing its job, or emulating it, letting the basic urges and drives pull its owner around, and then explaining to them why it was the most logical thing to do. Always try and observe in which mode the person of your interest is functioning at the moment: the reason mode, or the body mode? (Since primal urges are normally born of the body.)

This is where some religions find its concept of sin: their followers are basically required to always put their reason first, and suppress the cravings of their body. What happens if the computer tries to fight the monkey and subdue it? Results vary, but we can certainly tell such behavior is destructive.

Does a human being possess a freedom of will? This question is rather philosophical – is there multiple choice, or is the Universe linear, every state of it predetermined by the state that came before? We cannot know. What we can know reviewing every decision taken by us or someone else we analyze is, was reason involved in making it, or were feelings, "the heart" involved?

In practice, if a decision was taken more or less instantly, it will be an unconscious "lizard mind" decision, the choice our monkey made without consulting with the computer.

And if we look into our own daily choices, we'll see in 98% of the cases the monkey-made choice was indeed mundane, very typical, repetitive – perhaps inherent to this particular place and/or time. We know our monkey is trained to carry out this part of our daily routine, so we gladly entrust our actions to this "autopilot", and keep our reason preoccupied with something else.

But this also means our actions become more direct, simple, and predictable; our monkey is after all but an animal following a simple pattern of well-learned repetitive behaviors: brush teeth, wash face, use towel, go to kitchen, put kettle on. If there's suddenly an accident at this point, something's on fire or falls on the floor and smashes, then we're suddenly "back on earth" – the computer switches back from its screensaver showing distant lands, and quickly runs the analysis routine: what must be done? What to take care of first? At the same time, the monkey holding it may panic, and then the computer's attention will be switched to pacifying the panicking animal, taking control of it.

In any case, after the danger is gone, we suddenly feel more alive, more present in the moment. This happens because our body and mind both entered the mode of behavior we shall call an "alert" mode. This happens when our reason, our active attention, is concentrated on here and now, the beautiful moment of full self-awareness, full internal agreement, when as much of ourselves is under our control as possible. This is when we become lethal, war-ready, and totally unpredictable for an observer. What actually happens is, our reason, our common sense, takes the full hold, and the animal is happy to follow it into the fray.

Explains The Masks That People Wear

I t so happens we do wear masks, and many of us have to change their mask twice or even thrice a day – just to put bread on our table – and we don't even call ourselves actors!

Because it's basic survival.

And this is something quite important to remember: basic survival instincts predate everything in a person. They are the primary directives, the ultimate priority calls of the wild. There's a popular book by Eric Berne call Games People Play which talks a lot about role models, the patterns of behavior we love seeing in others – sometimes in a favorite cartoon character! – which we then copy and think of as inherent to our own unique, authentic selves.

One thing is definitely true: each personality is built upon this primal, absolutely wild, fight-or-flight creature buried inside each of us, the creature we become when we hit rock bottom, when we are reduced to our lowest, and our survival becomes the only thing we care about. Think werewolves.

Now imagine someone who, instead of a wolf, becomes a Chihuahua scared of its own shadow. And this someone, who remains quiet and careful while at the brink, may turn out to have a much higher survival potential. You never know how someone's survival mode persona looks until you find yourselves together between a rock and a hard place, hence a wise observation of old: homo homini lupus est, which is again, the werewolf theme, the Beware of Evil Mr. Hyde! theme, which is not how it has to be, mind the Chihuahua!

A good manager or military commander takes mental notes of their team members' behaviors during a crisis, pretty much like a captain would take their team through at least one storm prior to real adventures, because this "panic mode" personality is what you want to know about a person you entrust certain things with.

Post-apocalyptic and survivor movies and books often display people driven to the brink suddenly becoming paranoid, randomly aggressive, selfish, escapist, and so on – but mostly the theme remains the same: as if a thin veil of civilization was swept away by this catastrophe or another, and you behold a human being's terrible true face, and it's a snarling grimace of a cavemen, or an animal of even more basic kind. So this book of Eric Berne, the one we highly recommend, Games People Play – finds an interesting application when we are speaking of this borderline character, the animalistic side exposed, the Mr. or Ms. Hyde pole of the personality spectrum of a given human being.

If you ever read fables and think about the masks people wear, then you'll remember what the art of fable is all about: a fable is a human social situation played out on animals. And this is a very interesting observation, for indeed, this "survival mode" will often manifest as behavior resembling that of some animal: in a crisis situation, the person may jump at people and roar like a lion, or retract into a shell like a mollusk, etc.

Another strange yet beautiful application of the role model idea of Eric Berne: for human beings, especially speaking of cultural symbolism, it's very natural to mimic certain behavior of animals, or, say, cartoon characters they liked as little kids. We primates are great mimics, and, finding ourselves amidst the wild we will often unconsciously put on a mask of whatever crazy thing we think represents our true character best. This is the factor that could make horoscopes relevant – never ignore a person's Zodiac sign if the person in question believes in Zodiac signs!

When everything is quiet and boring though, when our inner animals are well-fed and fluffy – this is when they turn back human. And the faces of humanity are . . . yet again, according to Eric Berne, Erich Fromm, Irwin Yalom – the faces of humanity are shaped and molded by cultures through fairytales and visions of our childhood. Little kids watch life in all its many facets; they pick their role models from the heroic, epic characters of their childhood, and create their first romantic ideals. Will these ideals stand the test of time, or will this childish personality be swept away and replaced by a more practical mindset, picked up from books and movies for adults, or live role models of adulthood? Or, perhaps, the character of this child will be reborn in the streets, in the concrete jungle, each mutation of it a dose of harsh street wisdom?

In any case, through simple and direct social lessons, both lived through and seen/read about somewhere – the entity we call a human character, or a personality, is born, and by now we see sometimes this personality has more than a single side. Our society is still happy to present a single person with many roles that may require a totally different character, so we normally only become the true ourselves when driven to the brink. Only forced into the game of survival – or into any other primal activity, like a sexual act – the human being dons all masks and becomes a singular creature driven by basic instincts. We may safely state one may never truly know a person until this part of their personality is revealed, observed, and known.

And the truth must be said: the multitude of masks people otherwise wear is endless, and fluidity of them is extreme. This is because all higher level habits, so-called "social instincts" – they are learned instincts, and learned things could be unlearned in a wink of an eye. Someone may eat bread all their life, then hear about glutens and quit gluten products forever, which leads them to change their entire lifestyle, which ultimately turns them into another person, someone their relatives hardly even recognize – and it happens as easy as that, a small article on glutens.

Speaks Of Empathy And Compassion

We all know what compassion is – it's a feeling of mutual care and attention found in mammals and birds but not found in many reptiles, for instance, found in rattlesnakes but not in tortoises or lizards.

Compassion is something we need to develop to become a good person to be around: it's your mindfulness of other people's wishes and needs, responsiveness to them (for compassion doesn't make sense when it doesn't involve action on one's part).

For the purposes of analysis, compassion is harmful.

You remember how Sherlock Holmes is normally portrayed – a rather cold and restrained character, even ready to risk the lives of the people he is supposed to care for in order to prove some theory of his? And it's not like Sherlock is a bad person – he can do little about this feature of his character, as it's only a side effect of his "deductive method", or rather, the reverse, dark side of his highly observant and analytical mindset. It's merely the nature of the game: a good analyst stays out of the picture to preserve it from their own interference, or at least limit this interference to the actions dictated by logic: the criminal must be stopped, who cares if a young widow suffers from a PTSD as a result!

This doesn't mean, however, that people analysis doesn't involve empathy. Quite the opposite: this analysis is based on empathy, or at least on something called "cognitive" or "cold empathy", merely because a compassionate detective sobbing and hugging the victim is of no use to anybody.

"Mentalizing" is exactly what we need; it's the concept that implies people analysis, detective work. It means the kind of insight into another human being that doesn't sway you emotionally. And these modes, affective empathizing and cognitive empathizing, are so different we could even claim they are mutually exclusive, or at least affection is something you want to restrain from while analyzing people, because the saying love is blind is very true, same as blind rage is.

How does it work? Imagine seeing a charity worker asking for money, carrying a sign with a picture of a traumatized child. Your affective empathy tells you: it's terrible, to be this child. The life of this poor baby is sheer torture. It's horrible, what happened to this poor little thing. And this charity worker, such a noble person, doing such a righteous job! And so, your compassion pushes your hand toward your wallet.

Cognitive empathy keeps you clear of these powerful feelings though. Yes, this child must have felt terrible when they photographed it. Yet the logic protests. How do we know who took this picture? And when? Is this child related to the money in the charity worker's box somehow? Is this charity worker a real deal, or is it a con artist who uses shock imagery to trigger people into donating money? This is something cold empathy is about, looking to understand another person's motives without being carried away by emotions.

Empathy has nothing do to with sympathy, although they are often being confused, and you see people who like to imagine themselves in place of someone else calling themselves empaths, although this is an absolutely wrong, inverted understanding of empathy. "Walking in someone else's shoes", imagining ourselves in the position of another person, is called sympathy. It normally resolves in us saying things like: "Don't worry, it happened to me a lot, it's fine", or "In your place, I'd go and see a doctor immediately." This way, we learn nothing about another human being, because we sympathize, not empathize with them.

Empathy is your ability to put aside your own self, your own worldview, experience, your own angle, and accept the world of this another human being, truly understand what moves them. How do we know if we truly understand another person? Easy! Remember how they say lovers and fools think alike? It happens exactly because lovers and fools empathize with each other easily, open up to each other the way their thoughts, feelings, and actions become synchronized to a degree they exclaim the same phrase in a certain situation.

Empathy is your ability to become another person and replace your own world with someone else's. It's like playing someone else on stage – except the stage is your imagination. How well can you empathize with me? 100% empathy means you can predict my words and actions perfectly.

Remember how a detective retraces the criminal's steps through the scene of the crime, touching something, pretending to drop something? This is about how his or her empathizing with the criminal would look – except of course there's no absolute need to move around in precise motions of the criminal, just getting into the criminal's mood and looking around the room would be enough.

Cognitive empathy becomes possible because of mirror neurons: the part of our brain responsible for learning new behaviors through observation of another human beings (or higher animals), no matter if we observe them physically or review conscious mental images of them. We watch how it's done, we try to do it ourselves (mentally or physically), we fake it till we make it, and sooner or later we learn how it's done (creating new neuron connections) or abandon hope (and let the whole thing fade away). If you look carefully into this learning process, you'll see it looks very close to how cognitive empathy works: copying and striving for a perfect match. Lovers and fools think alike.

Muscular Core, Posture And Breathing

The best way to find out is to copy your subject's muscular core state, just look at how their muscles are arranged and try to arrange yours the same way. There's a good expression, "to carry oneself", and your goal will be to carry yourself just as them. Your copy doesn't have to be identical, just close enough so you feel close enough to themselves – imitate them as close to perfection as your present acting skills allow (to be a good judge of character, a good analyst, you don't have to be a good actor, but it helps – remember Sherlock Holmes and his transformations?) It isn't hard – just contract whatever they have contracted and keep it that way!

Now, as we learned to carry ourselves like our subject of study, we must learn to walk like them and breathe like them, or at least pretend to do it, deep inside.

Much can be learned from a human posture and walk: people with bad eyesight recognize and spot their relatives and friends by their silhouette, their posture, their walk in the crowd of hundreds of people, alone, as easy as a person with keen eyesight would. Can you stand or sit exactly as your subject does, and feel as comfortable as they seem? Can you breathe like them, at the same rate, with the same depth, following the same intervals?

Try and practice it alone at first, looking at a video of someone else. Soon you'll be able to perform it mentally, running the process almost completely in your imagination. As soon as your musculature and posture imprint will feel identical to that of your subject; as soon as your combined breath sounds like one, it's time to analyze their non-verbal message.

Are they demonstrating the will to move closer, shorten the distance between you – or are they trying to distance themselves from you? Is their posture open towards you (face, chest, and groin unobstructed by limbs) or closed from you? (Folded arms, crossed knees, etc.) If their posture is closed, don't jump to conclusions: they may position themselves this way merely for comfort, not because they'd like to lock themselves away from you. If your object's posture is closed and is comfortable – they are likely an introvert. With extroverts, expect abrupt changes in posture, quick movements ahead (lean towards the person they're speaking to, or reach for them), meant to shorten the distance between them.

Body language is a nation-specific feature of communication – in some countries it's hardly used, while in the others two conversing people may resemble two windmills. Still, you can normally detect the heat of discussion by the amount and smoothness of gesturing, even when watching the speakers from the distance. The rougher, sharper gestures become, the less controlled they are, the higher the likeness of a conflict.

A conflict is something often provoked by the opposition, or a third party, with intent to unsettle us, upset us, or make us lose our temper and act out. Our goal in this situation will be to retain control of ourselves. This doesn't mean suppressing our anger or bottling our frustration. This means dissolving the heat of emotions in the cold presence of our reason. This means starting with controlled breathing, restrained posture, and slow relaxation of the muscle core, resetting it to absolute calm.

A person in control is not someone gritting their teeth, holding reins back – it's the person showing calm restraint and conscious choice of their words and actions. Remember the monkey and the computer? The last one is the analyst; the first one lives for battle, and spots a good fight miles away. There's a good use for this quality too: your instincts will tell you when the situation is about to heat up a bit too much, so your reason could be there in time to prevent unnecessary drama before it has a chance to happen!

The point is neither of the two parts of one's consciousness must be restrained or removed from the interaction. When the reason is cast aside, no civilized communication is possible: any conversation will quickly derail and devolve into something childish, silly, and virtually useless for any purposes but socializing itself. If the emotional part is suppressed, the person starts feeling discomfort.

This is a very important point, and it happens to be twofold: whenever you spot manifestations of discomfort in either yourself or your object, you will know it happens because the primal part, the emotional part, is subdued by reason. This may happen when the person's reason doesn't want to give something away, yet their body – heartbeat, breathing, perspiration – seems eager to betray them, so they try and shut it off using reason, forcing themselves under control for a period of time, after which their animalistic part will inevitably act out. You must have seen how, leaving the room after a difficult meeting, people will be overly childish and agitated, exclaiming loudly, pushing each other, craving some sort of physical gratification – it's all the backlash of self-control imposed by reason, now lifted.

Hence, to stay comfortable, to remain in full control of oneself – which is something you want to practice in order to become a good restrained analyst – one must never suppress their inner feelings! It's hard to give advice on how your computer could keep your monkey in check, as this is a personal thing, inherent to your own character. There's a huge number of venting and confidence-building techniques out there, and you're free to try them all! Just remember this simple rule: by indulging a certain whim of your animal, you grow it, not reduce it. For instance, aggressive behavior does not deplete aggression, in contrary, it increases your aggressiveness – same as being afraid will not deplete your fear.

Still, there are techniques helping you to drop the level of aggression and overcome fear, from the most basic things like counting to ten, naming objects around you mentally, or drinking a glass of water – down to counseling and transcendental meditation. In this book, we'll merely say the solution is out there, and self-control is essential if you want to stay an involved yet unbiased party.

On the other hand, this is what you want to notice in the behavior of your subject: not their controlled, reasonable actions, but their slips, their subliminal telltales; the small movements, expressions, and changes in posture that happen without the subject noticing. How to interpret this body language? The problem is, it's not only inherent to a particular culture, but also varies from one individual to another.

Many sources claim they're able to teach you some kind of universal list of telltales, enabling you to tell truth from lies, present you with recipes of telling an act from the real deal – but these sources are at best-generalized information, sometimes applicable to many people, enough to make it seem true, but definitely not to be applied to just everyone. The truth is, only your own experience, attentiveness, and insight will help you to read another person's body language, for there are as many body languages as there are different people.

For instance, when someone is trying to touch or hide a part of their face – lips, the nose, an ear – it's normally considered a sign of secretiveness, the telltale of a person lying or trying to hide some information from the listener. In many cases it's indeed so – and still, be careful not to call someone a liar just because they tend to rub their three-day stubble while they're thinking.

Another popular facial feature to be pointed out as a telltale: a genuine smile would cause crinkles around eyes, while a fake smile normally wouldn't. Yet again, in many cases it may be true – we often hear about "someone smiling while their eyes remain cold". Then again, the experiments show the "smiling eyes" can be faked more or less easily, and if you were to encounter a sociopathic person, someone good at mimicry – you'd never catch them faking a smile.

Approach tendencies in the posture of your subject may mean aggression – or they could mean affection, and only your judgment may discern between the two. If your subject demonstrates avoidance tendencies – this, yet again, could mean an entire spectrum of emotions: apathy, fear, disgust, mistrust, submission, meekness, and so on.

A good analyst would always view the non-verbal signals of their subject as a part of the bigger picture, applying to them the knowledge of this person as a whole. Even a habit as simple as biting one's fingernails – are you sure I bite mine when I'm nervous? It may happen a person tends to stick their thumb in their mouth while they're thoughtful, relaxed, their attention directed inward – miles from feeling nervous!

Always remember: what you see is only half of the picture. Another half, no less important, is what you hear.

The Importance Of Knowing How To Read People

Y ou analyze people so that you may understand them and be able to relate to them better. From the academic point of view, it may not be very important but it could be interesting to analyze others. However, from the perspective of life in general, it is more than just analyzing. When we understand ourselves and other people better, it becomes a lot easier and we end up being more successful in dealing with situations and other people and thus, ensuring we get it right.

We look at psychology as an academic discipline but we need to know how we use it to understand personalities which is a more practical subject. This is about using psychology on a daily basis in order to understand them, influence them, support and help them in order for you to get your points across in the best way possible so as to comprehend more and influence decision making, manage and motivate people, for conflict resolution and also to manage and understand our personal influence on other individuals.

It is important to differentiate between the subject of psychology and the subjects of psychology which are the people. Using character analysis, it helps break down different elements into situations that are observable. For instance, you may want to know or may want to understand if a person prefers to hold back and think things through before responding or just speak out, whether they like to start from the beginning or with available possibilities, do they approach situations bluntly or do they have tactical diplomacy? Do they like to relax before doing a job or do the job then relax and so forth. A lot of times it is possible to get it wrong. You may have thought a particular person was extravagant simply because they were outspoken well, in fact, they could be introverted and had been asked a question on a matter that was important to them and they felt passionate about it. It takes practice and with time it is possible to analyze people more correctly.

As human beings, we all practice applied psychology. We have friends and family, we socialize, we may find ourselves in teams and in these different situations, we make decisions concerning people often and often we get it wrong. It is therefore important to get it right when it comes to understanding people since it is more rewarding and avoids many problems.

The Need to Analyze and Understand People

The ability or the skill of understanding other people and being able to predict their behavior, as well as share experiences, is what is known as social cognition. Social cognition is also important in understanding different challenges in daily speech reasons being that people are prone to saying one thing while they mean another. For instance, you may have heard a person claim a place to be hot but what the statement truly means or what the person expects is to have the windows open. This is basically the intention or the meaning behind their remark.

Social cognition, therefore, represents specialized skills in the brain to understand people and are separate the skills needed for non-social tasks like realizing that your dress is dirty or the car is out of gas. This means that social cognition may be affected by brain disorders regardless of the non-social skills which in many cases may remain the same or intact.

Studies have shown that a person with brain damage, especially to the frontal lobe, develop poor social skills as well as interpersonal behavior despite their good intellect. At the same time, autism persons also seem to have inordinate challenges with any social information. With these examples, it can, therefore, be concluded that social cognition could have evolved separately from non-social abilities or skills.

Human beings are social animals that rely on competition and cooperation within groups for their survival. Therefore, their ability to understand social cues as well as understand different social behaviors may be evolutionary and important, hence, the separate development of non-social information skills.

How does it work

Social cognition basically involves you being able to understand the mental states of people by putting yourself in another person's shoes. By doing this, you are able to understand their beliefs, experiences, intentions, and feelings. This enables you to empathize and think through situations from a different point of view. Social cognition also helps us to be able to be more flexible in moving from our own perspective to another perspective. Of interest to note is that social cognition depends on information that may not be observed directly but concluded from information that is incoming and the knowledge we have on the social world.

Increasing evidence seems to suggest that social cognition involves mimicking or simulation of others' experiences in an effort to understand them better. This is evidenced by how we experience and react to other people's emotions in various situations. For instance, when you are watching a person's face, you are likely to mimic or copy their facial expression, smile when they do, frown when they do and so forth. It may not be obvious that you are mimicking a person but one can detect small muscle movements especially while getting exposed to emotional expressions. Sometimes, you also get your eyes to dilate when looking at the other person when having emotional expressions. When we concentrate on the actions of others, the mirror neuron systems in our brain are activated. This means that we not only copy thoughts but we also copy actions. However, it is important to note that mimicking of the facial expressions can be impaired as a result of brain injury.

Understanding social cognition and how different types of brain disorders can disrupt it gives a better promise for much better assessment and solution of social challenges. It also promises to open knowledge of how the brain is wired to enable functioning in a social world.

Explains Why People Throw Themselves Into Toxic Relationships

A healthy relationship is going to involve an equal amount of giving and take between the people who are in it. But if you are in a relationship where it feels like you are always the one giving, and never actually receiving something, you may be in a relationship that has someone who is manipulative in it. A manipulative relationship is going to be really tough to identify because the manipulation is going to be more subtle compared to some of the other relationship types that are toxic.

Psychological manipulation can happen when one person tries to create a power imbalance in the hopes of exploiting another person. Manipulation is going to have several methods that it can manifest, but the one theme that is going to keep on showing up between them all is that one person, the manipulator, is going to be the one who benefits, and the other person, the victim, is not and may even get harmed.

There are a lot of times when someone is going to end up in a toxic relationship, and not even realize it. The relationship may have started out perfectly normal, without any of the drama or the issues that you will later have to face when dealing with the manipulator. This is going to be part of the process that comes with the manipulator because it allows them to get in with target, and take control, without the other person realizing.

Of course, the relationship is not going to start out with the drama or the drain on self-confidence or any of the other tactics that the manipulator is going to use later on. If they started out with this, then the target would see right through them in the beginning and would run the other way. the manipulator is going to take a different approach. One that is slower and more thought out.

In the beginning, they will have no problem with love bombing and showing lots of affection. When the target is invested in the relationship, and often in love, then the manipulator will start to switch tactics. This will not be overnight and can take place over many weeks so that the target doesn't really notice the changes until it is too late. By this point, the target is so invested in what is happening in the relationship and around them that they will tolerate more of the manipulation and the problems than they would in the past.

There are actually a few different signs that can come up that show a manipulator may be at work in your own relationship. If you are uncertain about whether someone in your relationship is toxic and causing problems for you, or if they are a manipulator, it is important to take a look for these signs:

They push you to go out of your comfort zone in many different manners. The manipulator is going to do this financially, physically, and emotionally in order to make sure their target is off balance. This allows the manipulator to be the one with the upper hand, and then they can be the one in control along the way.

They will try to get rid of your confidence. When we start to have low self-confidence, we are going to be more easily manipulated because we are looking for ways to make ourselves feel better. This is why a manipulator is so interested in chipping away at our confidence levels to make us feel smaller and like we are never good enough. The manipulator can take our vulnerability and use it to their advantage.

The silent treatment. This is where the manipulator is going to take any small slight that you do, and turn it into a big deal. And to punish the target, they are going to use the silent treatment and ignore them. This includes all emails, chances of talking, phone calls, messages, and more. The manipulator gets to maintain all of the control with this, and they will decide when the silent treatment is done.

The guilt trips. None of us want to feel guilty about something, and if we are feeling this guilt, then we are going to do every action we can think about in order to make that guilt go away. The manipulator is counting on this and will throw as much blame and guilt on the target as they can, even blaming the target for things that they had nothing to do with.

They will ignore or gloss over problems that are unresolved. Unhealthy relationships are going to thrive with lots of unresolved conflicts because there is no communication, or because the manipulator will deliberately not want to solve these conflicts. This is because manipulating you into thinking that the discussion was over and done with is going to be easier and more convenient for them than working to resolve that problem with you in the first place.

Now, we can imagine that this is not that healthy of a relationship type to be dealing with. None of us want to get caught up in this kind of relationship where we feel trapped and like the other person is always in control, taking advantage of us and doing what they want in the process. We want to be able to have control over our own lives. And we want to find a partner who is willing to let this happen, without taking full advantage of us in the process.

Before we go too far into all of this though, there are a few questions that we need to ask ourselves in order to help establish were we stand in a relationship if we think our partner is a manipulator. The questions that you should ask yourself here include:

Am I being respected?

Are the expectations and the requests set upon me by my partner reasonable? Would I let someone else give me these same requests and be fine with it?

Is the giving and the receiving equal in the relationship? You don't have to go out and do a tally sheet, but there shouldn't be an obvious disparity here.

Do you feel good about yourself when you are around this person?

By the time we have gone through this guidebook, you should already be pretty sure about whether your relationship is a manipulative one or not. If you are in one of these types of relationships, some of the things that you can do to protect yourself include:

Know your rights. If you have been in this kind of relationship for a long period of time, it is sometimes hard to remember how to stand up for yourself. Remember that, no matter what the manipulator has said to you, you do have some fundamental rights that need to be respected. These rights include the right to have others treat you with respect, the right to express some of your own feelings, needs, and opinions, the right to set your own priorities without someone else controlling you, and the right to tell another people no. It is also your right to have an opinion that is different than another person, to help make sure you are protected physically, mentally, and emotionally, and that you are able to have your own life apart from someone else if you choose.

These are rights that the manipulator is going to try and take away from you in the long term. This allows them to maintain the control that they want and will ensure that you are able to do what they say. But the next time that you are around your partner who is a manipulator, remember your own rights, take in a deep breath, and then try to execute them. You are the only one who gets to be in control of your life.

Stay away. The next thing that you need to focus on doing here is to stay away from the other person. It is always best if you can keep your distance from someone who is manipulative. If it is too late for this one, see if you can at least get a bit of distance between the two of you. Every time that you do need to have some engagement with someone who is manipulative, you are simply giving them another chance to learn about you, figure out your weaknesses, and find a way to get into your life.

Staying away from this person is the first and the best way to protect yourself from someone who is manipulative. If you start to feel some kind of impulse to try and help them, run the other way. Remember that the manipulator wants you to fall for this, and they want you to feel bad for them so that they can get you back into the relationship and can take advantage of you again. Remember your own worth and stay away from the manipulator, and don't fall for the trap of wanting to feel bad for them or wanting to help them.

Remember that it is not your fault. One thing that a manipulator is going to work with is trying to look for the best ways to exploit the weaknesses that you have. When the manipulator finds what these weaknesses are, they are going to be able to take full advantage of these and will use it against you. This makes it easier to feel inadequate and the target will often end up blaming themselves on a regular basis for how much you end up disappointing the manipulator.

The manipulator does this on purpose. They know that you are going to be looking for ways to avoid guilt. And they know that they can always move the goalposts so that no matter how hard you work, and how long you work for it, you will never meet the standards that are set. This allows them to keep control the whole time, and to take advantage of their target for as long as possible.

Don't allow the manipulator to keep going with this. They want to blame you for having weaknesses, and they want to make sure that you feel bad all of the time so that you stay around and search for validation from them to feel better. The thing to remember here is that none of this, and none of what the manipulator is blaming you for, is your fault. You have just been manipulated in order to feel really bad, and this is done so that you are more likely to give up your agency and your rights. When you realize that things are not your fault, the manipulator is going to lose some of the control over you.

Learn how to say no. The manipulator in the relationship has started to rely on the fact that their target is always going to say yes to everything. They go through a lot of information and a lot of tactics in order to make sure that their target will say yes and do what they want. And they often do this so well that the target feels like they are never allowed to say no.

Learning how to say now is one of the fundamental rights that we talked about above, but it is still something that we need to look at is a bit more and expand out because it is definitely something that many of us, whether we are in a manipulative relationship or not, struggle with saying on a regular basis to those around us.

Whether we are worried about hurting the feelings of someone else, or we have concern over how the opinion of another person could change if we refuse to help them, simply saying no to another person is going to be enough to make us sweat, and it often takes a lot of courage.

This is in a regular occurrence. Imagine what it takes to say no when you are dealing with a manipulator. Saying no firmly and learning how to stand your ground with this one is going to be a crucial skill that is going to help you pull some of the power away from the manipulator, and back over to your side. Of course, they will not like this, and you are going to need to fight it and stand your ground a bit. Being able to say no without all of the guilt, whether you are dealing with a manipulator or not, is going to be the key to having a freer and happier life overall.

Being in a toxic relationship is never a good thing for the target. It is a whole relationship that is going to focus on giving the manipulator what they want, and the target is going to end up losing everything in the process. The target has been conditioned though to think that this is the right way to do things, and they won't realize that they are in such a toxic relationship until it is too late and they have been in it for a long time.

Learning how to recognize when the deception, the manipulation, and the other issues are going on in your relationship can be the first step to fixing the problem. It takes time and a lot of courage, especially since the target has been in that relationship for a long time, and they have to start working on gaining their confidence and self-esteem back to help them get through this tough time. but when it is able to come together and the target finally realizes the relationship they are in and how to make it better, they will find that things can really improve in their life without the manipulator.

Speak Of Macchiavellism

Strictly defined, Machiavellianism is the political philosophy of Niccolò Machiavelli, who lived from 1469 until 1527 in Italy. In contemporary society, Machiavellianism is a term used to describe the popular understanding of people who are perceived as displaying very high political or professional ambitions. In psychology, however, the Machiavellianism scale is used to measure the degree to which people with deviant personalities display manipulative behavior. Machiavelli wrote The Prince, a political treatise in which he stated that sincerity, honesty, and other virtues were certainly admirable qualities, but that in politics, the capacity to engage in deceit, treachery, and other forms of criminal behavior were acceptable if there were no other means of achieving political aims to protect one's interests.

Popular misconceptions reduce this entire philosophy to the view that "the end justifies the means." To be fair, Machiavelli himself insisted that the more important part of this equation was ensuring that the end itself must first be justified.

Furthermore, it is better to achieve such ends using means devoid of treachery whenever possible because there is less risk to the interests of the actor.

Thus, seeking the most effective means of achieving a political end may not necessarily lead to the most treacherous. In addition, not all political ends that have been justified as worth pursuing must be pursued. In many cases, the mere threat that a certain course of action may be pursued may be enough to achieve that end. In some cases, the treachery may be as mild as making a credible threat to take action that is not really even intended.

In contemporary society, many people overlook the fact that Machiavellianism is part of the "Dark Triad" of dark psychology and tacitly approve of the deviant behavior of political and business leaders who are able to amass great power or wealth. However, as a psychological disorder, Machiavellianism is entirely different from a chosen path to political power.

The person displaying Machiavellian personality traits does not consider whether his or her actions are the most effective means to achieving his or her goals, whether there are alternatives that do not involve deceit or treachery, or even whether the ultimate result of his or her actions is worth achieving. The Machiavellian personality is not evidence of a strategic or calculating mind attempting to achieve a worthwhile objective in a contentious environment. Instead, it is always on, whether the situation calls for a cold, calculating, and manipulative approach or not.

For example, we have all called in sick to work when we really just wanted a day off. But for most of us, such conduct is not how we behave normally, and after such acts of dishonesty, many of us feel guilty. Those who display a high degree of Machiavellianism would not just lie when they want a day off; they see lying and dishonesty as the only way to conduct themselves in all situations, regardless of whether doing so results in any benefit.

What's more, because of the degree of social acceptance and tacit approval granted to Machiavellian personalities who successfully attain political power, their presence in society does not receive the kind of negative attention accorded to the other two members of the Dark Triad—psychopathy and narcissism.

Signs of Machiavellianism

In today's world, you can observe most of the people carrying the torch of Machiavellianism. Even you can also be a Machiavellian yourself but you would not even aware of this fact. The ideology of Machiavellianism is based upon ambiguous cunning, fraudulent, controlling, and manipulation. It is the selfish conduction of selves to acquire other people to do what you want them to do.

Machiavellians do anything to get what they desire for even they walk over the people if it is in need. They are very much focused on their interests and never think about the hazardous and troubles they can create for others.

The person with Machiavellianism possesses the following traits.

Signs of Duplicity

Machiavellian has a sporadic personality. They show duplicitous behaviors depending upon what they need from others or whom they are talking with. You can find them completely different persons in every new day according to the situations and circumstances. It is better to give an example of politicians to make you aware of duplicity.

Tactical People

They had better know how to get methodical with their manipulation techniques. They are incredibly tactical to achieve their goals.

Charming Indeed

They know how to grab attention and generate trust. They choose the bunch of so many rights from dressing, facial and body expressions, tone, and words to obsess people with their charming personality. All these qualities make them master manipulator also.

Intimate Toxic

They can bring so much negativity and noxious in anyone's life. Their presence generates a feeling of being heavy and overwhelmed. They simply suppress the whole environment around them due to their toxicity.

All's Well That Ends Well

They just do not believe in ethics, morals, and rules. The only rule they follow is manipulation. They carry themselves in a very utilitarian way and feel free to do whatever they can to get favorable results. Philosophically they believe in "all's well that ends well".

Extremely Narcissist

Machiavellians always look for their interests and try to fix their problems and own paths of life. They never show any kind of magnanimity, amplitude, and conscientiousness for others.

Signs of Psychopathic Tendencies

Machiavellians may suffer from mental illness of any kind that leads them only towards distraction. They may be only having the desire to destroy and ruin the lives of people around them only to calm down their evil deeds.

Try To Get Ahead

The only result they expect is an ultimate success. They continuously work to get ahead of everyone, and for this, they follow no rules and ethics at all.

Talk Little About Sadism, Macchiavellism And Anti-Social Behavior

Humans have this fixation on the concept of "evil". We are obsessed with it. Most world religion condemns it. Most human society tries to avoid it. Most people who act in a way that offends us earns the evil label. We try and base our lives around its existence, and around avoiding being anything like it.

However, "evil" does not exist anywhere in nature. No animal concerns itself with whether killing its food or its enemy is ethical. No animal worries whether its power comes from righteous means. They do not care if they are being good or being evil. It is an exclusively human concept.

So, what do we humans mean by this word? Often, we are quick to label an action "evil" when it comes from a strange human, which we would not consider evil if it came from a known person, or an animal. When someone we know does an "evil" thing we look for a motivation, for something to excuse them, to make sure they did not intend to cause harm.

If they hit a dog, but the dog was attacking their child, that is fine. If they stole food from a store because they were starving, that is fine. If they threw a stone through a window for no reason at all, we start considering them "bad" or "wicked", and if someone repeatedly does harmful things without cause, then they are "evil". Indeed, even if they are generally good people, if they do a particularly heinous thing for no reason, such as murder, they are automatically evil at the first offense. In short: what we consider "evil" is harm for the sake of harm itself. It is impossible to go through life without causing any harm at all, so we all strive to cause the least harm possible. We justify harm when there is no other way. When someone causes harm for no reason, or causes harm when there was a better way, we consider them to be evil.

We also base our definition of "evil" on our own personal ethics. This happens because although we generally agree on what we consider harmful, we all place the severity on a different scale. For example, to an informed vegan, the lives of thousands of animals are more valuable than the quality of life of one human. To an informed omnivore, the quality of life of a human is more valuable than the lives of thousands of animals. If someone risked a human life to save an animal, the vegan would consider them good, but the omnivore would consider them bad, if not evil.

Very few people actually set out to cause harm for no reason! This is why it is easy to call strangers evil, but not friends. When someone is a stranger, we rarely know their motivation. When they are a friend, we can see that they were doing their best.

Nevertheless, there are some people who do set out to cause harm just because they want to hurt others. Even if you could ask them directly, their honest answer would be "I wanted to hurt someone." This desire to hurt others for no other reason than to see them squirm can be loosely divided into the sexually motivated desire and the socially motivated desire.

Sadism is the name we give to the behavior of someone who likes seeing others in pain because it brings them sexual pleasure. Although the term is used often, there are actually not many true sadists in the world. Most people are not sexually aroused by pain, no matter how much they strive to cause it. In fact, most people are actively turned off by seeing others suffer.

That said, sadism is based on natural behavior. On some level, pain and pleasure are deeply connected. Love bites, scratching, and other acts of primal lovemaking are things we would not tolerate outside of sex. We would consider it abusive if a partner choked and bit their lover as they did the laundry.

Some adventurous people make an exception in the bedroom to indulge their primitive urges to bite and scratch and bruise. Not only that, but the hormones released during sex make these things feel pleasant, rather than painful. Sadism is just a more extreme form of this natural urge.

A healthy sadist is someone who can compartmentalize their sadistic urges and only act them out with a willing, masochistic partner. They make special time for sex, find someone who enjoys the feeling of pain, and indulge in private, safely, without intent to cause lasting damage.

Schadenfreude, or epicaricacy, is a term used to describe when someone simply finds the pain of others to be amusing.

We all experience this urge on some level. It usually manifests as either good-natured or vindictive. Sometimes we see a friend hurt themselves, or do something that cannot possibly end well, and so long as they are not badly hurt, their suffering amuses us. Sometimes we see someone do something we consider to be bad, or evil, and the consequences affect them in such a way we find it entertaining.

A healthy way of living out schadenfreude is when we simply enjoy the "karma" that others have earned, without doing them harm, and preferably helping them at the end. There is nothing evil about laughing when someone falls into the pool after trying to push you in. There is nothing wrong with feeling satisfaction when someone hurting a dog gets hit back. So long as we are not actively harming others for no reason, a little bit of schadenfreude is healthy and natural.

A toxic form of schadenfreude is when someone will actively hurt others for their own amusement. This usually manifests as bullying, though it can be more serious. The person who pushes others into the pool, insults their appearance, or tries to make them do things against their will is probably experiencing schadenfreude.

Whether it is sadistic or just for fun, taking pleasure in the suffering of others is a key component to many Bad Guys' behavior. Of course, some Bad Guys just don't care. But the ones who enjoy seeing you suffer are even more dangerous. A Bad Guy who does not care will at least stop causing suffering when they have what they want. A Bad

Guy who enjoys your pain will keep on hurting you no matter how much they get.

Antisocial personality disorder is the official psychiatric term for what the rest of us call a psychopath. We often talk about psychopathy like it is some sort of a "serial killer mental illness" which will make a person go around committing serious crimes, but the reality is not that simple.

Psychopathy is defined by a complete lack of empathy and too much impulsivity. This doesn't mean they are ready to go out and hurt people any more than you go out of your way to kick rocks. But it does mean that to them you are nothing more than a rock, and that if hurting you crosses their mind, it could happen. Which actually makes a real psychopath more dangerous than a stereotypical movie psychopath.

The DSMV says that psychopaths have certain behaviors. However, it is again important to remember that any of these behaviors can be dangerous and that a person who does any of these things regularly is a risk, even if they are not a true psychopath!

A strong emphasis is placed on legal versus illegal behavior because obviously this impacts society the most, and in our culturally varied world, what is a social norm for one person may be a strange custom for another. The key thing to remember is that a psychopath does not follow the rules. Whether it's the law, social expectations, office rules, or civilized behavior, they do not conform. They live and act only for themselves.

When someone does not care about any rules or norms at all, they will break them if they want to. This means a psychopath is more likely than a normal person to do something illegal, dangerous, or unpleasant.

Quite simply: they do not care about the truth. The truth is a social norm that almost every society values, but because it is a norm, it doesn't matter to the psychopath.

Telling the truth ourselves and being able to tell when someone is lying are important cornerstones of socializing. With a psychopath you are always in the dark.

Impulsivity or failure to plan ahead

This trait is not related to their lack of empathy. It is actually the other key trait of a psychopath. It may not be obvious, but they are continually in what we call fight or flight mode, always running on adrenaline. This can be confusing because often they look like they are planning everything so carefully. In reality? That calm, collected face and that "I planned this all along!" speech are lies. Because they are used to adrenaline, they may be able to hide their energy, but they are always looking for their next rush.

When we enter fight or flight mode it is usually for survival reasons. An animal attacking us, a loud sound in the middle of the night, or a fight are good examples. Our body then tells us to run or to fight, and we do it without thinking. This is a good response because thinking would waste valuable time where we could be in danger. Now imagine if every decision was split-second, you followed through on almost everything you considered doing, and you had to second-guess everything decision because you acted rashly. Chances are you would do a lot of risky things.

Many psychopaths adapt as they grow up, and eventually learn to pause and force themselves to think instead of act on impulse. But even the best-trained psychopath slips up, so they will eventually do something dangerous on an impulse.

Again, this is because of their increased stress response. All it takes is a slightly tense situation and they break into aggression like they were being attacked by a bear.

Obviously, someone being ready for a fight as soon as you bump into them is not a good thing for society.

Reckless disregard for safety of self or others

Again, fight or flight is to blame. In a dangerous situation we rarely have time to calculate the least dangerous option. Instead, we just focus on getting rid of the threat.

Because the psychopath is acting completely on impulse, they will not be able to stop and consider everyone's safety. They may not even care. This, in day to day life, is definitely not a good thing.

Again, when you are an impulsive person you do not think about long-term things. Psychopaths are unable to consider how they need to act for the next day, let alone weeks, months, or years. Some psychopathic people are able to act like psychopaths and still plan ahead, but a true psychopath, under the DSMV definition, would not be able to do so. Because they treat people like they will never need them, spend like money will never be scarce, and treat work like it will be there forever, they are completely unprepared for when these things disappear. This not only affects them, but everyone around them.

Going back to their lack of empathy, a psychopath does not feel bad about the results of their actions. Someone could do all the above and although they would be a dangerous person, they would not be a psychopath. Psychopaths are genuinely comfortable being who they are. They do not mind hurting people. Much like the solipsist, the only time they regret their actions is when they are suffering the consequences. And even then, when the consequences end, they rarely learn from their mistake. They often do the same things repeatedly.

This means that everything a psychopath does to hurt you will happen repeatedly. You can never correct them. No matter what you say or do, as soon as they are free, they will repeat their behavior and cause the same damage again.

At this point, you are probably starting to see why psychopathy was renamed Antisocial Personality Disorder. It is literally a threat to society. Civilization was built by people looking forward, putting aside their primitive animal instincts, and looking out for one another, to build a better future for all. Psychopathy is literally the opposite of civilization and, in that sense, the opposite of humanity. Everything that makes us different from animals is missing in a psychopath. They are the raw, primitive human beast that we all wish had been left behind.

A lot of us, especially those of us who are a bit less emotional, like to think we are pragmatic. Even if you haven't heard the word "pragmatism" before, chances are you are familiar with the ideas behind it:

Pragmatism is the belief that a good solution, or the best possible solution, is the noblest goal for any thought or action.

In a pragmatic mindset, the universe is continually changing and evolving. Justice is not an end goal but something that's always one step away from us, and logic is a tool to help us reach true goodness and happiness.

For example, under pragmatism you might accept a job you don't want to give you time to work toward the one you do want Pragmatism means taking your experience of the world and accepting some compromises in order to reach the best possible end for all.

However, the Bad Guys like to corrupt things to suit themselves. Much the same way that they corrupted self-respect into narcissism, they corrupted pragmatism into Machiavellianism. Machiavellianism, if you have not heard the word before, can be summed up in one sentence:

The ends justify the means.

Of course, there is a bit more to it than that. But that belief lies at the core of Machiavellian philosophy. It has one distinct difference from pragmatism. Under pragmatism we see the world holistically. For example, we take the job we do not want because we understand that in the short term we have less money, but in the long term we have some money and more time. A pragmatist would not accept a job that stopped them getting their ideal job completely, and they would not lie to get their ideal job instead.

Under Machiavellianism there is no big picture. There is just the end result. A Machiavellian person is more idealistic than pragmatic. To them, the ideal job is the only good outcome. So not only will they turn down the job they do not want, but they will lie and cheat and do anything it takes to get the ideal job, even if this means they are not ready for it.

Machiavellianism allows Bad Guys to convince us to do their bidding. Deep down we all want to reach our goals eventually, and we all understand that other people want to reach their goals, too. Deep down we all want to be pragmatic about it. We want to make the decisions that hurt as few people as possible, help as many people as possible, and slowly but surely move us toward our end goal.

As we have seen, the line between "The noblest goal is chasing the best solution" and "The ends justify the means" is very, very fine. The main difference is that the pragmatic noble goal involves everyone's well-being, whereas the Machiavellian ends involve only the success of the ideal.

To push us into following their Machiavellian plans and not our own pragmatic ones, the Machiavellian person must, therefore, persuade us that their goal is also our goal and everyone else's goal.

This theory comes from Niccolo Machiavelli's book "The Prince". He explained the ways in which someone who wanted to be a ruler could manipulate society to convince people to side with their goals. There is a big debate about whether Machiavelli actually believed this was good or was just trying to avoid being killed by angry rulers, but one thing is undeniable: a Machiavellian approach to power works.

Most politicians rise to power and stay in power by convincing us that they are acting selflessly. When we vote for someone we are not thinking, "this person wants to be in power for status and money", we are usually thinking "this person has some good points about important topics and will look out for my best interests". Likewise, cult leaders and dictators avoid being overthrown, even though they are outnumbered, because the followers believe the leader is looking after them.

A Machiavellian person always tries to get money, power, and love from people, no matter what it costs. But because they need you to make sacrifices for their goal, they will try to convince you that their goal is your goal, too.

Pathological Liars

You can learn to detect dishonesty in others. This can be a useful skill when your job mandates that you do such.

Interpersonal matters can also be improved with the ability to seek out the truth. Below, you will find a list of features to watch in order to know when you are being lied to:

The Eyes: Clues to Revealing the True Intention

The eyes are one of the most principal expressive areas of the face. They may act as deception detectors. Reading dishonesty is dependent on the non-verbal cues, and thus through the eyes, it becomes easy to reveal the exact intention that an individual has. The eyes also communicate the next action that someone is likely to take, whether bad or good.

A break in eye contact is one determinant of deception. This occurs when an individual refrains from directly looking at the other party. This action is associated with no emotion other than shame.

In most cases, it is essential to understand that those who tell the truth are able to directly look at the other individual. They don't feel ashamed of their actions. Whenever someone breaks the eye-contact sometime after the conversation starts, then this is a clear indicator that they have changed their intention. This shift is evidence that such individuals are lying.

Consequently, detecting deception through the use of eyes is complex since it requires the interviewer or the investigator to continuously ask various questions. It is applicable whenever an investigator applies a series of questions to a particular subject, which requires the person to conform to the process.

To determine if these individuals are lying, they are allowed to diverge from the main subject, which is an indicator of deception. In the session which involves questions and answers, it is the principal role of both parties to maintain eye contact. Keeping this gaze could allow the liar to avoid detection, but they are likely to be unable to manage their movements. It is essential to note that as a principal organ, the emotion of an individual is directly tied to the movement of their eyes.

Body Language

Body language is a vital aspect of detecting deception. We all gesture unconsciously while we speak. Watching someone's movements may allow you to discern if they are being honest on the subject matter. These motions are composed of various components: including head movements as well as breathing.

Body language is essential because it portrays exactly what an individual feels. Whenever someone's movements (such as that of the head) do not complement the various affirmations and verbal denials, then it is a clear indication of deception. Consistency is imperative during this process.

A good example is a consistency in the head movement. Whenever an individual's head steadily moves, it indicates that they are telling the truth. Whenever they nod their head erratically, they are lying. Most of the investigators fail in the determination of dishonesty because they don't correlate the inconsistencies which are observed between the nonverbal behavior and also the spoken words. It is vital to note that whenever someone is comfortable about what they are saying, the body movements (specifically the head) conforms to their words.

One essential element of body language which can be applied in the detection of deception is the aspect of breathing. Individuals who lie are often burdened with fast breathing due to the increased speed of their heartbeat. Interestingly, other than rapid breaths. Whenever an individual starts lying, they are plagued by fear. This eventually results in a change in the breathing pattern. Deception is detectable through watching these features.

The Hands

Hands also act as a determinant of deception since truthful individuals are not nearly as worried. They can easily spread their fingers. Those who are insecure, due to their lying nature, need to fold their palms and also tend to try to occupy a minimum amount of space.

Interestingly, liars are also known to fold their legs since they strongly believe whenever they occupy too much space, they could be easily detected. Furthermore, deception can be determined whenever an individual's fingers or hands tremble without any climate change noticed. They may also attempt to cover their appendages with a sleeve.

Most of the individuals that are experts in the art of dishonesty will barely move their hands or bodies. They speak in a measured tone and are very careful not to give away any extra information with their motions. Someone who is tasked with interviewing a known conman would be wise to watch for this lack of change. No one sits completely still.

Slouching may also serve as an indicator that a person is lying; it directly helps in boosting confidence. While yawning, those who are being deceptive also stretch their hands to ensure they can confuse the parties that they are addressing. Watch for motions that could be used to misdirect attention. Liars are either going to have a decent poker face, an issue with fidgeting or weird and disjointed gestures.

The Face

Facial expressions also play a significant role in the determination of lies. There are several types of facial movements that clearly indicate that an individual is dishonest. This is the most expressive region of the human body and should be watched intently.

Facial expressions may be caused by various emotions (like nervousness) and other physical reactions. They can be identified to act as a scale for detecting dishonesty. One of the common ways to identify that a person is lying is when someone blinks their eyes between four or five times, within less than a minute.

The closing of eyes can also be used as a way to show that someone is lying. Under normal circumstances, an individual should not close their eyes when they answer a certain question. Whenever an individual shuts their lids for more than two seconds, it is a clear indication that they have not told the truth.

Based on the facial expression, deception can also be detected whenever an individual who is right-handed is asked a question regarding what they had seen in the past, and they look to the left side and upwards. They are directly lying to you and they are trying to diverge your attention. However, whenever they look right side but upwards, they are sincere. These are some of the facial expressions which clearly show an individual is lying.

The Voice

Variation in the voice is also one of the ways to determine whether a person is lying or not. In most cases, the trembling sounds are associated with fear. Under normal circumstances, it is essential to note that an individual's tone should not vary in every answer that they give.

Whenever an individual's voice trembles as they answer complex questions, it is essential evidence that they are lying. The shakiness is an indicator that people are applying various kinds of defense mechanisms. This is mostly observed among those who cannot justify their claims. It is essential to conclude that someone's voice gives a direct glimpse of whether they are lying or not.

Big Lie vs White Lie

You may have encountered people telling lies in their everyday life. Some of these are categorized as "big lies and white lies". In the two forms of lies, a person intentionally deceives the other person or groups of persons by communicating misleading information.

There is a big difference between big lies and white lies. In big lies, the deceptive person tries to gain something from the deceived person. This means that the dishonest individual seeks to exploit the other party, out of self-interest.

Telling a lie to gain personal benefit is condemned across all cultures of the world. For example, a used electronics dealer may mislead his/her customers about the condition of the TV he/she is selling. The salesperson will pass the device off as being in a good working condition, even when they know too well that the TV is faulty. He/she will then sell the TV at a high price in order to maximize the profits.

On the other hand, white lies involve manipulating information in order to motivate or please the deceived. Sometimes situations may compel you to mislead others. You may be forced to say what the other person is expecting to hear, even when the situation is different. For example, you may have told your friend how great their new hairstyle was, even when you secretly loathe it. You do this to make your friend happy.

White lies usually don't harm the other person's feelings. In fact, when you tell a lie in order to please the other person, you are just exercising an innocent part of your daily interactions. These are sometimes necessary to keep the peace.

The difference in the two types of deceptions lies in the motives of the deceiver. While the big lies are often condemned, the white lies are sometimes encouraged depending on the context. There some scenarios where white lies cause harm, especially when you use it to foster relationships and connections. When you desperately want to bond with others, you tend to agree with all of their opinions in order to please them or to gain favor from them. This may greatly hamper your decision-making skills.

Look Inside Yourself

In order to accurately read other people, we must first know how to read our own emotions and thoughts. After all, what is the goal behind analyzing others? It's to develop a deeper understanding of humanity, and this desire is incomplete if it doesn't include ourselves. Understanding your own emotions is important for countless reasons: career success, healthy relationships, and living a peaceful existence in general. But it will also help you in understanding all social dynamics you are surrounded by. Let's look first at the consequences of not understanding yourself.

What do Unrecognized Emotions Result in?

When we bury or repress our feelings, by not taking the time to understand them or ourselves, serious issues exist not only mentally, but physically as a result. Not taking the time to pay attention to and deal with your emotions will affect your mentality, ability to develop and grow as a person, and your personal relationships.

•Physical Consequences: Repressing or ignoring your emotions on a long-term basis will lead to serious issues, such as permanent fatigue, arthritis, or lowered immunity. Studies show that your mentality directly relates to your ability to heal from serious illnesses. People with serious physical health issues have trouble with everything in life, including accurate judgment when it comes to interpreting the behavior, thoughts, and moods of others. If you wish to get better in this area, you must first notice your own emotions.

•A Lowered Ability to Accurately Read Others: When you don't pay attention to your own feelings, you cannot accurately judge what you observe in other people. If your goal is to analyze other people and understand what they think and feel, you must first have a logical perspective about yourself. For example, if you struggle with insecurity and don't believe in yourself, you will likely interpret someone else's actions as negative towards you when they don't necessarily show this.

To have sharp perceptive skills of observation, you need mental energy and keeping emotions buried burns off this mental energy. This means that you don't have the stamina necessary to perform other mental tasks, even something as simple as accurately gauging what others are thinking or feeling.

How to Learn More about yourself:

A person who decides to get healthy on an emotional level and understand themselves truly is committed to this path and willing to do whatever it takes. Although this is not always comfortable or easy, you will become much smarter and observant about others once you undertake it. Feelings are the most reliable way to figure out what is happening inside your mind. Many methods exist for identifying your emotions, meaning that you can pick the method that works best for you.

While some people find that it's easiest to do this alone, others find it helpful to combine it with observing other people. Some people may find journaling helpful, while others prefer not to write about emotions. For most people, a combination of multiple methods works best. What follows are some general guidelines for figuring out your own thoughts about feelings regarding a particular situation or person.

Becoming Aware:

In order to understand and analyze others, you first have to become aware of yourself. This is the first step to making progress in any pursuit in life. Here are some steps to doing this:

•Paying Attention to Thoughts: The best way to start getting to know yourself better is to start paying attention to your own thoughts throughout the day. Most people get so used to thinking a certain way that they don't notice what is going on in their own heads. Pay attention to every little detail and stay aware of what your thoughts are. This is a great way to learn more about the way your mind works, how you truly feel about your relationships, and what you like and dislike. Although many believe that they already know these things about themselves, looking a bit deeper may surprise you, and there is always more to learn.

•Journaling: One great way to stay aware of your thoughts is to start keeping a journal and write every day, even if it's only a small amount. You can then look back on these entries and learn a great deal about yourself and the way your thoughts and feelings function. This will help you recognize the thoughts and feelings of others and become better at analyzing their behavior. The better you get at reading your own thoughts and feelings, the better you will be at reading the thoughts and feelings of the people in your life who you wish to analyze.

• Figure out what "Doesn't Matter" to you: Most people have a list of things in their life that they claim don't matter or are not a big deal when, in fact, something is bothering them quite a lot. This leads to repression and denial of your own feelings and thoughts and makes it hard to digest the information. This leads to confusion and turmoil inside and makes it hard to tell right from left. Start by making a list of those small things that "don't matter" but actually keep popping up for you.

Anything that seems to appear repeatedly but cannot be easily explained away should go on your list. A lot of people have a long list of items from the time they were children, which leads to mental issues and health problems later in life — taking the time to identify these "small and meaningless" matters will help you learn about your own emotions and the best way to deal with them.

•Notice what Elicits Strong Feelings in you: Start paying attention to different matters in your life that elicit strong feelings in you for a few weeks. This can be a person, certain weather, or politics; anything that makes you have strong emotions, good or bad, must be recorded. This is a great way to become emotionally healthy and understand yourself as well as others in a deeper way. Once you recognize what makes you feel strong and know how to identify when this happens, you will be able to recognize the same feelings in those around you.

Recognizing emotions is part of what analyzing people is all about, since you have to know how to identify emotion in order to notice that it's there in the first place. Once you can label and deal with your own feelings, you will be better equipped to label and deal with the feelings of others. This includes both positive and negative emotions and everything that lies in between.

• Pay Attention to Memories: Everyone has recurring memories that never seem to go away, no matter how much time has passed. This could be related to a situation or a person from your past. Although it isn't comfortable to do, you should intentionally remember these incidents and allow yourself to feel the pain surrounding them. Write extensively about what this is like since these memories are likely contributing to mental distress that you are not even aware of.

•Get Specific about your Feelings: Before you can be any good at identifying other people's emotions, you first need to learn how to identify your own. This begins with getting specific. Ask yourself not only what you are feeling, but why, and any details about it. Many people get confused trying to become familiar with their feelings since they are too general in describing them.

Staying general about feelings doesn't really help at all because it doesn't offer a solution. Once you figure out specifically what you feel and why you feel it, you can effectively deal with your emotions. This will help you recognize the feelings of others and also help them deal with them, which is part of the appeal of learning how to analyze people.

•Know your Positive Feelings: It's important that you know how to pay attention to your positive feelings as well as your negative ones. Most people are generous, forgiving, and compassionate multiple times throughout their days. Make sure that as you get to know your own mind, you are giving yourself credit for these emotions, which will allow you to see a fuller picture of who you are as a person. Once you can identify these feelings in yourself, they are easier to see and recognize in the people around you. Remember to keep a balance by accurately looking at the entire spectrum rather than being biased toward either positive or negative thoughts and feelings.

•Hone your Intuition: You are already an expert at analyzing the thoughts and feelings of other people due to the way we have all evolved as humans. It is simply a matter of getting in touch with this innate wisdom. Set aside some time each day to get in touch with your own instincts, learning how to listen to them, and believing what they are telling you. This will make you a lot more perceptive and observant when it comes to reading yourself and others.

The best time to start doing this practice is during the morning when you have some quiet time to think undisturbed. This allows you to get in touch with your mind before the chaos of the day begins or your schedule and work duties catch up with you. If you take the time to get in touch with silence and your own mind, this peace will follow you throughout the rest of the day and your judgments and observations will be much more accurate, thorough, and keen.

• Talk with Friends: Friends are a valuable resource when it comes to both understanding ourselves and others better. If you have a friend who is also interested in learning how to analyze people accurately, that's even better. You can compare your findings, observations, and notes with each other and practice together. Throughout the day, stop a few times to try to read what your friend is thinking or feeling and confirm whether you were correct.

Have them do the same to you; it will provide great practice for both of you in learning how to analyze people better.

Conclusion

It's been an eventful journey. Where we explored the common verbal cues, this is the "encyclopedia" for all your people-reading skills.

This book revolves around learning the inner mechanics of the thousands of facial expressions you could come across in the course of your daily activities. This skill is indispensable and applicable to many situations.

It's the main factor to give you an A-game when you attend that interview or when you are visiting your in-laws. Perhaps it might come in handy during parenting. There's no doubt that there's a benefit to learning how to analyze people, although I'll advise you to keep your newfound "superpowers" under wraps since others might not feel comfortable if they think you are trying to constantly observe and analyze them.

It can make people clamp up around you, and this can deny you of the opportunity to practice these skills.

The essence of this book is to help you blend and survive better in a complex and largely unpredictable environment and not for you to become isolated. So carefully observe the gestures stated in this book. Remember, the only way for you to fully grasp this information is for you to practice and refer back to the book as needed. By doing this, you will quickly get familiar with the common nonverbal and verbal cues from those around you.

It's important for you to know that there are some nonverbal cues that are not covered in this book. So practice reading people and observe the context in which they exhibit nonverbal and verbal cues. Remember, never stop learning. I wish you the best in your endeavors. Human behavior is like the life script of an individual by which he/she can learn the art of reading people. Every human being whether the situation is bad or good tries to analyze people, and what they think regarding that issue. And up to some extent you may be right in reading people. Actually, it depends upon the type of human behavior we have.

The main purpose of this book is to help and aware readers to understand the importance of analyzing people through varied tricks like facial expression, body language, and numerous others.

However, we are grown-up individuals and have tremendous options to read people by learning and practicing different methods like by developing our personality, through social and communication skills, verbal communication, by analyzing different attractions, and many more.

Furthermore, there is so solo secret to analyze people, rather it comes only through learning and practicing. This concept makes your life more interesting and different which you will never think of. So, give your best in order to read people's mind and become an eminent personality.

In this book, all the concepts are explained related to how to read people, which ought to help the person to self-assess and understand the other people's behavior and why they react like this. Moreover, an individual would find this very beneficial to develop the art of observing and analyzing people so that over the period of time they easily understand people try to offer a suitable solution for their problems.

HOW TO ANALYZE PEOPLE

Learn how to read People and Improve your Empathic, Mind-Control and Body Language Skills to Develop a Deeper Understanding of Human Relationships and to Hack Others' thought.

ADAM JOHNSON

Introduction

Tthere are many professions that not only make use of the art of reading people but absolutely rely on the ability in their everyday activities.

In the performance art called mentalism, practitioners exhibit what appears to mind reading or clairvoyance using tricks and illusions. This differs from other forms of stage magic in that with magic everyone is aware that these are tricks that play on your imagination. The performer invites the audience to pretend with them for a while. With a mentalist, every effort is made to convince the audience that their mental powers are real. Thus, you'll never see stage magic in a mentalism show, but you might see mentalism tricks in a magic show.

A mentalist will claim to possess the powers of telepathy, clairvoyance, precognition, mind control, and hypnotism. Their performances can be extremely convincing because they present information that seems impossible for them to have without mental powers to help them. But the truth is that these performances are just what the name implies: mental tricks. These tricks can be learned by just about anyone and don't require any amount of flexibility or sleight of hand skill to accomplish, which can take years of practice to master. Learning how these are done can rob the magic of them, so don't go looking for the explanations if you want to be able to enjoy these performances in the future. For the rest of us who are interested in what mentalism techniques can teach us in people reading, here are some examples.

If you've been working on your observation skills, you're already on your way to learning mentalism like the pros, because the first step is to practice extremely sharp awareness of details and information about your subject. But with these first few tricks, you won't even need this skill, just remember a few simple steps.

The Triangle in a Circle

Ask your subject to think of a shape that "is like a square but not a square." You're working off of probabilities here, as most people will think of a triangle. If you subtly trace a triangle in the air when you're asking them to think of a shape, you'll increase the likelihood that they'll think exactly that. Next, ask them to think of another shape to go around the first shape. Since most people won't immediately come up with anything else for this aside from a circle you can pretty much count on that being the outcome. Now, you can freak your audience out by drawing the image out for them, maybe after some fun embellishments like appearing to focus really hard with your fingers at your temples.

This next trick requires you to enlist the help of a friend to perform this for your audience. Before you do this in front of other people, tell your friend, who will be your plant in the audience, that you'll be asking the audience to tell you a number between 1 and 20, and that you will read their mind when you place your fingers on their temples. When you do this, your friend will clench his jaw the number of time equal to the secret number he was given. Muscles in your temples naturally jump when you clench your jaw, and the motion is strong enough to feel with your fingers tips. This way your plant can communicate the number to you in a way no one can possibly see from your audience, even if they are right next to you.

You can put thoughts into your subjects easily with subtle suggestions they'll have no idea you're feeding them. For example, if you ask a person to think of a specific card in a deck, you can put the three of diamonds into their head with two simple tricks. As you explain what you want to do, subtly move your hands in the shape of a diamond. Also, make other small gestures in series of threes. They won't have any idea that these gestures mean anything but they'll absorb the suggestion anyway and almost always will decide on this card. It's unlikely anyone will notice your gestures or attribute them any meaning and you'll wow them all.

This guide aims to teach you techniques to best analyze people. Read On!!

It All Starts with the Brain

H ave you ever asked yourself these questions: "Why do I react a certain way to different emotions even without thinking?" "Why do I cross my arms and lower my chin instinctively when I'm trying to shut people out?" "Why do liars often tend to cover their mouth or put their hands to their face unconsciously?" "Why are these gestures consistent with specific reactions?"

Well, look no further as the answer lies in your brain. Once you learn how your brain makes your body to react in certain ways, you will know how to properly observe these behaviors in other people. So let's take a closer look at the cranial matter that's responsible for your nonverbal responses.

You Have More than One "Brain"

Let's kill a misconception about the human brain. In reality, you have more than one brain, with each part revealing an evolutionary trend. The brain consists of three "brains," each performing specialized functions that work together to act as the command center for all our actions.

In 1952, this research was pioneered by a scientist named Paul McLean, who spoke of the brain as having a triune structure: the reptilian part (the brain stem), the mammalian part (the limbic brain), and the evolutionary advanced human part (the neocortex).

In this book, we will concentrate on the limbic part of the brain since it is responsible for the expression for nonverbal signals. We use the neocortex, which is the advanced part of the brain, to analyze and decode the limbic reactions of those around us. It is vital for us to know that the brain controls all our reactions from the conscious to the unconscious ones. Therefore, understanding the limbic part of the brain is the secret in unlocking the reason why we express nonverbal signals to those around us.

Understanding the Limbic Brain

In December of 1999, a US Customs Officer, Diana Dean, was able to thwart a terrorist attack in the Los Angeles Airport. Taking notice of Ahmed Raheem's extreme nervousness and excessive sweating as he came into the States from Canada, she decided to ask him to step out of his car for further questioning. This action, I believe, saved countless lives that would have been lost if the bombs were detonated at the Los Angeles Airport.

At this point, Ahmed Rasheed jumped out of the car and attempted to flee but was quickly captured. Here are questions for you: Why was Ahmed Raheem extremely nervousness and sweating excessively? Why was he not able to control those gestures to avoid detection? How was Officer Dean able to detect and analyze those gestures as signs of extreme duress? You will discover the reason as you read further.

The limbic brain is the part that reacts to the world instinctively in real time without any conscious thought. It is that part of the brain that gives off a "true response" to the environment, and it never stops functioning since it is crucial for our survival. This part of the brain serves as our emotional center, and it sends signals to other parts of the brain, which in turn controls our behaviors as they relate to emotions. These behaviors can be decoded as they are expressed physically in our face, legs, hands, torso, and arms.

This part of the brain is referred to as the "honest brain" since its nonverbal gestures don't lie. The limbic signals that control our behaviors are hardwired into our nervous system and cannot be faked or hidden. We can trace the limbic part of our brain to the days of the early men that roamed the savannas of Africa.

The third and largest part of our brain is the neocortex. It is a recent evolutionary addition to our brain. The neocortex is the part of the brain that distinguishes us from other primates. It is the part of the brain that's responsible for our cognitive and intellectual capacity. It's that part of the brain that enables you to compute, analyze, and interpret external stimuli from the environment. It is referred to as the lying part of the brain since it is capable of complex thought.

Conversely, the neocortex, also called the thinking part of the brain, is quite capable of allowing him to lie during questioning. This part of the brain will compel him to say, "There's nothing in the trunk of my car," should the customs officer inquire as to what's in his vehicle.

Therefore, the neocortex is not a reliable source for getting accurate information about people since it is capable of dishonesty. You should focus on the signals from the limbic system since it is responsible for nonverbal cues.

How the Limbic System Helps You to Deal with Threats?

The limbic part of our brain is the vestige of our evolutionary origins, and it has always served as our survival guide in the face of danger. These limbic responses are freeze, flight, and fight. I know most people are only familiar with the "flight or fight" response.

Recent studies have shown this is inaccurate as there are actually three main responses to danger: freeze, flight, and fight.

Freeze Response

What happens when you shine your headlights on a deer? The deer will freeze immediately before bolting off into the woods. Just like animals, humans use the freeze response in the face of danger. Since movement attracts attention, the limbic system enables us to freeze to effectively survive in the face of danger.

In today's society, you observe the freeze response in people who are caught bluffing or lying. People often tend to freeze when they feel exposed or threatened. Sometimes this response occurs innocently, such as when a person walking down the street suddenly stops and hits himself with the palm of his hand before turning around to turn off the stove.

This response also happens during interviews. When the interviewee feels exposed or under pressure, his breathing becomes shallow. This response is also common in people being questioned about a crime that will put them in big trouble.

Most times, people who exhibit the freeze response may place their feet in a secure position. That is why security agencies are trained in the art of detecting these responses and discerning if this response is from guilt or fear.

Sadly, this response is also exhibited by children that are being abused or molested; they often tend to freeze at the touch of an adult. Abused adults also display this response.

Remember, these are clues you need to consider when analyzing people. Another way the limbic brain utilizes the freeze response is an attempt to diminish our exposure in the face of danger. There's one thing that stands out during the surveillance of shoplifters; the thieves will always minimize their presence by hunching over as if trying to be invisible or by restricting their motion. Ironically, these behaviors make them stand out further since it's a deviation from the normal shopping posture. Psychologically, these shoplifters are trying to master their environment by "hiding" in the open.

Flight Response
The freeze response is to avoid detection or minimize exposure in the face of danger or scrutiny. This response gives you the opportunity to pause and assess the situation before determining the right course of action to take.

When the freeze response is not enough to ward off danger, the limbic part of the brain switches to the flight response. The aim of the flight response is to distance oneself from the danger. Humans have discovered a modification of the freeze response since it's impossible to run away from a threat or those you are not comfortable with.

We have learned the art of evasion or blocking. Just as a child turns away from an unfavorable food at the dinner table, you might turn away from someone you don't like or a conversation you are not interested in. These evasive or blocking actions include placing the hands in front of the face, rubbing the eyes, or closing the eyes momentarily.

The person might place an object on their lap or point their feet toward the exit. The flight response is also common in negotiation talks. An individual may lean away from the counterpart if he is not interested in the offer. He may lean away from the table or point his feet toward the exit if he's not interested.

Fight Response

Imagine coming across a snake while hiking in the woods. After the initial freezing response to your presence, the snake will try to move away from you. It will turn to attack if you walk toward it, and that is what we call the fight response.

The brain's final tactic to danger is the fight response. Just as an animal turns to attack once it's cornered, we confront danger by resorting to aggression. Mind you, this is a modern world, where your rage might not be practical or legal. Therefore, the brain's limbic system has come up with practical ways of showing aggression.

Arguments are a modern form of aggression. When you think about it, civil lawsuits are also a form of modern warfare in which the litigants aggressively argue over opposing viewpoints.

Although we engage in far less physical aggression than centuries before, it is not uncommon for people to resort to aggressive responses that involve punching, and kicking. Sometimes, an invasion into a personal space can trigger the fight response.

The main reason why I'm explaining this is to help you detect and analyze people who show these signs. One benefit of reading body language is that they can sometimes warn you when someone intends to harm you physically.

How the Limbic System Helps You to Recover from Threats

Thus far, we have observed how the limbic system shields us from threats through the freeze, flight, and fight response. Though this is just half of the equation. Just as Newton's third law states, "To every action, there is an equal and opposite reaction," the response following a freeze, flight, and fight action is always accompanied by a comforting behavior or adapter.

These adapters help to calm us down after we experience a negative stimulus. Comforting behavior or adapters are easy to read and are an indispensable tool for analyzing people. Most people are unaware of the immense significance of adapters in revealing a person's thoughts and feelings. To become a successful reader of nonverbal behavior, you need to know how to decode and analyze these adapters. Why? Adapters reveal a person's thoughts and feelings with uncanny precision.

Types of Adapters You Need to Know

There are different types of comforting behaviors or pacifiers. For example, when we are stressed, we often massage our necks, play with our hair, or touch our face. This is your brain's way of shouting, "Please pacify me now." Sometimes, we touch our lips or leg or give off different nonverbal cues to calm ourselves. Below are some of the common comforting behaviors people use.

Touching or Stroking the Neck

This is a frequent and significant comforting gesture people commonly use to respond to stress. One person might decide to stroke the underside of his chin; another may massage or rub the back of his neck. Some might go further by tugging the flesh of the neck above the Adam's apple. Studies reveal that this area has a high number of nerve endings, which when stroked, lower the heart rate and reduce blood pressure.

Over the course of studying and analyzing people, I've noticed that men and women have different ways of using their neck to pacify themselves. Women are less obtrusive in their comforting behavior; some will twist or touch their necklace repeatedly if they are wearing one. She may cover her neck dimple (the region between the neck and the collarbone) if she feels stressed, insecure, threatened, anxious, uncomfortable, or threatened.

Touching or Stroking the Face

This is a common comfort response to stress. It involves a motion such as tugging or stroking the beard; rubbing, licking, or nibbling on the lips; massaging and pulling on the earlobe with the fore and middle finger; and stroking the forehead. Some people will even puff out their cheeks and slowly exhale when responding to a stressful situation. There are lots of nerve endings in the face, and this makes it an ideal place for comfort behavior in response to negative stimuli.

Whistling

It's common for people to whistle when they are walking down a dark street corner or alley. Whistling is a comforting behavior to an individual when faced with a stressful or scary situation. Some might even talk to themselves as a way of creating an assurance that they are not alone.

Leg Cleansing

When people are stressed, especially during a long, gruesome interview, they often try a comforting behavior by placing their palm down on the top their legs and repeatedly sliding them down the thighs toward the knees. This behavior often goes unnoticed because it frequently occurs under the table or desk. Some individuals will do the leg cleanse activity only once, but it's often done repeatedly. Sometimes, people do the leg cleanse to get rid of sweaty palms caused by anxiety.

People do the leg cleanse mainly to get rid of tension, and it's a good indicator to watch out for when analyzing people.

So how can you detect this nonverbal clue without peeking under the table? I'll advise you not to peek underneath the table for obvious reasons. The best way to watch out for this behavior is to observe people who place one or both hands under the table. You will see the shoulder and upper arm moving in tandem with the hand as it moves along their leg. In my experience, the leg cleanse is an important clue for gauging how stressed and disturbed the other person is.

Security agents are trained to watch out for this behavior, and it's usually an indication of guilty knowledge in an investigation. Marriage counselors are also trained to observe this comfort behavior. If the intensity of this leg cleanse increases, you can deduce that the question is of great discomfort to the person.

We examined two of the three main parts of the brain that is responsible for generating your nonverbal responses. We also looked at the impact of the limbic system of the brain in generating survival mechanisms in the face of danger.

I'm sure you are now familiar with the basics of how the brain sends out stimuli to the environment. However, your work is not done yet. Once you are through with the book, you will become adept at reading many of the nonverbal cues from those around you.

So are you ready to delve into the language of hands and palms?

Reading People Through Their Handwriting

Every person's handwriting is known to be as unique as their personality. You can make an in-depth analysis of everything from their behavior to personality to the thought process. Graphology is the science of studying an individual's personality through how they write. Handwriting goes beyond putting a few characters on paper. It is about glimpsing into an individual's mind to decipher what they are thinking and how they are feeling based on their handwriting.

Here are some little-known secrets about speed reading a person through their handwriting.

Reading Letters of the Alphabet

How a person writes his or her letters offers a huge bank of information about their personality, subconscious thoughts, and behavioral characteristics. There are several ways of writing a single letter and every person has their own distinct way of constructing it.

For example, putting a dot on the lower case "I" is an indication of an independent-spirited personality, originality, and creative thinking. These folks are organized, meticulous, and focused on details. If the dot is represented by an entire circle, there are pretty good chances of the person being more childlike and thinking outside the box. How a person constructs their upper case "I" reveals a lot about how they perceive themselves. Does their "I" feature the same size as the other letters or is it bigger/smaller compared to other letters?

A person who constructs a large "I" is often egoistic, self-centered, overconfident, and even slightly cocky. If the "I" is the size of other letters or even smaller than other letters, the person is more self-assured, positive, and happy by disposition.

Similarly, how people write their lower case "t" offers important clues into their personality. If the "t" is crossed with a long line, it can be an indication of determination, energy, passion, zest, and enthusiasm. On the other hand, a brief line across the "t" reveals a lack of empathy, low interest, and determination. The person doesn't have very strong views about anything and is generally apathetic. If a person crosses their "t" really high, they possess an increased sense of self-worth and generally have ambitious objectives.

Similarly, people who cross their "t" low may suffer from low self-esteem, low confidence and lack of ambition. A person who narrows the loop in lower case "e" is likelier to be uncertain, suspicious, and doubtful of people. There is an amount of skepticism involved that prevents them from being trustful of people. These people tend to have a guarded, stoic, withdrawn, and reticent personality. A wider loop demonstrates a more inclusive and accepting personality. They are open to different experiences, ideas, and perspectives.

Next, if an individual writes their "o" to form a wide circle, they are most likely people who very articulate, expressive, and won't hesitate to share secrets with everyone. Their life is like an open book. On the contrary, a closed "o" reveals that the person has a more private personality and is reticent by nature.

Cursive Writing

Cursive writing gives us clues about people that we may otherwise miss through regular writing. It may offer us a more comprehensive and in-depth analysis of an individual's personality.

How does a person construct their lower case cursive "I?" If it has a narrow loop, the person is mostly feeling stressed, nervous, and anxiety. Again, a wider loop can be a sign that the individual doesn't believe in going by the rule book. There is a tendency to rewrite the rules. They are laidback, low on ambition, and easy-going.

Again, consider the way a person writes cursive "y" to gain more information about their personality. The length and breadth of the letter "y" can be extremely telling. A thinner and slimmer "y" can be an indication of a person who is more selective about their friend circle. On the other hand, a thicker "y" reveals a tendency to get along with different kinds of people. These are social beings who like surrounding themselves with plenty of friends.

A long "y" is an indication for travel, adventure, thrills, and adventures. On the other hand, a brief cursive "y" reflects a need to seek comfort in the familiar. They are most comfortable in their homes and other known territories. A more rounded "s" is a signal of wanting to keep their near and dear ones happy. They'll always want their loved ones to be positive and cheerful.

They will seldom get into confrontations and strive to maintain a more balanced personality. A more tapering "s" indicates a hard-working, curious, and hard-working personality. They are driven by ideas and concepts. Notice how cursive "s" broadens at the lower tip. This can be a strong indication of the person being dissatisfied with their job, interpersonal relationships, and or life in general. They may not pursue their heart's true desires.

Letter Size

This is a primary observation that is used for analyzing a person through their handwriting. Big letters reveal that the person is outgoing, affable, gregarious, and extrovert. They are more social by nature and operate with a mistaken sense of pride. There is a tendency to pretend to be something they aren't. On the contrary, tiny letters can indicate a timid, reticent, introvert, and shy personality. It can indicate deep concentration and diligence. Midsized letters mean that an individual is flexible, adjusting, adaptable, and self-assured.

Gaps Between Text

People who leave a little gap in between letters and words demonstrate a fear of leading a solitary life. These people always like to be surrounded by other folks and often fail to respect the privacy and personal space of other people. People who space out their words/letters are original thinkers and fiercely independent. For them, they place a high premium on freedom and independence. There is little tendency for being overwhelmed by other people's ideas, opinions, and values.

Letter Shapes

Look at the shape of an individual's letters while decoding their personality. If the writing is more rounded and in a looped manner, the person tends to be high on inventiveness and imagination! Pointed letters demonstrate that a person is more aggressive and intelligent. The person is analytical, rational, and a profound thinker. Similarly, if the letters of an alphabet are woven together, the individual is methodical, systematic, and orderly. They will rarely work or live in chaos.

Page Margin

If you thought it's only about writing, think again. Even the amount of space people leave near the edge of the margin determines their personality. Someone who leaves a big gap on the right side of the margin is known to be nervous and apprehensive about the future. People who write all over the page are known to have a mind full of ideas, concepts, and thoughts. They are itching to do several things at once and are constantly buzzing with ideas.

Slant Writing

Some people show a marked tendency for writing with a clear right or left slant while other people write impeccably straight letters. When a person's letters slant towards the right, he or she may be affable, easy-going, good-natured, and generally positive. These people are flexible, open to change, and always keen on building new social connections.

Similarly, people who write slanting letters that lean towards the left are mostly introverts who enjoy their time alone. They aren't very comfortable being in the spotlight and are happy to let others hog the limelight. Straight handwriting indicates rational, level-headed, and balanced thinking. The person is more even-tempered, grounded, and ambivalent.

There is a tiny pointer here to avoid reading people accurately. For left-handed people, the analysis is the opposite. When left-handed people have their letters slanting to the right, they are shy, introverted, and reserved. However, if their letters slant to the left, they may be outgoing, gregarious and social extroverts.

Writing Pressure

The intensity with which an individual writes is also an indicator of their personality. If the handwriting is too intense and full of pressure (there is indentation), the individual may be fiery, aggressive, obstinate, and volatile. They aren't very open to other people's ideas, beliefs, and opinions. There is a tendency to be rigid about their views.

On the contrary, if a person writes with little pressure or intensity, they are likely to be empathetic, sensitive, and considerate towards other people's needs. These people tend to be kind, enthusiastic, passionate, lively, and intense.

Signature

A person's signature reveals plenty about an individual's personality. If it isn't comprehensible, it is a sign that he or she doesn't share too many details about themselves. They fiercely guard their private space and are reticent by nature. On the contrary, a more conspicuous and legible signature is an indication of a self-assured, flexible, transparent, assured, confident, and satisfying personality. They are generally content with what they've accomplished and display a more positive outlook on life.

Some people scrawl their signature quickly, which can be an indication of them being impatient, restless, perpetually in a hurry, and desiring to do multiple things at one time. A carefully written and neatly-organized signature is an indication of the person being diligent, well-organized, and precision-oriented.

Signatures that finish in an upward stroke demonstrate a more confident, fun-loving, ambitious, and goal-oriented personality. These people thrive on challenges and aren't afraid of chasing these dreams. Similarly, signatures that finish with a downward stroke are an indication of a personality that is marked by low self-esteem, lack of self-confidence, low ambition, and a more inhibited personality. These folks are likelier to be bogged down by challenges and may not be too goal-oriented.

Stand Out Writing

If a particular piece of writing stands out from the other text, look at it carefully to understand an individual's personality.

For example, if the text is generally written in a more spread out and huge writing, with only some parts of the text stuck together, the person may most likely to be an uncertain, dishonest, or mistrustful individual, who is trying to conceal some important information.

Concluding

Though studying an individual's handwriting can offer you accurate insights about his or her personality, it isn't completely fool-proof. There are several other factors that are to be taken into consideration to analyze a person accurately. It has its own shortcomings and flaws. At times, people may write in a hurried manner, which can impact their writing. Similarly, the way people construct their resume or application letter may dramatically vary from the manner in which they may write a to-do list or love letter.

If you want an accurate reading of someone's personality, consider different personality analysis methods like reading verbal and non-verbal communication techniques. Various techniques may offer you a highly in-depth, insightful, precise, and comprehensive method of understanding a person's inherent personality.

Body Language and Voice Basics Revealed

D o you know that people communicate much more through what they leave unspoken than what they actually say? Body language accounts for around 55 percent of the entire message during the process of communication. In a study conducted by Dr. Albert Mehrabian, it was revealed that only 7 percent of our message is communicated through words, while 38 percent and 55 percent is conveyed through non-verbal elements such as vocal factors and body language, respectively.

Generally, what people say is well-thought and constructed within their conscious mind. This makes it easier to manipulate or fake words for creating a desired impression. Our body language, on the other hand, is guided by more involuntary movements of the subconscious mind. It is near impossible to fake subconsciously driven actions that we aren't even aware of. When you train yourself to look for non-verbal clues, you understand an individual's thoughts, feelings, actions and more at a deeper, subconscious level. Try controlling the thoughts held within your subconscious mind and you'll know what I am saying.

People are perpetually sending subconscious signals and clues while interacting with us, a majority of which we miss because we are conditioned to focus on their words. Since primitive times, human communicated through the power of gestures, symbols, expressions and more in the absence of a coherent language. You have the power to influence and persuade people through the use of body language on a deeply subconscious level since it's so instinctive and reflex driven.

Here are some of the most powerful body language decoding secrets that will help you unlock hidden clues held in the subconscious mind, and read people more effectively.

Establish a Behavior Baseline

Create a baseline for understanding a person's behavior if you want to read him or her more effectively. This is especially true when you are meeting people for the first time, and want to guard against forming inaccurate conclusions about people's behavior. Establishing a baseline guards you against misreading people by making sweeping judgments about their personality, feelings and behavior.

Establishing a baseline is nothing but determining the baseline personality of individual based on which you can read the person more effectively rather than making generic readings based on body language. For instance, if a person is more active, fast-thinking and impatient by nature, they will want to get a lot of things done quickly.

They may fidget with their hands or objects, tap their feet or appear restless. If you don't establish a baseline for their behavior, you may mistake their mental energy for nervousness or disinterest, since the clues are almost similar. You would mistakenly believe the person is anxious when he/she is hyperactive.

Observe and tune in to an individual completely to understand their baseline. This helps you examine both verbal and non-verbal clues in a context. How does a person generally react in the given situation? What is their fundamental personality? How do they communicate with other people? What type of words do they generally use? Are they essentially confident or unsure by nature?

When you know how they normally behave, you'll be able to catch a mismatch in their baseline and unusual behavior, which will make the reading even more effective.

Look For a Cluster of Clues

One of the biggest mistakes people make while analyzing others through non-verbal clues is looking for isolated or standalone clues instead of a bunch of clues. Your chances of reading a person accurately increases when you look at several clues that point to a single direction rather than making sweeping conclusions based on isolated clues. For instance, let us say you've read in a book about body language that people who resort to deception or aren't speaking the truth don't look a person directly in the eye.

However, it can also be a sign of being low on confidence or possessing low self-esteem. Similarly, a person may not be looking at your while speaking because he/she is directly facing discomfort causing sunlight. You ignore all other signs that point to the fact that the person is speaking the truth or is confident (a firm handshake, relaxed posture etc.) and only choose to look at the single clue that he/she isn't maintaining eye contact to inaccurately conclude that the person is lying. Look for at least 3-4 clues to arrive at a conclusion. Don't make sporadic conclusions about how a person is thinking or feeling based on single clues.

For all you know a person may be moving in another direction, not because they aren't interested in what you are speaking about or looking to escape, but because their seat is uncomfortable.

If you think the person is disinterested, look for other clues such as their expressions, gestures, eyes and more to make more accurate conclusions. Include a wider number of non verbal clues to make the analysis more accurate.

Look at the Context, Setting and Culture

Some body language clues are universal – think smile or eye contact. These signals more or less mean the same across cultures. However some non-verbal communication signals may have different connotations across diverse cultures.

For example, being gregarious and expressive is seen as common in Italian culture. People speak loudly, gesticulate with their hands in an animated manner, and are generally more expressive.

However, someone from England may decipher this behavior as massively exaggerated or a sign of nervousness. Enthusiasm, delight and excitement are expressed in a more subtle manner in England. For the Italian, this retrained behavior may signify disinterest. While the thumbs-up is a gesture of good luck in the west, in certain Middle Eastern cultures it is viewed as rude. If you are doing business with people from across the world, understanding cultural differences before reading people is vital.

Similarly, consider a setting before making sweeping conclusions through non-verbal signs such as body language. For example, a person may display drastically different behavior when he's at work among co-workers, at the bar and during a job interview. The setting and atmosphere of a job interview may make an otherwise confident person nervous.

Head and Face

People are most likely experiencing a sense of discomfort when they raise or arch their eyebrows. The facial muscles also begin twitching when they are hiding something or lying. These are micro expressions that are hard to manipulate since they happen in split seconds and are subconscious involuntary actions.

Maintaining eye contact can be a sign of both honesty and intimidation/aggression. On the other hand, constantly shifting your gaze can be a non-verbal clue of deceit.

The adage that one's eyes are a window into their soul is true. People who don't look into your eyes while speaking may not be very trustworthy. Similarly, a shifting gaze can indicate nervousness.

The human eye movements are closely linked with brain regions that perform specific functions. Hence, when we think (depending on what or how we are thinking), our eyes move in a clear direction. For example, when a person is asked for details that he/she is retrieving from memory, their eyes will move in the upper left direction.

Similarly, when someone is constructing information (or making up stories) instead of recalling it from memory, their eyes will shift to the upper right direction. The exact opposite is true for left-handed folks. When people try to recall information from memory, their eyes shift to the upper left, whereas when they try to create facts, the eyes move towards the upper left corner. A person who is making fictitious sounds or talking about a conversation that didn't happen, their eyes will move to the lateral left.

When there's an inner dilemma or conflict, a person's eyes will dart towards their left collarbone. This is an indication of an inner dialogue when a person is stuck between two choices. Increased eye movement from one side to another can signal deception. Again, look for a cluster of clues rather than simply analyzing people based on their eye movements.

Expanded pupils or increased blinking is a huge sign of attraction, desire and lust. A person may also display these clues when they are interested in what you are saying. If a person sizes you up by looking at you in an upward and downward direction, they are most likely considering your potential as a sexual mate or rival. Similarly, looking at a person from head to toe can also be a sign of intimidation or dominance.

When you are observing a person's face, learn to watch out for micro expressions that are a direct involuntary response based on feelings and thoughts. These reactions are so instinctive and happen in microseconds that they are impossible to fake. For example, when a person is lying, their mouth slants for a few microseconds and the eyes slightly roll.

How can you tell apart a genuine smile from a fake one? Pay close attention to the region around the person's eyes. If someone is genuinely happy, their smile invariably reaches their eye and causes the skin around the eyes to crinkle slightly. There are folds around the corner of the person's eyes if they are genuinely happy. Another clear sign of a genuine smile is a crow's feet formation just under the person's eyes. A smile is often used by people to hide their true feelings and emotions. It is near impossible to fake a smile (which is so involuntary and subconscious driven).

Even the direction of a person's chin can reveal a lot about their thoughts or personality. If their chin is jutting out, he/she may be a stubborn or obstinate about their stand.

Posture

When a person maintains an upright, well-aligned and relaxed posture, he/she is most likely in control of their thoughts and feelings and is confident/self-assured. Their shoulders don't slouch awkwardly, and the overall posture doesn't sag. On the other hand, a sagging posture can be a sign of low self-esteem or confidence. It can also mean placing yourself below others or subconsciously begging for sympathy.

When a person occupies too much space physically by sitting with their legs apart or broadening their shoulders, they are establishing their dominance or power by occupying more physical space.

Limbs

Pay close attention to people's limb movements when you are reading them. When a person is bored, disinterested, nervous or frustrated, they will fidget with an object or their fingers. Crossing arms is a big signal of being, closed, suspicious, uninspired or in disagreement with what you are saying. The person isn't receptive to what you are speaking about.

If you want to get the person to listen to what you are saying, open them up subconsciously first by changing the topic of conversation. Once they are in a more receptive state of mind, resume the topic. When a person crosses their arms or legs, they are less likely to absorb or be persuaded by what you say.

A person's handshake can reveal a great deal about what they think about themselves or their equation with the other person. For instance, a weak handshake is a sign of nervousness, low self-esteem, lack of confidence, submissiveness and uncertainty. Similarly, a crushing handshake can be an indication of dominance or aggressiveness. A firm handshake implies self-confidence and a sense of self-assuredness.

Observe the direction in which a person's feet are pointed. If they are pointed in your direction, it means the person is interested in what you are saying. On the other hand, if they are pointed away from you, the person is looking for an escape route. Feet pointing in your direction or leaning slightly towards you are huge non-verbal signals of attraction.

Tone

The tone of a person's voice can communicate a lot about the way a person is feeling or thinking. Look for any inconsistency in a person's tone. Does the tone and pitch vary throughout the conversation? This can be a signal that the person is experiencing a surge of emotions. Listen to the volume of a person's voice. Something may not be quite right if they are speaking in a softer or louder than usual manner. Observe if the person is using filler words rather than concise phrases or sentences. It can be a sign of nervousness or they may be buying time to make up stories.

A person's tone can convey emotions they try to conceal or are unable to express. They may say something flattering to you but their tone may be slightly sarcastic or bitter, which can be a giveaway to what they are truly feeling. It can indicate a more passive aggressive personality. The meaning of exactly the same words can change drastically when delivered using a different tone, volume and inflection.

Let's say the person ends their sentence on a higher note. Doesn't it sound more like a question than a definitive statement? Similarly, if the person finishes their sentence on a flat note, he/she is making a confident or assured statement. The former can indicate doubt, uncertainty or suspicion, while the latter can be an indication of authority.

Proxemics

Proxemics refers to the physical space maintained during communication between people, which reveals volumes about how they relate to each other. Haven't you experienced a feeling of discomfort when someone tried to invade your personal space or come closer than you appreciate? This person is most likely seeking acceptance from you or trying to make their way into your inner social circle.

On the other hand, if a person comes closer than intended during negotiations, he/she may be trying to intimidate you or subconscious coax you into accepting their conditions. The ideal distance to test a person's comfort level is to stand at a minimum distance of four feet from them. If the person appears open, they are welcoming into their personal space. Similarly, if they are rigid, don't jump into their personal space immediately. They may not be ready to include you into their personal zone.

Mirroring

Mirroring a person's body language is a wonderful way to establish a rapport with a person on a subconscious level. Closely observe a person's body language while they are interacting with you. How is their posture? What are the words they typically use? If they are leaning against the bar or table, follow suit. Similarly, if they sip on their drink, mirror their action. If you spot them resting their elbow on a table, mirror their action.

Mirroring a person's action gives the other person an impression that you are one among them. It works on a primordial level to create sense of affiliation, likeliness and belongingness even before spoken language was invented. Adapt your actions, posture, gesture and movements with the other person to give a feeling of "being one among them." If the person is following your actions, they are seeking acceptance or validation from you.

How Are They Breathing?

There are different ways you can read someone's body language. It can be read by their leg and arm movements, facial expressions, eye contact, or smiles. Do you realize that how a person breathes has meaning, too?

Emotions and how you breathe are connected. You could read a person's feelings by watching the way they breathe. If emotions change, how they breathe might be affected. See if you can notice breathing patterns in your family, friends, coworkers, or significant other. They may not tell you exactly how they are feeling and it might depend on certain situations.

- Deep breathing might indicate excitement, attraction, anger, fear, or love

Deep breathing is the easiest pattern to notice. If somebody suddenly starts to hold their breath, they might be feeling a little scared. If someone takes a deep breath and then shouts, they could be angry. People who are excited, are experiencing shock, or are surprised might suck in a deep breath. They might also take in a deep breath and hold it for a few seconds. If their eyes start to glow this might indicate that they are surprised or excited. A person might start to breathe deeply if they feel an attraction toward another person. You may notice someone take a deep breath in, suck in their stomach and push their chest out in order to try and impress somebody they are attracted to.

- Sighing might signal hopelessness, sadness, or relief

When you sigh, you are letting out a deep, long breath that you can hear. Somebody might sigh if they are feeling relieved after a struggle has passed. They are thankful that their struggle is over. A sign might show sadness or hopelessness like somebody who is waiting for a date to show up. It could also show tiredness and disappointment.

- Rapid, heavy breathing might show fear and tiredness

You may have just seen a person rob a place and they are being chased by the police. You notice they are breathing very rapidly. This is because their lungs need more oxygen since they are exerting a lot of energy because they are running. Their bodies feel tired and their lungs are trying their best to keep up. We feel the exact same effects when we feel scared. This will happen when we experience fear; our lungs need more oxygen, so we begin to breathe faster. You will be able to easily see when somebody has been scared or running by noticing the way they are breathing.

Another interesting fact about breath is that smells can influence breath. Any odors that are tied to emotions can change a person's respiration rate. There have been several studies that have shown that the body will respond to bad and good smells by breathing in a different way. If you were to smell something rotten, you would end up breathing in a shallow and rapid manner. But, if, instead, you smelled baking bread and roses, your breath would be slow and long. The really interesting part of this is that the breathing rate will change before the brain has ever been able to conscious register if the smell is good or bad.

According to *Scientific American*, the emotions that we have with smells and scents are extremely associative. We started learning about these different smells in the womb, and then during our lives, our brains learn to refine our views of emotional rewards, pleasures, and threats that are contained within a certain odor. If a person breathes deeply, then they feel that something is safe, and it creates a pleasurable emotional state. This means if you notice a person's breathing rate suddenly change, let your sense of smell catch up first. It could be that they have gotten a whiff of something they either like or dislike.

The interesting thing is that while we can learn how a person feels based on how they are breathing, the way a person breathes can also affect their emotions. In a 2006 study, published in *Behavior Response & Therapy,* they discovered that undergraduates who practiced slow-breathing exercises for 15 minutes had a more positive and balanced emotional response afterward than the group who were faced with 15 minutes of unfocused worrying and attention.

And it doesn't even have to do with just being calm. In a study by the French scientist Pierre Phillipot, he asked some participants to identify the pattern of breath that they connected with certain emotions such as sadness and joy. They then asked a separate group of people to breathe in a certain manner and then they probed their emotions. The results they got were amazing. If the subjects were told to breathe in a particular manner, even if they were unaware of it, they said that they felt the feeling associated emotion, apparently, out of nowhere.

This is something that you can't readily do, but it is still interesting.

A new idea that is being studied about emotions and breath is that what you exhale also plays a role in emotional response, and that the chemically analyzed exhales were able to figure out how the person felts. In an article from *Science News,* the chemical makeup of the air within a soccer stadium varies when people begin cheering and the same is true in movie theaters. They studied 9500 people as they watched 16 different films that ranged from rom-coms to horrors, and then they studied the air composition of the room to see if it changed during certain scenes that were rather emotional in one way or the other.

The crazy thing is that it did. In suspenseful moments, there were more CO_2 and isoprenes in the air, which are chemicals associated with the tensing of muscles. Every type of emotion came with its own chemical makeup.

Facial Microexpressions

Learning to decode facial expressions is similar to having superpowers. The face with all its expressions which are called microexpressions could be a window into their soul. Knowing how to read them could help you to understand a lot about how someone is feeling.

Methods of Nonverbal Analysis

For you to perform any type of nonverbal behavior analysis, you have to use techniques that can help you describe the behavior in a way so it can be trusted. The advantages of scientific analysis are:

- To select a person's weaknesses and strengths during normal relations.
- To expose lies by using a combination of facial and verbal expressions.
- To anticipate a person's behavior.
- To identify another person's state of mind and emotions.

It doesn't take long to learn these techniques with an interactive and focused program that is based on specific exercises.

Scientific Based

The very first text that was written about emotional expressions was written by a French neurologist, Guillaume Benjamin Amand Duchenne de Boulogne. This text was written in 1862 and demonstrated the method of using electrodes on the facial muscles to establish their relationship between the movements of the facial muscles and the subsequent emotional expression. To honor him, a true, authentic smile can sometimes be called the Duchenne smile.

The Expressions of the Emotions in Man and Animals was written by Charles Darwin in 1872. In this, he says that emotions are just another evolutionary product and are inherited. Body and facial expressions go hand in hand with emotions and look to be the same in people who live in different parts of the world and in other animals and primates. Darwin's studies didn't continue after he died because of the hostility within the scientific community toward his theories and him. He was criticized for saying animals actually have emotions. According to his critics, only humans have the capability to feel things. His theories were based on observations rather than science.

This concept of emotional expressions being universal was discovered one more time in the late 1950s. Researchers like Birdwhistell, Izard, Ekman, Ellsworth, and Friesen tried to get Darwin's theory validated. All of them worked together to develop a set of theories, tests, and methods that created the "Facial Expression Program." They believed the origin of emotional expressions and emotional experiences would be a specific number of inherited neurological programs. We know now that there are certain paths for every emotion that causes a facial expression that is associated with that certain emotion. According to the theory of evolution, emotions have adaptive functions that will let a human react through immediate responses to various stimuli for survival.

There are two groups of nonverbal techniques:

- Decoding technique: This interprets and will give meaning to movements.
- Coding technique: This describes body and facial movements.

Facial Expression Techniques

- ISFE or Interpretative System of Facial Expressions

This was developed by Jasna Legisa in the NeuroComScience laboratory in 2013. It is a table of what facial movements mean. It is comprised of a set of descriptions and tables that order and integrate facial expressions according to the emotions they are related to.

Other than secondary and primary emotional expressions, other facial signs get described as regulators, illustrators, and manipulators. According to Ekman, Izard, and Hjorstjo, emotional expressions get grouped into "big families." All of these "families" include many facial expressions that, even though they mean slightly different things, get united because they receive the same emotional range. Within the "surprise" family, you will have annoyed surprise, face surprise, a real surprise, awe, and many more.

Primary emotional movements get put into three categories:

- The first category includes muscular movements that belong to certain emotions.
- The second category includes movements that might belong to primary emotions.
- The third category includes minor variations to emotions that could be part of many emotional families.

These categorizations make the interpretation and accuracy of the whole analysis.

- Mimic Language and Man's Face or the Hjorstjo Method

An anatomy professor at Lund University located in Sweden, Hjorstjo during 1969 tried to systematically categorize certain facial movements with their meanings into eight emotional families. His handbook reports the decoding and coding of facial expressions so it is possible to determine the facial muscle contractions either in combination or by themselves.

- MAX or Maximally Discriminative Coding System

This system gives meaning to the facial movements instead of just describing them. Izard developed MAX in 1979. Later in 1983, he worked with Hembree and Dougherty to create an advanced version of MAX that was named AFFEX. The created facial configurations that were based on normal expressions of emotions like shame, disgust, pain, surprise, happiness, interest, fear, sadness, and anger. Basically, for every emotion and expression gets classified.

- EMFACS or Emotional Facial Action Coding System

Friesen and Ekman worked to describe the expressions of six emotional families: fear, surprise, anger, disgust, sadness, and happiness. Hager has been working at Ekman's laboratory since 1994 studying facial expressions by using an automatic computer to identify their techniques. This database has created the FACSAID or FACS Affect Interpretation Dictionary system.

- Hanest

During the same year that the first version of FACS was published, the Hanest Manual was also published. The Hanest Manual was created by Gergerian and Emiane who are two French scientists. It has the same agenda of FACS to describe facial movements.

- FACS or Facial Action Coding System

Vincent W. Friesen and Paul Ekman in 1978 introduced FACS or the Facial Action Coding System. In 2002, while working with Hager, they release another version. This one is a descriptive facial coding system and it doesn't ascribe meaning to facial expressions. It contains detailed descriptions of changes that happen because of facial movements.

- BabyFACS or Baby Facial Action Coding System

The exact same structure that is used for adults can be used for small children and babies. During 1993, Oster looked at babies' facial expressions and changed up the descriptions as needed. These are only descriptive and don't give any meanings to the emotions.

Using Interrogation to Detect a Lie

It is important to be smart when trying to detect signs of lying. People easily pass off signs of stress as that of lying because the signs look similar. This is why it is important to look for clusters—meaning, three or four signs—before concluding that someone is lying. When people are shy, embarrassed, stressed, ashamed, or feel inferior, they might appear dishonest.

This is why to detect a liar, you should not just watch out for nonverbal cues. You will need to engage the person in conversation to establish further that they are lying.

Make the Person Feel Comfortable

Create a stress-free environment and build rapport. This is not the time to start interrogating the person or make it obvious that you are out in getting them to spill out the truth. This is the stage to make them feel relaxed if possible. Offer them a glass of water and mirror their body language. With this, the person will likely feel relaxed, and you can see them for who they really are. This will help you read the signs clearly.

Set a Baseline

This is the normal behavior (in terms of talking, gesticulating, etc.) when they are not stressed. With this, you get to know whether the person is putting up a different act from their normal self. You do this by asking simple questions, questions in which they have no reason to lie. We recommend asking something that you already know the answer.

Look for Differences

At times, a liar will not answer your question directly but will give you another correct information, just not what you asked for. Hence, this sort of deviation is a tactic not to answer the question. Most often, they would supply the information they wanted you to ask. This is a typical sign that someone is hiding information.

Ask Them to Repeat Their Story

When you are lying, it is mentally tasking to keep track of information to ensure that the things you supply do not contradict. As a result of this, ask the suspect to repeat the information many times. In the process of repeating the information, a liar might deviate or give inconsistent information that will rat them out.

Ask for the Story in Reverse

This one is mentally tasking. Even psychopaths and professional liars will flop when asked to do this, especially if it requires precise details.

Stare at the Liar in Disbelief

Fake the look of disbelief and give a cold stare. A liar will often get uncomfortable. A sincere person might likely get angry or frustrated and avoid your gaze.

Employ the Power of Silence

This is a good one. Most liars are never comfortable with silence as they get nervous. In desperation to make themselves sound credible, they will fill the silence with information in a bid to appear credible. The silent tactic leaves them anxious as they are confused whether you believed them or not. Without even asked anything, a liar will keep spilling out information that might hurt them in the process. Be sure to give a cold, expressionless look as you use this tactic. This is because a liar is constantly watching out to see whether you bought what they sold you.

Posture and Body Orientation

E xpectedly, posture, and body orientation should be interpreted in the context of the entire body language to develop the full meaning being communicated. Starting with an open posture, it is used to denote amicability and positiveness.

In this open position, the feet are placed openly, and the palms of the hands are facing outward. Individuals with open posture are deemed more persuasive compared to those with other stances.

To realize an open stance, one should stand upright or sit straight with the head upright and maintain the abdomen and chest bared. When the open posture is combined with an easy facial expression and good visual contact, it makes one look approachable and composed. Maintain the body facing forward toward the other person during a conversation.

There is also the closed posture where one crosses the arms across the chest or crosses the legs or sits in a facing a forward position as well as displaying the backs of the hands and closing the fists are indicative of a closed stance.

The closed posture gives the impression that one is bored, hostile, or detached. In this posture, one is acting cautious and appears ready to defend themselves against any accusation or threat.

For the confident posture, it helps communicate that one is not feeling anxious, nervous, or stressed. The confident posture is attained by pulling oneself to full height, holding the head high, and keeping the gaze at eye level. Then bring your shoulders backward and keep the arms as well as legs to relax by the sides. The posture is likely to be used by speakers in a formal context such as when making a presentation, during cross-examination and during project presentation.

Equally important, there is postural echoing and is used as a flirting technique by attracting someone in the Guardian. It is attained by observing and mimicking the style of the person and the pace of movement. When the individual leans against the wall, replicate the same.

By adjusting your postures against the others to attain a match, you are communicating that you are trying to flirt with the individual. The postural echoing can also be used as a prank game to someone you are familiar with and often engage in casual talk.

Maintaining a straight posture communicates confidence and formality. Part of the confidence of this posture is that it maximizes blood flow and exerts less pressure on the muscle and joints, which enhances the composure of an individual. The straight posture helps evoke desirable mood and emotion, which makes an individual feel energized and alert. A straight posture is highly preferred informal conversations such as during meetings, presentation, or when giving a speech.

Correspondingly being in a slumped position and hunched back is a poor posture and makes one be seen as lazy, sad, or poor. A slumped position implies a strain to the body, which makes the individual feel less alert and casual about the ongoing conversation.

On the other hand, leaning forward and maintaining eye contact suggests that one is listening keenly. During a speech, if the audience leans forward in an upright position, then it indicates that they are eager and receptive to the message.

Furthermore, if one slants one of the shoulders when participating in a conversation, then it suggests that the individual is tired or unwell. Leaning on one side acutely while standing or sitting indicates that you are feeling exhausted or fed up with the conversation and are eagerly waiting for the end or for a break.

Think of how you or others reacted when a class dragged on to almost break time. There is a high likelihood that the audience slanted one of their shoulders to left or right direction. In this state, the mind of the individual deviates to things that one will do next. In case of a tea break, the mind of the students will deviate to what one will do during or after the tea break.

By the same measure standing on one foot indicates that one is feeling unease or tired. When one stands on one foot, then it suggests that the person is trying to cope with uncomforting. The source of uneasiness could be emotional or physiological.

For instance, you probably juggled your body from one foot to help ease the need to go for a short call or pass wind. It is a way to disrupt the sustained concentration that may enhance the disturbing feeling.

If one cups their head or face with their hands and rests the head on the thighs, then the individual is feeling ashamed or exhausted.

When the speaker mentions something that makes you feel embarrassed, then one is likely to cup their face or head and rest the face on the thighs. It is a literal way of hiding from shame.

Children are likely to manifest this posture though while standing. When standing this posture may make one look like he or she is praying.

Additionally, if one holds their arms akimbo while standing, then the individual is showing a negative attitude or disapproval of the message. The posture is created by holding the waist with both hands while standing up straight and facing the target person. The hands should simultaneously grip on the flanks, the part near the kidneys. In most cases, the arms-akimbo posture is accompanied by disapproval or sarcastic face to denote attitude, disdain, or disapproval.

When one stretches both of their shoulders and arms and rests them on chairs on either side, then the individual is feeling tired and casual. The posture is akin to a static flap of wings where one stretches their shoulder and arms like wings and rests them on chairs on either side. It is one of the postures that loudly communicates that you are bored, feeling casual, and that you are not about the consequences of your action.

The posture is also invasive of the privacy and space of other individuals and may disrupt their concentration.

If one bends while touching both of their knees, then the individual is feeling exhausted and less formal with the audience. The posture may also indicate extreme exhaustion and need to rest.

For instance, most soccer players bend without kneeling while holding both of their knees, indicating exhaustion. Since in this posture, one is facing down, the posture may be highly inappropriate in formal contexts and may make one appear queer.

When one leans their head and supports it with an open palm on the cheeks, then it indicates that one is thinking deep and probably feeling sad, sorrowful or depressed.

The posture is also used when one is watching something with a high probability of negative outcomes such as a movie or a game. The posture helps one focus deep on the issue akin to meditating.

Through this posture, an individual tries to avoid distractions and think deeper on what is being presented.

If you watch European soccer, you will realize that coaches use this posture when trying to study the match, especially where their team is down. However, this posture should not be used in formal contexts as it suggests rudeness. The posture should be used among peers only.

Then there is the crossing of the legs from the thigh through the knee while seated on a chair, especially on a reclining chair. In this posture, one is communicating that he or she is feeling relaxed and less formal.

In most cases, this posture is exhibited when one is at home watching a movie or in the office alone past working hours. If this posture is replicated in a formal context, then it suggests boredom or lack of concentration.

For the posture where one crosses the legs from the ankle to the soles of the feet while seated, it communicates that one is trying to focus in an informal context such as at home. For instance, if a wife or a child asks the father about something that he has to think through, then the individual is likely to exhibit this posture. If this posture is replicated in a formal context, then it suggests boredom or lack of concentration.

Analyzing People Through the Nonverbals of the Hands and the Palms

hereas the key to success when it comes to both professional and personal relationships lies in the ability to communicate correctly, it is not necessarily the words that one uses but the body language and nonverbal cues that speak volumes.

Hiding behind a barrier is one of the typical responses that we learn at a tender age. We usually do this as a way of offering protection to ourselves. As kids, it was reasonable to hide behind particular solid objects like furniture whenever we realized that we had gotten into hot soup or threatening situations.

As we continue to advance in age, this behavior of hiding becomes sophisticated, as just another behavior pops in. Since hiding behind an object was one of the prohibited behaviors, folding the arms tightly across the chest is also another behavior that came in during threatening situations. As teenage checks in, kids will learn how to make the gesture of crossed arms more evident by relaxing the hands and arms just a little bit. They would also accompany the signals with legs that are crossed.

Defensive Arms Display

The gesture of folding the arm has been upgraded to the extent where now people try to make it even less evident to others who are seeing them. When a single or both the arms are folded, maybe across the chest, a barrier is then created. This is one of the ways of blocking all that might be perceived as threats or situations that are undesirable. When arms are neatly folded across the regions of the lungs and heart, it is a sign of protecting these very vital organs. That shows that the behavior of crossing the arms could be inborn.

One thing that is for sure is that when a person has a defensive, or nervous attitude, there are possible chances that he will have his hands tightly on the chest as a sign of feeling threatened.

Self Hug

Hugging is one habit that has evolved with time. As kids grow up, their parents or caregivers will hug them when they are in tensed or distressed situations. As adults, there is usually an attempt to recreate these very comforting gestures each time we get to stressful circumstances.

Apart from taking a whole arm-cross sign that could reveal to all that we are in a fearful circumstance, there is a subtler version that women usually substitute. A Partial Arm-Cross is a situation where a person's single arm is made to swing across the body to or even make contact to the remaining arm that forms a boundary and appear like she's hugging herself. In places or events where a person might appear stranger to the group or does not have the self-confidence, the use of partial arm barriers is always very rampant. Any female taking her full place in a stressful circumstance will usually make claims that she is just okay, which could be so untrue.

Men, on the other hand, use a partial arm barrier that is known as Holding-Hands-With-Yourself. Men who stand right in front of a crowd to give a speech or receive an award commonly use this. The other name for this kind of self-hug gesture is Broken Zipper Position. The gesture gives the man a sense of security since he will be able to safeguard his expensive items and can also bar the consequences of getting a very unwelcome frontal blow.

It is the exact place that men take in a line at a food court or to get social security advantages and goes ahead to reveal their vulnerable and depressed feelings. This brings on the feeling of having another person holds your own hands. Adolf Hitler, for instance, used this gesture so frequently as a way of masking the sexual inadequacy that he felt as someone who just had a single testicle. He did this in public.

It is evident that the man's hands were shortened by evolution to enable them to take up some of these errands and reach some places without straining. This is due to the fact that when chimpanzees, which are our closest primate cousins, assume the very similar situation, their hands usually cross at their knees.

The Territorial Arm Displays

Status can also influence one to use a given arm folding gesture. A superior kind of person can make his superiority evident by failing to fold his hands, saying that they are not afraid of anything.

For instance, if a general manager of a firm is introduced in a company function, he will usually stand back from them, with his hands in his back or by his side or in a superiority position. At times, he can also put one of his hands in his pockets, which is a sign of non-involvement. In very rare cases will such a person fold his arms across the chest as an indication of the tinniest sign of being nervous.

Once they have shaken hands with the boss, the new employees might also opt to cross their aims either fully or partially because of their main apprehension of being in the company of the highest leader of the company. Both the company's GM and the new workers will feel very comfortable with their respective gesture clusters as each one of them is signaling his status that is relative to the other.

However, things might get a different twist when the GM meets a young and upcoming male individual who might display some superiority and even signal that he is as important as the general manager. What happens is that after the two have given everyone a dominant handshake, the upcoming young officials may be forced to fold their arms as a signal with both the thumbs folding in the upward direction.

The gesture shows two arms that are crossed and all the thumbs facing up, indicating that the individual is in control and feeling just okay. As he continues to speak, he will gesture with his thumbs as a means of displaying to others that he has a self-confident kind of attitude, and the arms that are folded still provided a sense of security.

A person who is not only feeling submissive and also very defensive will sit in symmetrically implying that the other part of their body is the best mirror to the other side. They will show the tone of a stressed muscle and appear like they are sensing an attack, while someone who is dominant and defensive will just opt to sit in an asymmetrical way, where one part of the body does not mirror the other.

How To Spot Insecurity In The Rich And Famous

People who are usually exposed to others, such as movie stars, TV personalities, politicians, and royalties usually don't intend their audience to realize that they either nervous or unsure of what they are doing or saying when they are on the limelight. When on display, these people usually prefer to project a controlled, calm, and cool attitude each time they are on display. However, their apprehension or anxiety normally comes out in not so good forms such as the crossing of arms. Like it is the case with all arm-crossing signals, a single arm swings across the body in the direction of the other arm, but instead of the arms getting to cross each other, one hand touches or hold on to a watch, or a handbag on or close to their other arm. For another time, the boundary is created, and the feeling of security is attained.

Men who wear cufflinks are usually captured fixing and adjusting them when they cross the dance floor or a room full of people. Adjusting the cuff-links was one of the trademarks of Prince Charles, who applied it to feel secure each moment he walked across an open place fully aware that there are other people who are watching them.

One would be deceived to believe that after close to a whole century of being confronted by large crowds and scrutinized in public, royals like Prince Charles will try to resist some of the nervous feelings that are revealed by his small arm-crossing.

A self-conscious and anxious man will usually find himself trying to adjust the band on his wristwatch, rubbing his hands together or checking what are contained in their wallets. At times, they can also be seen playing with the buttons on their cuff or even using any gestures that enable his arms to cross in front of their body.

One of the most favorite gestures for a businessman who is insecure is making in ways to an official event holding a folder or briefcase in front of their bodies. To someone who has some training, these signals are just giveaways since they achieve no definite aim as opposed to a try to hide their nervousness. If there is a better place of observing these body signals, then it has to be at any place where individuals walk past a large group of bystanders. A good example would be a man who moves to the dancing podium to look for a female dancer who can join him on the dance floor or a person who cross the stage to go and get an award.

The use of hidden arm barriers by women is not easily noticeable as that of men. This is because women will be able to grasp into things such as purses or handbags if they are unsure of themselves or become self-conscious. Princess Anne and other loyalties would usually clutch some flowery items each time they are making inroads in public. The flowers and handbag clutch are the favorite for Queen Elizabeth. There are very limited chances that she would be carrying lipstick, theatre tickets, and credit cards in the purse.

Instead of that, she applies this as a kind of safety blanket when necessary and as a way of sending out a strong message. The royal watchers have recorded a total of twelve signs that she sends to her minders whenever she wants to leave, go, or be taken from a conversation she does not enjoy.

There is a very usual means of creating a strong barrier is to carry up a glass of cup with two hands. Usually, one would only need one hand to hold the cup, but two hands will enable the insecure person to create a nearly invisible boundary. These kinds of signals are applied nearly by everyone, and there are some of us who are fully aware that we are applying them.

The Legs Reveal The Mind's Intentions

The more distant from the human brain a body part is placed, the less awareness the human being have of what is really happening with the body. Most people, for instance, are much aware of their face and the kind of signs and expressions that they are showing to the public. As a matter of fact, there are certain expressions that we can practice, such as putting on a brave face or looking unhappy when disappointed by a close friend or relative. After our face, the body parts that we are much less aware of got to be our hands and arms. They are closely followed by our stomach and chest, and we are also not so much aware of our legs and nearly oblivious to our feet.

This implies that the legs and the feet are a very vital information source regarding the attitude of a person since most people are not so much aware of what they are doing with these body parts and do not think of faking gestures with them in the manner they might apply with their face. Someone who is appearing composed and in full control while the foot is taping repeatedly or making short jabs in the air shows their frustrations at being unable to escape away from the trap they are.

Knowing Me, Knowing You

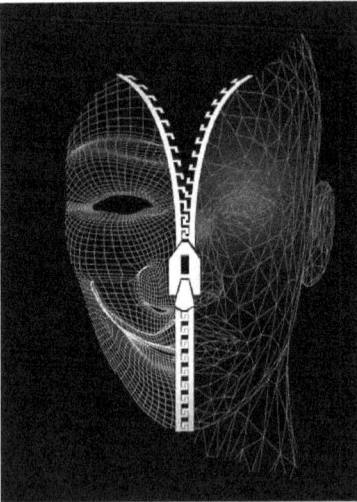

I t is an intriguing prospect, isn't it? The idea that you could precisely decipher how and what someone is saying without them having to utter a word? The second body language that they are giving off which others might miss. But not you. Because you're perceptive, and you know exactly what to look for when you begin analyzing someone.

When was the last time you stopped to analyze yourself, though?

Before you can begin analyzing someone else, you need to learn how to analyze yourself first. Self-awareness is one of the core principles and a sign that someone possesses emotional intelligence. This key trait is what helps you understand who you are as a person. What your beliefs and your values are as well as the way that you react and respond to others.

When you look at yourself in the mirror, how well do you know the person who is looking back at you? Learning to analyze people is an important skill to have because it can help you strengthen the relationships that you have with them. But there is one relationship you need to work on strengthening first - the relationship with yourself.

Why It Is Important to Understand Yourself Before You Can Analyze Others

If you don't learn how to recognize and identify with yourself, you'll never be able to do that with others, too. At least, not entirely. When you're attempting to learn how to analyze someone else, you're attempting to look for clues which will be indicators about who they are and what they're feeling. However, it is equally important to do the same thing with yourself. When you're looking for clues as to why people react the way that they do, you also need to look for clues about why you react the way that you do. Only when you understand yourself entirely, can you then begin to understand others.

To understand and build better connections with the people around you, you need to first understand yourself. If you don't have the necessary self-awareness to begin understanding why you do or say the things that you do, how can you begin to understand someone else's intentions and where they're coming from? Remember, someone else could be reading and assessing your body language, too. Analyzing you the way you may be doing to them. What message do you want them to read?

So, if self-reflection is so important, why don't more people do it? There could be several reasons for that, including:

- *They're Unsure about What Needs to Be Done.* Many people don't necessarily spend enough time in self-reflection because they're simply unsure about what needs to be done. We are quick to analyze others, but when it comes to ourselves, that's where many fall short.

- *They Don't Particularly Enjoy It.* Self-reflection is not always the easiest process, especially because it forces people to confront all the emotions and thoughts that they would prefer to ignore. In fact, it is one of the most difficult skills to master personally. Weaknesses, vulnerability, fears, and more are all the emotions that many people prefer to keep buried or hidden, and self-reflection is a process that is going to force all these unpleasant qualities to the surface, which is why many people don't enjoy this process. For many people, acknowledging the flaws is the most difficult part of the process. Nobody likes to admit they've got faults which they need to work on. Pride and ego get in the way. This is largely responsible for why many people suffer from denial, completely blind to their own faults.

- *They Don't Understand How It Can Help.* As people, we tend to be motivated to do something only if we can see what is in it for us. We need the motivation to get us to do something we may not necessarily like or enjoy. Only if we can clearly see the benefits do we then take action. This is why many people don't spend enough time self-reflecting, because they don't see how this process is going to help them. They don't view it as a good use of their time, especially when they have a busy schedule.

- *They Don't Have Time.* It's a common phrase that is uttered these days. *I don't have time.* There never seems to be enough time to get things done. To those who feel like they are constantly on the move from one task to the next, asking them to spend several minutes in quiet self-reflection doesn't make any sense because they don't see it as a good use of their time.

When you understand yourself and your personality a little better, you'll naturally become more understanding of others, too. If you notice the way that you behave and the body language signals that you emit, you'll be able to understand why someone else might be doing the same thing. If you're an introvert, for instance, you'll be able to acknowledge why other introverts may be displaying certain signals, because you will recognize them in yourself. It works the same way for extroverts, too. Understanding others begins, very simply, with understanding yourself first.

Self-Awareness and Emotional Intelligence

Human emotions remain the driving force of a lot of the things we say, think, and do. Emotions can be a very powerful, volatile force within us that may sometimes have difficulty trying to control. This is why emotional intelligence is linked to self-awareness. A clear sign that someone possesses a high level of emotional intelligence is when they can master and control not just their own emotions, but they can also exercise influence over the emotions of others, too.

Yes, emotional intelligence allows you to influence the way other people are feeling. In fact, you'll be able to understand the people around you even better when you've got emotional intelligence on your side. Made of five core principles, emotional intelligence involves self-awareness, self-reflection, motivation, social skills, and empathy. These five traits are the tools which are going to help you analyze others even better than ever because each of these qualities is working in a way that encourages you to be more observant about a person's body language.

Self-reflection, which is what this chapter has largely been focusing on, is first understanding your own emotions so you can then regulate your responses and reactions (self-regulation). To begin developing a deeper understanding of the people around you is where social skills and empathy come into play. Empathy is the ability to put yourself in someone else's shoes, to see things from their perspective, and to understand where they are coming from and why they feel what they feel. When you can connect with them on this level without them even realizing it, your social skills will then play a role in getting them to open up more and be comfortable around you.

Identifying Your Strengths and Weaknesses

People are quick to talk about strengths, but not everyone likes to admit they have weaknesses. However, the only way you're going to begin developing a great understanding of yourself is by recognizing both your strengths and weaknesses together. It isn't going to work if you just acknowledge one, but not the other. Understandably, it's never enjoyable to admit that you have weaknesses. It makes you feel inadequate, and for some people, it feeds into their deep-rooted fear about not being good enough. Others may have a lot of pride, and they simply do not like to admit they have weaknesses because they don't want others to think any less of them.

When you embrace both your strengths and your weaknesses, you begin opening yourself to even greater potential for personal growth. Weaknesses are nothing to be ashamed of. It just means that there are areas for you to work on and you're getting there eventually. This is why self-awareness is so critical.

It puts the power of change in your hands, and you are in control. You are the one who gets to decide if these traits continue to remain weaknesses, or whether you're going to work on them and turn them into strengths.

Everyone should make time to get to know themselves better. The benefits of being more aware of who you are and what makes you tick include:

- *It is the Key to Being Happier.* Chances are if you're not happy, you're mind is going to be too preoccupied to effectively analyze and decipher someone else's body language anyway. The more you understand yourself and your emotions, the happier you will be. It also makes it much easier for you to express your desires.

- *It is the Key to Less Internal Conflict.* Another happiness barrier that many people experience is internal conflict. Understanding yourself allows you to connect to your mind, body, and soul, and when your external actions work in tandem with your internal emotions, the internal struggle that you face becomes significantly less.

- *It is the Key to Tolerance and Understanding.* Analyzing what other people feel is a lot better when you've got tolerance and patience on your side. Your awareness about the emotions and challenges that you face will make you more perceptive towards the plight of others, that they may be going through the same thing you are.

- *It is the Key to More Self-Control.* Knowing yourself also means your values are grounded and you know what your preferences are. It affords you better decision-making abilities because you know what you're willing to put up with, what's acceptable, and what isn't.

- *It is the Key to Succeeding at Work.* Excelling at your job goes beyond just being good at what you do. It involves the way you communicate, the way you relate to others, how well you present yourself and of course, the secret messages that you're revealing through your body language. An employee, for example, may say that they love their job, but their body language could be conveying something completely different. If they aren't self-aware, they won't even realize this is happening. But you know who will notice? The bosses (and your other colleagues who are paying attention).

Effective Tools and Strategies to Help You Analyze Yourself

Most people spend far too much time trying to think about what someone else's body language might be saying and not enough time on what their own body language is saying. Becoming too preoccupied with trying to say all the right words makes it easy to forget that your body could be saying something entirely different. If the person you're in a conversation with is perceptive enough, they'll quickly pick up that your body language and your words are not a match.

Consider this scenario, for example. You've just had a long, hard day at work. You're exhausted, drained, and just looking forward to changing into your pajamas and spending some quiet time alone. Then, the phone rings and your best friend wants to talk to you and she sounds upset over the phone. Because you care deeply about your friend, you meet up with them like they requested and agree to talk it out. However, throughout the conversation, you're constantly stifling your yawns, sitting back with your arms crossed over your chest, and constantly checking your watch every couple of minutes while thinking you're being subtle about it. Your friend picks up on these signals and comes to the conclusion that you're either bored or disinterested and they might become even more upset because of that. They leave, visibly upset while you're wondering if you've said the wrong thing. Obviously, you didn't say the wrong words. In fact, you said everything that your friend wanted to hear. Your body was just telling a much louder different story without you even realizing it.

Analyzing yourself is an exercise which is easier than you might think. Start applying these strategies below to help you master your self-reflection process:

- *Taking Note of Your Feelings Daily:* How often do you find yourself noticing your thoughts? Probably not very often up to this point. That is about to change though because your thoughts are a very important part of who you are.

These thoughts drive you more than you realize. It shapes your perceptions, your attitudes, and your responses to the people, situation, and circumstances you find yourself embroiled in. Start spending several minutes a day just pausing to notice and monitor what's on your mind. Are the things that you're thinking positive? Negative? Are you empowering yourself and feeling happy? Or stressed, worried, and imagining a lot of worst case scenarios?

- *Writing It Down:* A thought journal can be your greatest asset in your self-awareness reflective exercise. During these moments when you're stopping to monitor your thought process, think about writing them down. Like a daily log journal of your thought process. Write about everything that you're feeling and don't hold back. Your happiness, sadness, frustration, anger, how you reacted today, and what you thought about doing. Anything and everything goes. Each time you've got a thought, put it down.

- *Evaluating Your Thought Patterns:* Another reason why a thought journal comes in handy is that it gives you a chance to look back and evaluate your thought patterns. At the end of the week when you look back on everything you wrote down, what's a common pattern that occurs? What's a train of thought which tends to repeat itself? We've got so many thoughts running through our minds daily that by the end of the day or week, we've forgotten most of the thoughts we had. With a journal, however, you can go back anytime and evaluate everything that went on, anytime. Even something that happened a few months ago.

- *Noting Your Perceptions:* Did you know that the way you perceive people and situations could sometimes lead you to misread things? Or draw on conclusions and assumptions which may not be entirely accurate. For example, if you were having lunch with a friend and you noticed that their body language or facial expression was signaling that they were in a bad mood. Or perhaps feeling irritated and angry. The way you perceive situations could lead you to believe that perhaps she is angry with you or you did something wrong, even though that may not necessarily be the case. When faced with these types of situations, this is where self-reflection once again proves its importance. By analyzing your beliefs, taking note of what you heard, what you saw and what you felt that led you to perceive a situation in a certain way, you will come to realize that situations are often affected a lot by factors which we may not necessarily be aware of.

- *Knowing Your Values:* Your values provide a crucial insight into who you are as a person at the very core. A lot of your current values are based on the experiences that you've been through. Values change as your life experiences change, and rarely do they stay stagnant throughout a person's life. When you can pinpoint and identify each of your values, it brings you one step closer to connecting with yourself. To deepen your understanding and acceptance that this is who you are as a person, and this is what you value in your life. When you know what you want, achieving your goals becomes much easier.

- *Reflect On Your Past Experiences:* Does the way you behave and react to certain situations now a result of your past experiences? A lot of the signals and subconscious messages that we give off is a reflection of our beliefs, values, and attitudes. Even though we don't realize we're doing it. Which is why, it is important to conduct this self-analysis to get to know yourself on a deeper level.

- *Reflecting On Your Self-Esteem:* This is another challenging aspect for many to confront, especially when they suffer

119

from a lack of confidence. What is the status of your health esteem right now? Do you believe you are confident? Worthy? Worthwhile? Or do you struggle with a crippling belief that people are constantly judging you? That you're never good enough? The levels of your self-esteem will affect your body language and the way that you are perceived by others. If you notice when someone is feeling shy or awkward because they're hunched, nervous-looking, and exhibit nervous mannerisms, you can be sure someone else will notice the same thing about you. No matter how well you believe you may be concealing your true feelings.

- *Be Honest with Yourself:* Be completely honest with yourself, even if you may not like what's reflected back at you. You're not going to be doing yourself any favors if you aren't. It's okay, this is an opportunity for you to work on improvements, and there is nothing to be ashamed of if you realize that you have some less than desirable areas that need to be worked on. Even if you try to pretend those shortcomings don't exist, remember that your body isn't capable of telling a complete lie all the time. Someone, somewhere out there is going to be able to analyze your hidden messages. Learning to understand yourself is how you learn to spot the same signals in someone else when you analyze them.

Types of Liars

In the same way, there are different reasons why people tell lies. There are different types of liars too. Some people might lie because it is the easiest thing to do, while others might be sick. The following are three of the common types of liars you might encounter as you go about your day:

- pathological liars
- sociopaths
- compulsive liars

Pathological liars are individuals who lie as a response to anything. They have perfected lying down to an art, such that it comes so naturally to them. It might not be easy to detect their lies.

One of the defining characteristics of a sociopath is that they don't empathize. Their lies must persist whether people get hurt in the process or not.

Compulsive liars are very easy to identify because they lie for whatever reason that comes to mind. They are not the best liars and will, in most cases, lie to get out of a situation, often clumsily.

Let's take an in-depth look at each of these types so that we understand what makes them tick and how to identify them.

Pathological Liars

The scientific term for pathological lying is *mythomania*. You might already deduce from this that these are people whose lives revolve around myths. This is a chronic behavior to the point where it becomes a habit.

While most people can tell a white lie from time to time to prevent someone from getting hurt, pathological liars, on the other hand, don't need a reason to lie. Even when they don't have a reason to lie, they still do. Interacting with such people can be very difficult and frustrating because you are never sure whether to trust them or not.

Pathological liars tell tales that make them appear to be the hero of the situation or tales that evoke sympathy. There might not be anything for them to gain in telling a lie, but the attention matters to them anyway. The following are some of the characteristics that can help you identify a pathological liar:

Pointless Lies. Many people tell lies to get out of an uncomfortable situation or to avert a crisis or whichever reason. A pathological liar, on the other hand, is comfortable lying even when there is no clear benefit to the lie. It is very frustrating interacting with such people because even after you learn about the truth, you cannot reconcile their lie and any achievable gains.

As a result, most people who are victims of pathological liars are left wondering what their motivation might have been. Is there something they stand to gain from the lie in the near future? Are you still living part of the lie, or is it over? This level of uncertainty can be disconcerting and creates a painful experience for people who interact with pathological liars.

Complicated Lies. One of the defining characteristics of pathological liars is the lengths they go to sell a lie. They create stories that are too complicated, dramatic, and have a lot of detail. This is possible because they are also very good at telling stories. Their tales might be compelling because of how good they can spin stories in an instant.

Victim or Hero Stories. Another thing that defines a pathological liar is their desire for attention. They must be at the center of the story. In this case, they will either be the victim in the story or the hero, but never the villain. People should either applaud them or sympathize with them, hence their tales. They also tell these stories to gain approval and validation from their audience.

Strong Belief in Their Tales. The problem with pathological liars is that as the lie grows, so does the liar's belief in it. Pathological liars are known to be deluded with their version of the truth. It gets to a point where they strongly believe their lies are the truth.

The challenge comes in dealing with a pathological liar who is not aware of their lies. Some people lie too much to the point where medical experts who attend to them believe they might not be in a position to tell apart the reality from the lie they built their lives around.

Perhaps one of the key highlights of a pathological liar is the fact that they are naturals when it comes to pulling a performance. Their eloquence is amazing, and it is very easy for them to engage people and entertain the audience.

They tend to get away with many lies because of how convincing and surprisingly lovable they are. Ask them one question, and they will go into a verbal tirade that might charm you instead of addressing the question you asked.

Different Versions of One Tale. A pathological liar is so creative that they need to make everyone believe in their stories by any means possible. As a result, they tap into their creativity to keep the audience entertained whenever they can.

Quick Responses. We all love someone who can address our concerns as fast as possible. This is one of the traits of pathological liars. They will respond to any issues raised very fast. However, you might realize that their answers are vague, and instead of answering the question, they try to throw you off your line of thought.

Sociopathic Liars

The term sociopath sends chills down your spine. You might feel unsettled and afraid. There are very many descriptions that have been put forward for sociopaths, but they all agree on a few things; sociopaths lack moral capacity or standards, and they don't have a conscience, or if they do, it only exists to serve their needs (Lipman and Pizzurro, 2016).

To understand how sociopathic liars operate, it is important that we take a deep look at the definition of sociopaths. Sociopaths can be identified in four groups:

Affective. Sociopaths can't empathize. They don't feel or show emotions at all. It is pointless expecting a sociopath to see things from your perspective or to care about what you feel concerning their actions.

Interpersonal. They cannot form deep connections with people when it comes to social interactions. Most of their interactions are superficial. It is very easy for a sociopath to put on a show to impress someone, but it is no more than a smokescreen. They are the embodiment of antisocial beings. Their partnerships, friendships, and relationships are meaningless and can use deception when necessary to gain the advantage they seek.

Antisocial. The basic construct of a sociopath is that they are immune to normal social tendencies. They believe they are all alone in the world. This is how they live their lives, locking out any interpersonal connection or societal interactions. This also explains their penchant for breaking the law.

Behavioral. The behavior of a sociopath is unpredictable. They are unreliable, cannot be trusted to set goals, or take responsibility for their actions. They can't even understand the responsibility for their actions, let alone owning up to them. They are also very impulsive.

At this point, you can already understand how damaging sociopathic liars can be in your life. Sociopathic liars are extreme in everything they do. This is one of the main reasons why you should be wary of them.

They feel no pain or remorse. If they are out to hurt you, they will keep at it until they think they have gained as much pleasure from your pain as possible.

Sadly, they are also very good impressionists. This is how they get people to fall for their charm. The first time you meet them, they are very likable. They can easily lure you into a trap, and by the time you realize what's going on, you are so deep into the web that getting out can choke you to death.

Other than the fact that they cannot feel emotions, they also have no desire to understand what their actions do to others. Your pain might be thrilling to a sociopathic liar. They are manipulative people and will never reveal emotions unless they do to trick you. There is always an explanation for that ill deed they subjected you to. Their explanations are in such a way that you might even feel guilty and remorseful, yet you are the victim in the situation. The following are some of the characteristics of sociopathic liars:

Strained and Difficult Relationships. Sociopathic liars struggle to establish healthy bonds with people in their lives. Because of this, most of the relationships they are in are full of chaos and are always unstable. One of the reasons for this is that instead of trying to establish a relationship, they try to exploit people around them through intimidation, coercion, or lying to them. All this is done for their benefit.

No Empathy. Are you hoping for empathy from a sociopathic liar? You are looking in the wrong place. Lack of empathy is one of the defining traits that identify people with antisocial personality disorder. Because they cannot empathize, sociopathic liars are a very dangerous lot. Someone who cannot feel remorse or pain for their actions is capable of doing anything and, to any limit, without care.

Dishonesty. Deceit and dishonesty come so easily to a sociopathic liar. If they are in trouble, it is easier to tell a lie than to admit the truth. They will also lie for any reason, as long as they can get what they want.

Gross Irresponsibility. Sociopathic liars tend to be highly irresponsible. From social obligations to financial prudence, they don't care about anything. They don't believe in recourse for their actions, and this is why most of them end up on the wrong side of the law.

Aggression. When interacting with a sociopathic liar, you should watch out for aggressive outbursts. This is someone who might not care what you feel, but they know what they want. If they can be aggressive and threaten you into submission, they will do it. It is common for a sociopathic liar to cut your conversation aggressively and interject with whatever they want you to hear.

Manipulation. Sociopathic liars are master manipulators. Everything they do is about them. They can charm and seduce their way into your life, but all this is aimed at a personal gain or for their pleasure. They take a lot of pleasure in hurting you for entertainment. While most of the manipulative sociopaths can be charming, this does not always apply to all of them.

Hostility. Hostility is an interesting principle when discussing sociopathic liars. While they might not necessarily be hostile by nature, it is easy for them to create a hostile environment and have you as an active participant without your knowledge. How does that happen? A sociopathic liar can respond to your reaction or behavior by interpreting it as a hostile response. As a result, they will seek revenge, in which case they become more hostile than the perception they created of you. Since they feel you hurt them, they will only be satisfied when they hurt you back.

Affinity for Risky Behavior. Sociopathic liars are very dangerous, given their desire for risky behavior. They don't care about theirs or anyone else's comfort or safety. It is easy for them to initiate or engage in risky behavior like crime, drug abuse, unsafe sexual acts, or gambling. Be wary of people in your life who are drawn to such activities because they might be trying to lure you in.

You might also realize that in a very dangerous or scary situation, they are uncharacteristically calm. Everyone might be freaking out after an accident, yet there is one person in your midst who doesn't seem to be threatened or afraid.

Impulsive Actions. Everyone makes an impulse decision from time to time. The difference between sociopaths and normal people is that even in your moment of impulse, you are still aware of the consequences of your actions. On their part, they have no disregard for consequences.

Laughter, Smirks, and Smiles. Sociopathic liars will speak to you with an evil smirk on their faces. They enjoy your pain and are thrilled by the fact that you are willing to go along. This is because they cannot empathize. They cannot help themselves from enjoying your pain.

You Are Special. Be careful with someone who makes you feel so special. They treat you differently from everyone else. When they are around you, they are emotionally astute and deep in their conversations and seem to pay attention to everything you want. However, at the same time, everyone else has a very bad observation about them. These are signs that you might be interacting with a sociopathic liar.

Sociopathic liars are very tricky because they have also perfected the art of telling lies. Whenever they talk to you, they can be compelling and come off as sincere, yet this is not their true intention. What they are really after is getting you to let your guard down and see them as genuine, yet they are not.

Justify Wrongdoing. It is difficult for a sociopath to admit that they are wrong. Instead, they will try to make you believe that you are wrong. This is someone who can do something so bad, but when you confront them about it, they try to make you believe it is okay to do what they did, and something is wrong with you if you feel otherwise.

Compulsive Liars

There is too much exaggeration in the world today. Social media has made it very easy for people to live fake lives. They try to portray themselves as something else, often opposite of who they truly are. Outright lies, distorted information, convenient truths, and half-truths—all these are common experiences you will come across today.

There is not much difference between compulsive liars and pathological liars. They both lie on impulse and will try to be as persuasive as possible. You might come across some literature that uses both terms interchangeably.

Compulsive lying is a situation where someone is used to lying that it becomes a habit. Even when they have no reason to lie, they still do. Compared to pathological liars, it is very easy to spot a compulsive liar. While pathological liars are creative and charming, compulsive liars try to get by. They spring a lie and hope it works. When they are lying, they will exhibit most of the common signs that someone is dishonest, like avoiding eye contact, breaking a sweat, or rambling over their words. They get anxious, especially at the slightest hint that you have them figured out.

Most of the time, compulsive liars don't have an ulterior motive behind their tales. As a result, they end up lying even about things that will hurt them. It might be difficult for them to admit the truth even if they have been figured out already. Persistent compulsive lying might be a sign that someone is suffering from any of the following:

- narcissistic personality
- borderline personality
- substance abuse
- attention deficit hyperactivity

- bipolar
- impulse control issues

Experts believe that compulsive lying is not necessarily a sign of psychosis. This is because most of the time, these individuals are not withdrawn from reality. Most of them can tell apart their lies from the truth. Many compulsive liars become what they are as a result of their immediate environment. For example, an individual who is brought up in a house or neighborhood where people gain advantage through deception will soon catch on, especially if those around them do not impose consequences on lying. As a result, to them, the benefits always trump the risks involved.

Many of these are short-term approaches, which do not pan out well in the long-run. Keeping track of all the lies becomes a problem and stressful. There is also the risk of strained relationships if their lies unfold, and in some cases, they might have their day in court.

Given the closeness between pathological liars and compulsive liars, it is almost difficult to tell them apart. However, the following are some differences that can help you distinguish between the two:

Pathological liars:

- have a clear motive and intent
- show very few signs of lying
- appear to be in control of their lies
- might be defensive when their lies are challenged
- the lie is a function of their illusory reality
- extravagant and extremely detailed tales, which might be modified each time

Compulsive liars:

- are compelled to lie as a survival mechanism
- can admit to lying when confronted but might not stop lying
- are aware of the difference between their lies and reality
- tell stories that they believe the audience needs to hear
- spontaneous and don't put a lot of thought into their lies
- lie because they can, even when there's no benefit involved

To be safe, you have to learn to treat liars with caution. While most of the things they say might be lies, they might also tell the truth from time to time. The challenge lies in distinguishing the difference between their lies and truths. This is where your ability to read people comes in handy.

Study their body language carefully over time, and you will learn to know the signs of trouble. You can also learn some of the subjects that they love to lie about and dig deeper to understand why especially if these are people who are so close and dear to you. Understanding the context is important in helping you understand them and protect you from the impending risks. When dealing with liars, you must also try not to withdraw from reality. Irrespective of your affection toward them, you have to respect the fact that the lies will happen again. This is who they are, so try not to take things too personally. You can also recommend treatment for them, especially for liars whose plight is already diagnosed.

Rapport by E-Mail

The same principles as in face-to-face and telephone conversations also apply in correspondence, which has become part of our daily life due to such technical innovations as SMS, e-mail, and chat. The only difference is that you can no longer mirror the body language or the tempo of the person's speech, but you can still agree with his views, opinions, and expectations. Even in the letter, you can try to copy the "tone" of the interlocutor and his mood. Determine who you are dealing with: a serious or frivolous person? Is the writing style official (formal) or friendly? Does he write long sentences or short ones? Paragraphs or intermittent phrases? What words does he use— slang, terms, borrowings? Does he have "favorite words"? Determine the expression form of your addressee and copy it. Suppose you got this message:

"Hi ... getting ready for Friday ... is everything valid? / Sa.

It will be a mistake if you answer it as follows:

"Hello, Samus!

I did thorough research and concluded that it would be more efficient to schedule an appointment for the afternoon. Be so kind and let me know as soon as you have such an opportunity if the indicated time is right for you.

Respectfully,

Henrik Fexeus.

A more appropriate answer would be this text:

"Hello!

Friday is good. But maybe better after lunch?

Henrik.

This is very important when communicating by email. Emails did not replace the usual letters, as many of them feared. In any case, the manner of communication remained the same. Email replaced phone conversations. In the e-mail, we express our thoughts in a language close to the spoken. The problem is that spoken language is not always clear. Much depends on the context: on the tone of voice, the pace of speech, pauses, smiles, movements of eyebrows, nods of the head, etc. (hereinafter I will discuss in more detail facial expressions during a conversation). However, in electronic correspondence, we do not have this context. We use the same words as in conversation, but without the "canvas" that gives them shape. Hence the need for emoticons, or emoticons, of which the most common :-) and :-(, as well as: -P and many others. We have redesigned the whole alphabet of abstract characters to convey to the interlocutor what we mean. But this was not enough for us: a lot of abbreviations appeared, like plz (Eng . please—please), 4ever (forever—forever), lol (laughing out loud—laugh out loud), etc. Thanks to them, you cannot be afraid that they will take your joke seriously or your text will not fit into one SMS. It is important not only to create rapport but also easy to understand, to use the same methods of expression in electronic communication as your interlocutor.

The Old Workaround: Make Another Talk About Yourself

Since ancient times, it happened so that most of all we love to talk about ourselves. The old school guru, a professional in the field of rapport creation, Dale Carnegie wrote in his book How to make friends and influence people in 1936: to make someone believe that you are a wonderful interlocutor, you need to start talking about yourself and then just sit and nod from time to time.

By allowing a person to talk about himself, you will protect yourself from undue attention: he simply will not notice that you are trying to mirror him. Allowing your interlocutor to talk about yourself is the shortest path to establishing rapport.

Did it Work? How to Check if Rapport is Installed

There are many ways to check if rapport is installed. One of the goals of rapport is to lead the other. So why not try it? Change something in the signs of body language or in the voice and see: does the other person follow you? If rapport is established, people constantly follow each other. If you find that the person does not repeat your movements, then go back a step and try again to establish contact. Now, wait for a new opportunity to check. Most often, there is a constant exchange of movements between people, until both come to the conclusion that the conversation is over.

What to Look For

It would be nice to determine immediately whether you are interested in the interlocutor or not. Pay attention to how he sits: whether both feet are on the floor, or one is thrown over the other, and if the back is tense or not. Wide-spaced legs, thumbs in the pockets of pants indicate self-confidence. This "macho"—the pose is often used by men. If two legs are parallel to each other, then the person is neutral towards you. Crossed legs can talk about the need to visit the toilet or that the person feels insecure. But all these poses speak of interest in you and a desire to listen, a desire to determine your and your position on the social ladder.

The "cowboy" position, when one leg is slightly bent and the sock is looking to the side, indicates that the person is mentally far away from you.

A bit like tai chi. Do not confuse this position with the one where one leg is simply placed in front of the other. We often stand like this, but the center of gravity is shifted forward. The movement indicates a person's desire to leave. Maybe he was bored with you or he just thinks about something else and no longer listens to you. Maybe he had an appointment or he noticed someone with whom he needed to talk. No matter how hard he tries to listen to your words, his head is busy with other things, and you need to let him go. Do me a favor— end the conversation as soon as possible, without trying to cram important things into the farewell phrases: there is too much risk that the person will not remember anything. It is better to save an important conversation until the next meeting.

When talking, it is also worth paying attention to whether the interlocutor looks into your eyes. It is important that he looks exactly in your eyes, not in a window or to the side, and does not look around the room, as if in search of an emergency exit (for the mental and physical bodies). If you are sitting, the person you are interested in is usually leaning towards you.

Watch Your Pupils

Pupil size matters too. Watching the pupils is not as difficult as it seems. When we show interest, our pupils spontaneously dilate. Of course, the same thing happens in the range of brightness of light, and in a dark room, our pupils are dilated. Sometimes even dark clothes are enough for the interlocutor's pupils to widen when they look at you, so this fact does not always mean a person's interest in you. Therefore, we must first monitor the changes. If the illumination in the room remains the same, and the interlocutor's pupils widen, it means that he is showing interest in you.

Many textbooks give an example: in ancient China, jade traders were forced to wear soot-darkened glasses to hide the size of their pupils. Traditionally, merchants and buyers had to bargain, and if the merchant showed interest, the price could be too high. Therefore, he tried to keep a low profile, but one thing he could not control was the size of the pupils. For a long time, sunglasses were the trademark of jade traders in China.

Nowadays, poker players use the same trick. If you have to watch a tournament, note that many players appear in dark glasses in the final round. Other popular attributes are a scarf and hat. No matter how skillful a poker player you are, you still cannot control your nervous system. Whether you like it or not, your pupils live their own lives and expand when you are excited.

A person with dilated pupils shows interest to you, and you, in turn, show interest in him. We love those who love us, don't we? Pupil dilation is a powerful signal that our subconscious cannot fail to notice. In one test, men were shown two photos of the same woman. The photos were the same with only one small difference—on one the woman's pupils were dilated. Men (heterosexual) should have indicated which of the two photos they find more attractive. Everyone chose the photo where the woman's pupils are dilated, although they could not explain their choice. And they really did not see the difference, but their subconsciousness noted that in one photo a woman signaled her interest in a man-spectator, whereas in the other she was neutral. And this alone made her more attractive in the eyes of men. And who said that in a woman the most important thing is beauty?

Detecting Lying and Deception

Notably, each one of us would like to easily determine deception at any level such as personal, social, and organizational levels but it is not that easy. Some professions that rely wholly on determining the truth in personal and social contexts such as law agencies, health agencies, and media agencies invest heavily in determining the truth value of their productions, but they fairly fail despite having immense resources.

There is only one reliable way to determine lying and deception, and that is establishing a baseline for the target individual and comparing against this baseline as well as doing the adequate prior investigation before confronting the person. Unfortunately, creating a baseline for each and conducting relevant background study is not always assured due to the time factor and resource constraints and this implies that a speedy analysis of body language and verbal communication can help determine a likelihood of a truth or a lie.

Verbal Hints of a Liar

Liars Tend to Respond to Questions That Were Not Asked

If a person is lying, then he or she wants to cover as much ground as possible, and this includes answering questions that were not posed. By answering questions that were not asked, the individual is prompting the speaker to a particular direction and does not want to be caught off guard. Answering questions that are not asked may also give the individual lying an opportunity to deny the speaker adequate time to analyze the answers given by continuously bombarding the interrogator with new information and ideas. Lastly, answering questions that were not asked also helps the layperson to appear well prepared and knowledgeable in what is being asked.

Liars Tend to Answer a Question with a Question

Expectedly, most liars will respond to a question with another question to shift the burden of thinking and responding to the interrogator. Most politicians employ this tactic when being interviewed, and it is meant to buy them enough time to recall information to the main question. For most liars, not responding is akin to affirming that they lack memory of what is being asked or what happened. The other purpose of responding to a question with another question is to irritate the interrogator and derail his or her composure. Responding to a question with a question is a defensive tactic indicating attempts to hide something.

Most Liars Tend to Make Self-corrections to Avoid Sounding Uncertain

As indicated, most liars want to ensure that each area is covered to eliminate any doubts because allowing room for doubt may expose them. For this reason, most liars tend to self-correct to ensure the information given is irrefutable. In most cases, liars will repeat the correction to ensure that the interrogator and the audience also capture the self-correction. As expected, the liar will blame the need to self-correct on a slip of the tongue or the fast nature of the interview. Another reason for self-correction by a liar is that the individual has a premeditated script and outcome and keeps forcing everything to align with the premeditated picture.

Liars Tend to Feign Memory Loss

As expected, most liars need a safe escape button when cornered and feigning memory loss is a favorite excuse for most liars. When a liar is cornered, then he or she will cite memory loss and later institute self-correction to attain the preformed script. Try watching interviews with politicians to appreciate how they feign memory loss to escape explaining something and pretend to have recalled the information when there is an opportunity to sound believable.

Most Liars Tend to Report What They Did Not Do as Opposed to What They Did

People that lie will give an account of what they did not do to avoid being held accountable. If a liar dwelled on what he or she did, then the individual can be held accountable, and this is not something that a liar wants. However, if a liar dwells on what they should have done, \ he or she has a large degree of freedom to give any answer and avoid scrutiny. Again, try watching a recorded or filed interview with any politician to appreciate how this technique is employed.

Liars Tend to Justify Their Actions Even When not Necessary

Expectedly, most liars are insecure and are uncertain that they sound convincing. For this reason, they over-justify everything because they feel that no one believes them even when people have fallen for the lies. When examining a potential liar, look for signs of unnecessary justification, and again, politicians will provide a good case study of over-justification.

Most Liars Avoid Mentioning Emotional Feelings in Their Version of Events

Since a liar is faking everything, he or she will avoid mentioning feelings that were associated with what is being reported. Mentioning emotions may force one to show them. For instance, if you were talking about an exciting event that you witnessed, then your facial expressions and voice should manifest positive emotions, and this is not something a liar wants because he or she is not assured of the consistency of verbal communication and body language.

Most Liars Are Careful, and Will Insist on a Question to Be Repeated

Finally, liars focus more on what is being asked because they only want to accept a question that they are certain of responding to. Liars dwell more on what the question is and what the interrogator wants to help them generate convincing information. The other role of wanting questions repeated is to help the liar elicit a response by making up one because there is none.

Nonverbal Hints of a Liar

Liars Randomly Throw Gestures

The hand gestures are among the best indicator of positive and negative emotions and are difficult to fake in a consistent manner. If one is angry but is pretending to be calm, he or she will throw gestures randomly. Most liars get irritated when taken to the task of what they just said and are likely to throw random gestures in the air even as they try to sound calm.

Against the Norm, Liars Speak Faster than Usual

People that normally do not speak fast will suddenly speak fast when they are lying. Speaking fast helps, the person denies the audience adequate time to listen and analyze the information. Speaking fast also allows the liar to exhaust all of the rehearsed information, as any interjection will throw the liar off balance. Speaking fast also indicates that the person is uncomfortable with the audience or the message and wants to finish fast and end the experience.

Liars Sweat More Than Usual

People sweat, and it is normal. However, more than normal levels of sweating even when the weather is fine may indicate that one is panicking and feeling cornered. All these may indicate a sign of a liar.

Liars Avoid Eye Contact

Most liars shun eye contact or give a sustained stare to intimidate the target person. Shunning eye contact indicates that the person feels awkward or embarrassed about what he or she is presenting to the audience.

Pacing Up and Down

If one paces up and down more than necessary, then the individual is likely lying. All these indicate feeling uncomfortable with the message and the audience.

Destroy Perception and Build Understanding

Unfortunately, many missed opportunities, acts of violence, and lapses of judgment occur due to inaccurate perception. Many people lose the opportunity to connect with others because they rely so heavily on initial judgment. Perception is defined as, "the ability to see, hear, or become aware of something through the senses." We gather conclusions about people from the information we receive from them. If we have a negative encounter, likely, we will perceive that person in a bad light. Body language and perception are the two components that equal a conclusion. The way someone positions themselves, holds their hands, or even moves their eyes can be taken a certain way. Although perceiving body language is a natural part of social development, perception can always be altered. We have the grand ability to be able to acknowledge something without jumping to conclusions. Is this really possible when interpreting body language?

Absolutely! One of the primary keys to building understanding is letting go of preconceived associations. For example, a young woman is always standing with her hands crossed, eyes lowered, and mouth downturned. Upon looking at her, you could conclude that she is prudish, stuck up, and distant. This may prevent you from speaking to her. In reality, the young woman is far from stuck up. Rather, she suffers from social anxiety and is uncomfortable in large crowds. She has a fear of carrying on a conversation along with personal insecurities. She desperately wants to make friends but doesn't want to make the first move. This disconnect creates a whirlwind of false notions that prevents pure human connection. Since one person perceives her as being stuck up, they avoid sparking a conversation without truly getting to know her personality. This occurs often and is the result of misunderstandings.

Breaking down those preconceived notions about certain behavior involves eliminating one-way thinking. As opposed to assigning only one meaning to a specific body movement, open your mind to the possibility of other reasonings behind behavior. Environmental factors may even alter traditional body language meanings. Crossed arms usually translate to feelings of self-consciousness or disapproval. However, in an extremely cold room, does it have the same meaning? When talking with a friend during a sunny day, does their looking to the side mean they are lying? Or could the sun be extraordinarily bright? Situational factors are also imperative to drawing definite conclusions. Breaking eye contact doesn't automatically mean your friend isn't interested in your conversation. Perhaps they are fatigued or swamped with personal issues at the moment. It's important to be flexible with how you perceive behavior. By understanding that there is always a reason behind everything, you will learn to give others the benefit of the doubt.

The traditional saying, "You can't judge a book by its cover," is vital to making social connections. A woman with scrunched brows, a downturned mouth, and hooded eyes may give off the impression that she is always angry. However, upon getting to know her, you realize she is extremely friendly. Perhaps that is the natural structure of her face. The same rings true for a man who engages in deep eye contact, leans in towards his subjects, and touches hands as he speaks. These clues may indicate that he is romantically interested in whomever he is talking to. In reality, that may be his way of showing interest in the conversation. It could almost be likened to respect.

Cultural differences may influence how we perceive certain behavior. For example, in the United States, we typically nod our head signifying, "Yes." However, in Greek cultures, a head nod means "No." In Portugal, individuals may tug their ears when something tastes delicious. Comical, yet true, Italians interpret this as a suggestive move with sexual undertones. Europeans kiss openly in public, whereas traditional Asian countries view this as inappropriate in public. His mother, no doubt, taught him how to show respect and interest to those to whom he is speaking. Although his actions came off as flirtatious, he was simply acting on a natural impulse. When analyzing others, it's key to remember that everyone comes from a different family that implemented different expectations for behavior. Some families may communicate through touching and warm embraces while another maintains a respectful distance. Before taking offense, consider how they grew up in conjunction with their personality. Perhaps they truly like you, and they are showing you in their own unique way.

Another key way to destroy perception from initial judgment is to get to know the person. Sure, someone may come off as rude, shy, aloof, or even angry. However, are they less deserving of having a social connection with you? Have they done anything concrete that prevents you from associating with them? The initial breaking of the ice may be challenging, but the results are worth it. When approaching someone who gives off negative body language, it's important to consider these tips if attempting to make a connection:

• Ask them about their interests.

• Discuss commonalities and attempt to make a connection.

• Ask them about their family. Do they have siblings? Is their family near or far?

• Share something special about yourself. This may open the door for further conversation.

• Simply ask them how their day is going.

There are a plethora of ice breakers that can be used to approach someone who may seem unapproachable. By doing so, you will learn that, although perception is key, understanding is what shapes relationships. You could be passing up on a purposeful friendship because of a misunderstanding. By taking the additional time to understand someone else, you will then understand their body language. You will learn what encompasses their inner being. This will help you to develop an open mind when building relationships.

Manipulation and Neuro Linguistic Programming

What is Neuro Linguistic Programming?

Neuro Linguistic Programming, or NLP, in simplest terms is the programming language of your mind. We've all had instances where we attempted to communicate with someone who doesn't speak our language. The outcome? They didn't understand us!

You go to a restaurant abroad and ask for a fancy steak but end up receiving insipid stew owing to the misinterpretation of language and codes.

This is precisely what happens when we try to communicate with our subconscious mind. We think we are commanding it to give us happier relationships, more money, a better job and other, similar things. However, if that's not what is actually showing up, something is being lost in translation. The subconscious/unconscious mind has the power to help us accomplish our goals only if we program it using codes it recognizes and understands.

If you are asking your unconscious mind for steak and receiving stew, it is time to speak its language. Think of NLP as a user manual for the brain. When people master NLP, they become fluent in the language of the subconscious mind, which is excellent when it comes to re-programming their own and other people's thoughts, ideas and beliefs. This gives them the power to influence and persuade people, and on the downside, even manipulate them.

Neuro Linguistic Programming is a set of techniques, methods and tools for enhancing communication with deeper layers of our brain. It is an approach that combines personal development, psychotherapy and communication. Its creators (John Grinder and Richard Bandler) claim that there is a strong link between language, behavior patterns and neurological processes, which can be used for enhancing learning and personal development.

Influence versus Manipulation

So, do you believe a hammer is a tool of utility or destruction? Well, it depends on how you use it, right? Or what purpose you use it for.

NLP is potent when it comes to getting people to do what you want them to. It is the hammer that can be used to fix a nail in the wall or destroy a piece of wood. Similarly, NLP can be used to build something positive, or it can be used for a destructive purpose (manipulation).

NLP and manipulation have nearly the same meaning. Both are about generating the desired effect on other people without obvious exertion. However, one key difference between influence and manipulation is that the latter is meant to influence others to meet the manipulator's selfish goals through means that can be unfair, unlawful, sneaky, or insidious. Things are contrived through underhanded methods to turn out in favor of the manipulator. A manipulator often preys on the insecurities, fears and guilt of other people. In turn, victims of manipulation feed dissatisfied, frustrated, trapped and unhappy.

Conversely, influence is the ability to inspire people in an admirable, charismatic and honorable way. We are often inspired by influential people and aspire to model our life on theirs. There is a general feeling of positivity related to them, and we feel positively impacted in their company. Not every influence is positive, which is why we use terms such as "bad influence" to signify a person's negative effect on us. However, manipulation is never categorized as good or bad. It always operates with sinister motives. That is the primary difference between influence and manipulation.

Influence is a double-edged sword that can be used positively and negatively, while manipulation only operates with a negative, narrow and selfish perspective to meet the objectives of the manipulator.

While manipulation has self-centered and questionable motives, influence can also be positive. In contrast to manipulation, influence has positive connotations, which considers other people's needs, goals and desires. Don't we, as parents, want to influence our children to lead happier and healthier lives? Similarly, as a manager, we want to influence our team to put in their best efforts.

NLP is a mind control tool that can do both – build and damage.

How is NLP Used for Manipulating People?

NLP training is conducted in a pyramid-like structure, with sophisticated techniques reserved for high-end seminars. It is a complex subject (whoever said anything related to the human mind would be easy?). However, to simplify a complicated concept, NLPers, or people who practice NLP, pay keen attention to people they work with. They watch everything from eye movements to skin flushes to pupil dilation in order to determine what type of information people are processing.

Through observation, NLPers can tell which side of the brain is dominant in a person. Similarly, they can tell what sense is the most active within the person's brain. The eye movements can determine how their brain stores and uses information. It is also easy to decipher whether the person is stating facts (telling the truth) or making up facts (lying) by looking at his/her eye movements.

After gathering this invaluable information, NLP manipulators will subtly mirror and mimic their victims (including speech, body language, mannerisms, verbal linguistic patterns and more) to give a feeling of being 'one among them.'

NLPers will fake social clues to lead their victims into dropping their guard and entering a more open, receptive and suggestible state of mind, where they become ready to absorb whatever information their mind is fed. Manipulators will cleverly use language that focuses on a person's predominant senses.

For example, if a person is focused on his/her visual sense, the NLP manipulator will most likely use it to his/her advantage optimally by saying something like, "Do you see where I am coming from?" "Can you see what I am trying to tell you?" or "See it this way?" Similarly, if a person is a predominantly auditory person, the manipulator will speak to them using auditory metaphors like, "Just hear me out once, Tim" or "I hear you."

By mirroring their victim's body language and verbal linguistic patterns, NLP experts, or NLPer manipulators, attempt to accomplish a clear objective – building rapport. The objective is the same – to strike a rapport with their victims, which then makes it easy for the victims to let down their guard.

Once the manipulator uses NLP to build rapport and get the victim to let down his guard through clever use of body language and verbal patterns, the victim becomes more open and suggestible. Fake social cues are fed to the victim to make their minds more malleable.

Once they build a rapport, NLPers will begin to lead the victim into increased interaction in a sublime manner. After having mirrored the victim and establishing in the victim's subconscious mind that he/she (the manipulator) is one among them (the victim), the manipulator increases his/her chances of getting the victim to do whatever the manipulator wants. They will subtly change their behavior and language to influence their victim's actions.

The techniques can include leading questions, sublime language patterns and a host of other NLP techniques to maneuver the person's mind wherever they want. The victim, on the other hand, often doesn't realize what is happening. In their view, everything is occurring naturally/organically or according to their consent.

Of course, manipulators (however skilled) may not be able to use NLP to get people to behave in a manner that is completely out of character. However, it can be used to steer people's responses in the desired direction. For instance, you can't convince a fundamentally ethical and truthful person to act in a dishonest manner. However, you can use it to get a person to think in a specific direction or line of thought. Manipulators use NLP to engineer specific responses from a person.

NLP attempts accomplish two ends, eliciting and anchoring. Eliciting occurs when NLPers use language and leading to draw their victims into an emotional state. Once the desired state is accomplished, the NLPer will then anchor the emotion with a specific physical clue - for example, tapping on their shoulder. This simply means that an NLPer can invoke the same emotion in you by tapping your shoulder.

For example, let us say the NLP manipulator makes you feel depressed or unworthy using language, leading and other NLP techniques. This is followed by tapping the back of your hands in a specific manner to create anchoring. Thus, each time they want to create an emotion of being disillusioned, depressed and unworthy in you, they will tap the back of your palm. It is nothing but conditioning you to feel in a certain way with linked physical clues.

Now that you have a fair idea of what NLP is or how manipulators can use it for submission, what can you do to guard yourself against NLP manipulators?

Here are some tips to prevent NLPers from pulling their remarkably smart yet sneaky tricks on you:

1. Be wary of people mirroring your body language. Agreed, you didn't know this until now, but people imitating or copying your body language is one of the biggest red flags of them trying to manipulate, influence or persuade you to act in a desired manner. I really enjoy testing these NLP experts using subtle hand gestures and leg movements to gauge if they are indeed mirroring my body language to establish a rapport.

If they follow suit, that's my clue to flee! Experienced NLPers have mastered the art of subtle mirroring, which means you may not even realize they are imitating your actions. NLP beginners will instantly imitate the exact same movement in their eagerness to establish a feeling of oneness. Good way for you to call their bluff!

2. Confuse with eye movements. Another fantastic way to call an NLP manipulator's bluff is to notice if they are paying very close attention to your eyes or eye movements. NLP users often examine their target or victim's very carefully. The eye movements are scrutinized to gauge how you access and store information.

In effect, they want to determine what parts of the brain you are utilizing to gather clues about your thoughts and feelings. I say beat this by darting your eyes all around the place randomly. Move them upwards and downwards or from side to side in no clear pattern. You are throwing your NLP manipulator off course. Make it appear natural. Their calibration will go down the wayside.

3. Beware of people's touch. If you know a person practices NLP, and you are in an especially heightened or intense emotional condition, do not allow them to touch you in any manner. Just throw them off course by suddenly laughing hard or flying into a fit of rage. Basically, you are confusing them about the emotion they need to anchor. Even if they attempt to establish a physical clue to invoke certain emotions, they'll be left with a mixed bag of crazy laughter, rage and whatever else you did.

4. Watch out for permissive language. Typical language used by NLPers includes "be relaxed," "relax and enjoy this," and other similar statements. Beware of this NLP, hypnotist style language that induces you into a state of deep relaxation or trance to get you to think or act in a specific manner. Skilled or covert manipulators rarely command in a straightforward manner.

They will cleverly seek your permission to give you the impression that you are doing what they want you to do out of your own free will (one of their many sinister tricks). If you observe experienced hypnotists, they will never outright command you to do anything but seek your permission to make it appear as if it is being done organically, with your consent.

5. Guard Against Gibberish. Watch out for mumbo jumbo that just doesn't make any logical sense or twisted/complicated statements that mean little. For example, "As you free the feeling of being held by your thoughts, you will find yourself in alignment with the voice of your success." Does this make any sense? NLP manipulators won't say anything purposeful, but rather, they will program your emotional state to lead it where they want to.

One of the best ways to guard against this sort of hypnotism-NLP induced manipulation is to urge the manipulator to be more specific. "Can you be clearer about this?" "Can you specify exactly what you mean by that?" It won't just interrupt their cleverly set technique but will also force the interaction into precise language, thus breaking the trance brought about through ambiguous words and phrases.

6. Don't quickly agree to anything. If you find yourself being compelled to make an instant decision about something important, and it feels like you are steered in a specific direction, escape the situation. Wait a day to make a decision. Do not be swept or led into making a decision that you do not want to make on an impulse. Sales professionals are adept at manipulating buyers into purchasing something they don't need using sneaky manipulation and NLP tactics. When someone rushes you into a decision, it should be a warning signal to back off and hold on until you've thought more about the situation.

Conclusion

As I conclude this book, I will advise that you drop all the prejudice you have against anyone. In other words, be sure to meet people on a neutral ground. Make sure there is no bias, for it is when you have a clear and neutral mind toward everyone that you can accurately read a person. Any bias will end up clouding your judgment, especially if you want to ascertain if someone is a liar.

Humans, by nature, are complex beings. Whether we like it or not, our subconscious constantly gives out information even without our knowledge. That is why someone might say something at times but their body language reveals something else. Many times, the body language gives the true intent of people. If you, however, do not have the required skill of reading people, especially their body language, you will miss out on the signs even though it is staring right at you. This is one of the things you will gain from this book. Imagine the upper hand you will have if you are able to see past the words people voice out and know them for who they really are!

This is the book that will help and equip you with the skills to get the best out of every interaction. Be it a romantic, professional, and casual relationship, you can make it better. You will get to understand the relationship well and see past the veil and mask everyone you meet is putting up.

All in all, bear in mind that the art of reading and analyzing people is a skill not restricted to a group of people. You also do not have to go to some school or take up a course before you can analyze people. This book has detailed the psychology of reading people. All you have to do is read and practice what you have learned. You are not going to be a badass secret service agent overnight. It takes time, commitment, and practice. Moreover, make sure you are discreet. It makes no sense making it obvious that you are trying to analyze people. With this, you give them the opportunity to be defensive by faking their body language and giving you what they think you want.

DARK PSYCHOLOGY SECRETS

How to Master Mind Control, Manipulation, and Emotional Influence through NLP and Persuasion. The Beginner's Guide to Improve Your Skills to Analyze Body Language.

ADAM JOHNSON

Introduction

Dark Psychology is the art of manipulation and the control of one's mind. Personality scholars agree that there is a personality profile, the dark triad, that determines certain behaviors socially or extremely selfish that involve suffering from others and skip social norms, thinking only of their benefits over anything or person.

The dark triad (or the Dark triad) is a personality profile based on a combination of the following three factors:

Psychopathy (Psychopathy): is a person with a tough personality, "callous," cruelty behaviors, and a very limited empathy. They are people who have no remorse, moral, or ethical standards are indifferent, and are often cynical and insensitive.

Machiavellianism (Machiavellianism): people with superficial charm and very manipulative. For example, they are people who can use other people to get what they want; they lie, they take advantage of who they can cheat and cheat.

Narcissism (Narcissism) consists of belief of superiority, grandiosity and vanity, and high emotional explosiveness. They are people who want everyone to admire them and pay attention to them, who believe they deserve a higher status or a social prestige and who expect special and favorable treatment and who, if they are not treated as they think they deserve, can react with anger, rage or aggressiveness.

Also, they are usually people with an unpleasant treatment (even being superficially charming), with very limited self-control (they can be very nice and suddenly have a fit of anger); they are usually aggressive, not very responsible and are not honest.

There is a great difference between the sexes, because it is much more frequent to find this personality profile in men than in women, unlike other personality profiles (such as an anxious profile).

What is manipulative behavior?

Deception is central to manipulative behavior. Very manipulative people are experts in the game of deception and in combination with the general coldness that they (often) have, they are merciless.

People who manipulate a lot often do not see people as living beings, but rather as a means to reach a goal.

That often means that once they have arrived at their 'destination,' they will certainly not think twice about leaving you on the side of the road.

The worst part is that they sometimes want to play it so that you are the guilty one and they are the victim. That is the tricky thing with people with manipulative behavior.

From small things about insisting that you come to their office or take you by surprise and immediately make a choice that is also part of the manipulation. This is also in line with one of the other important parts of manipulative behavior: intimidation.

Manipulators like to intimidate and belittle because it puts them in their position of power and puts them above others.

People also manipulate for power and money, but also status and vanity. So manipulation is often the improvement of one's situation (at the expense of others!)

Causes of manipulative behavior

Unfortunately, the cliché that people who show manipulative behavior during their youth have been mistreated or have suffered trauma is true.

Being physically abused by parents or emotionally by, for example, narcissistic parents can have a huge effect on a child who can express himself in terribly nasty ways.

Another reason that people behave manipulatively is when there is a lot at stake, such as in politics.

A certain type of people will do everything to stay in power once they have experienced it, with all the consequences that entail.

Many narcissistic people, such as managers and politicians, do everything to maintain their power and status.

This is often also why a 'ladder' is created at schools and universities with a group of people who will do everything to stay 'at the top.'

The parties, luxury houses and cars, expensive watches, and designer clothing, everything is about them to convey a sense of authority. Often these people are also narcissists.

However, there are also people who naturally have the impulse to behave manipulatively, and they are often found in the situations mentioned above. These people are also called psychopaths.

Examples of manipulative behavior

Although this may all sound a bit far away and perhaps even unrealistic, manipulative behavior is more than enough in everyday life: You wrote an important file yesterday afternoon and gave it to a colleague so that they could look at it again and then send it.

When you came to work this morning, your boss was at your desk and started screaming angrily that you never wrote that file.

So after the boss was finished, you went on high legs to your colleague, and something very strange happened: your colleague claimed that you never gave him that file, but he did it in such a convincing way that you started your memory to doubt!

This is gas lighting and is a textbook example of manipulative behavior.

Manipulative people will also not accept guilt under any circumstances: You and a friend fought this week, and after thinking about it for a while, you also concluded that you might have reacted a bit exaggerated.

You determine to go to your friend's house to make it up, and after you apologize and get accepted, you notice that your friend did not apologize.

If you ask for it subtly, the answer is short: "No, of course, I don't have to apologize! If you hadn't done that stupid, I wouldn't have gotten angry. "

This is, of course, strange reasoning and is almost iconic for manipulative behavior.

There is one good example of manipulative behavior:

You were ill this week, and that is why you were sick at home all week. It was so bad that even walking from the bed to the couch was too much trouble.

Fortunately, one week later you feel a little better, and if you are down the line later that week to encourage your son to play football, you tell one of the parents along the line about it who took your son last week because was sick.

The answer was not what you expected:

"Is that all? That's nothing, man! Last year I was so sick that I bruised my lungs, I coughed so hard! And yet I stood along the line! Because you should be there for your children, you just don't have to put yourself up like that and just come along. You are a good parent, aren't you? "

Not only was this a bad answer (because you were sick last week and you really couldn't), it was also a manipulative answer.

The parent has not only minimized your problems and put them in the spotlight, but they have also belittled you.

Dark Personality Traits

Various researchers and psychologists have given different number of dark personality traits. According to Paulhus and his colleagues, there are four different dark personalities that one has to encounter in his everyday life. Those dark personalities are Narcissists, Machiavellians, Nonclinical psychopaths, and Everyday sadists. According to Paulhus, many psychologists confuse the traits of a mysterious personality. Every dark personality trait given by Paulhus and colleagues tends to be outgoing and extrovert, but on the other hand, they have clear cut significant differences.

However, the majority of psychologists have identified the three Dark Personality traits named "Dark Triad." The three traits which come under Dark personality are sociopathy, Narcissism, and Machiavellianism. People usually consider dark personality traits negative, however not every aspect associated with these traits is negative some come with positive characteristics as well. Therefore, you can say that these traits are both beneficial and harmful. In this section, the three aspects of Dark Triad are given along with an additional trait that is given by Paulhus.

To make you clear about these personalities, let's have a look on characteristics of these personalities.

Personality Traits in the Dark Psychology

1. Narcissists

Narcissists are the personalities holding the element of grandiosity and are high in attention and admiration seeking behavior. People often get easily annoyed with these types of personalities. Narcissists have a highly elevated sense of self-worth and possess a dramatic personality. There are many superstars in the media industry which possess narcissistic personality.

Narcissists consider themselves as the one who no other being can be. If these symptoms persist for long, it can result in the debris field of suffering.

Narcissists think that they are the most loved entity on the planet earth. They do not get ashamed of their doings and considers others to make apology them even if other people are not wrong. Narcissists don't make an apology; they think others must tolerate and accept them no matter what.

Narcissists do not consider them obeying the rules and regulations set by the authorities. They believe rules are only for others who are below average and not for them because they are above average.

"Everyone has to like and be interested in what you have achieved and what you wanted." On the other hand, narcissists themselves disrespect the achievements of others. They do not show much interest and anxiousness towards other's success as much they want others to show for them. They always remain on the "don't care" mode.

"You must appreciate me and appraise me for my achievements" kind of thinking prevailed in narcissists. They consider others to be normal with them even when they are rude or arrogant. One thing which continuously prevails in narcissists is that they think that others are below them and they are far above than them.

They expect everyone to be loyal and fair to them no matter what they do to others. They hope others to appreciate them or accept them even if they are criticizing them. On the other hand, no one can criticize them specifically in public or else they will be ready to murder you.

"To be in good relationship with me, you must obey me." Narcissists expect others to do good to them and obey every order they make and in return do not expect him to follow them.

Living, working, or spending time with a narcissist can make you psychologically and physically ill.

Dealing with narcissists

Being surrounded by narcissistic personality, it is essential to know about their traits. Only a person who understands the thinking patterns and the reason behind their thoughts can better live with narcissists. Moreover, you can get your relatives, partner, kids, or other immediate family members get out of this personality type. You can do this, only by understanding and knowing them well. The best thing the relatives, friends, children, colleagues, school-fellows, and coaches can do with a narcissistic personality is to support them.

There are various ways to deal with narcissists and to make the active living possible. You need to start accepting the following things:

• First and foremost thing you need to accept that you may feel degraded or devalued. Accept that! Because narcissists overvalue themselves and do not keep into consideration the values and self-respect of others; therefore, you may repeatedly feel devalued.

• Narcissists needs, desires must be fulfilled first, no matter what! Narcissists do not see how inconvenient is something to achieve or get. They go out of the way and ask you for the things which may be difficult for you to buy. Try your best to fulfill their needs.

• Always be ready to be treated the way you never imagined. Narcissists treat others very rudely and do not expect others to treat them likewise. In other words, you have to be nice with one who will never behave nicely to you. Narcissists get nice very rarely when they want to get something from you or when they seek something of their own good from you. So be wise while dealing with narcissists.

• Narcissists always think that they are prior than others and have no equals. Therefore, be prepared to accept that narcissists are above than you.

- Narcissists don't have any word "apology" in their dictionary. Don't expect them to apology or excuse for their wrongdoings or mistreatment.

- You may get feelings of shock, insecurity, and inconsistency. Believe that these feelings are real and you have to adapt to these feelings while being with narcissists.

- Narcissists will never obey the laws, rules, and regulations. They don't come up being the follower of ethics code or principles. They only follow them for their own good else these are just the words!

- Sometimes you may be the one to cheer them up even when you are the one who needs to be motivated.

- The only important word in the life of narcissists is "me." They can only think and talk about them. They only talk about their values, codes, and worthwhile ignoring the values of others.

- Narcissists always want to be authoritative and manipulate others. To manipulate people, they often come up with false sayings. When one will catch them lying, they will blame that person for the one who is lying. They don't accept what they do instead impose it on others. Therefore, always be ready to encounter such arguments.

- Narcissists often outburst in anger, therefore you may get the feeling of insecurity. Always be careful as you may get attacked from narcissists.

2. Machiavellians

Machiavellian personalities are referred to as the "Master manipulators" and have mastery degree in deceiving others. The victims realize the intentions of Machiavellian very late. The people who are highly focused on their goals, Machiavellians manipulate their thinking and deceive them. In this way, the purposes of the subjects get affected. Machiavellians don't need any mastery class to manipulate others instead they are predisposed with the qualities of deceiving others. They use others to achieve their goals. People who are at higher levels, status or at the positions of power choose to be the Machiavellians in order to gain power over others.

The term Machiavellians was derived from the name of famous Renaissance philosopher Niccolo Machiavelli. The Machiavelli became famous because of his book, which was of the view that those in higher authorities must be rude and harsh to their employees and subjects.

Machiavellians are usually aimed at conquering the world or achieving their goals by deceiving others. The term was named until the 1970s. During that period, Florence L. Geis and Richard Christie developed the Machiavellianism Scale, and this is from where the name was originated.

Different research studies have been conducted to check the gender differences in Machiavellians. It was revealed that the level of Machiavellianism is higher in males than in females. Males are more likely to deceive others to achieve their goals.

The Dark Triad describes three personality types: narcissism, sociopathy, and Machiavellianism. It was revealed that Machiavellians receive less attention than narcissists and psychopaths.

Characteristics of Machiavellians

- *Machiavellians tend to be charming and friendly with others. They use self-disclosure as a tactic to use against others. Machiavellians disclose them to make others share their feelings as well. Machiavellians then use those secrets and feelings of others against them to manipulate them or overpower them. These tricks are used by Machiavellians to hide their true intentions.*

- *People don't prefer Machiavellians to be in their peer group, at work environment or as the life partner. People might like them to be in their competition but don't want to be any relationship with them.*

- *Sometimes Machiavellians show as if they are guilty for their doings to get sympathies from others. Be aware of these harming tactics.*

- Machiavellians often use threats to persuade others.

3. Psychopaths

It is considered as one of the utmost dark traits of personalities and is equally dangerous as well. Various research studies done on psychopaths in prisons and in the community have shown consistent higher crime rate.

It encompasses the personalities which have a lack of empathy for others, involves manipulative behavior, shows antisocial behavior, and involvement in illegal activities (not always). In extreme cases, psychopaths can be your killer, they don't care whether you live or die. Some psychopaths can be murderers, killers, aliens, or violent offenders. It is very difficult to spot the psychopaths as they appear normal and have a very charming personality. It is considered difficult to treat adult psychopaths. Psychopathic personality traits are innate or genetic and a person is predisposed to act like a psychopath. Psychopaths and sociopaths come under the antisocial personality disorder of Diagnostic and Statistical Manual. An antisocial personality disorder is considered to be the root cause of both innate and environmental factors. Research studies have found that men are more victim of this disorder than women. Symptoms are prominent during the early 20s of the person and diminish during his 40s.

There are very little chances for an individual to encounter a psychotic person as according to research studies only 1% of the general population exhibits psychopathic traits. Another research study has shown that about 3% of business leaders come under the umbrella of sociopathy.

At starting when you come across psychopaths it would be very difficult for you to spot, whereas with time the nature and characteristics of them become apparent.

Psychopaths are unable to differentiate between the emotions. They may sometime mistake sexual interest with love or anger with irritability. In short, psychopaths come up with shallow emotions. Psychopaths usually talk more than normal people. They can be humorous or funny and engage in telling others stories. They don't make others feel the real side of them. They appear charming and attractive to others. Many times psychopaths talk about the things as if they are experts but in fact, they know nothing. Psychopaths are highly manipulative and can easily control the brains of others. They are truly the master manipulators.

Psychopaths come with elevated self-esteem and sense of self-worth. They have an element of pride and arrogance and always consider themselves right even when they are wrong. They engage in multiple marital relationships and have poor control over behaviors. Psychopaths usually lack long-term goals and deny reality.

Characteristics of psychopaths

In this section, there are various characteristics of psychopaths mentioned which will help you spot them easily.

- **Charming**

Psychopaths always seem normal and are liked by everyone. When they make small talks they seem like well-behaved and well-mannered. They often draw the attention of people towards them by their personality. They tell people interesting stories and are good at persuading others. Overall they got charming personality and are good at attracting others towards themselves.

- Lack of empathy

Psychopaths don't think of others before performing any action. They don't think that their actions can hurt someone's feelings. They blame others for hurting them instead of admitting that they hurt others. Psychopaths lack feelings of empathy, love, and care. They don't forgive people easily. They even get ready to kill someone for their own good and benefit.

- **Aggressive**

Psychopaths have aggressive tendencies and are involved in bullying. Psychopaths bully others wherever they go. First signs appear in their school life. Afterward, they are involved in aggression and bullying to their colleagues, family members, and peers. People who can't fight back or are down to earth are usually the victims of psychopaths. They easily get jealous of others and bully the people whom they get jealous of.

- Lack of remorse or guilt

The first and foremost sign that psychopaths usually show is the lack of remorse or guilt. Psychopaths are usually not guilty of their wrongdoings. If they hurt someone, they won't accept it. They may consider the victim as responsible for whatever has done to him. Psychopaths deny taking responsibility for doing wrong to others and get offended when someone tries to make them realize. Instead of accepting their fault, psychopaths blame others.

- Narcissists

Psychopaths have a high feeling of self-admiration and love. They don't think of other's good or harm even for a second. They always think that they are superior to others and every other person is inferior. They want others to admire them. Psychopaths consider that others are nothing and what they know is the best.

- Easily Bored

Psychopaths continuously seek change and thrill in their life. They get easily bored and want continuous change in their lives. They always search for something novel which can make their lives entertaining and full of fun.

- Seek power

Psychopaths always want to overpower people. They want others to work under them and obey them. They think they must be followed by others and others should obey rules and regulations defined by them. In short, they want to become CEO of everything where every other person works under him obeying his directions. They love to be the authoritative figure and control everyone.

- Risk Takers

Psychopaths don't think of the safety of them and others as well. They perform the actions whatever comes in their mind without considering that it could be harmful to them or others. Psychopaths engage in illegal activities such as robbery, stealing, killing other people and many other grand crimes. They engage in crimes with efficiency, they don't leave a clue for others to spot them. Psychopaths are intelligent and very well-organized.

- Deny rules and regulations

Such people don't obey rules, regulations or laws set by higher authorities. Psychopaths believe that rules or laws are unnecessary and don't have any genuine basis. Therefore, psychopaths are often seen involved in breaking laws, breaking signals, robbery, stealing, and many other illegal activities without feeling guilty. Moreover, they often deceive people in order to satisfy their feeling of envy.

- Master manipulators

Psychopaths get mastery in deceiving and manipulating others. They know hundreds of tactics to persuade people and manipulate them easily without making them know their (psychopath's) true intentions. Psychopaths don't show people the true emotions they experience for them instead they fake the emotions. Therefore, the peers and loved ones of psychopaths usually don't understand the true motives of the psychopaths. By using various manipulating tactics, they gain the sympathies of people to meet their needs. They trap people through their manipulating tactics.

- Involve in continuous lying

Lying is very easy for psychopaths. They lie even on very little things and matters. Psychopaths are often said to be two-faced. They hide their real self and deceive others by their fake self. The actions of psychopaths don't match their words. Their motive behind lying is to benefit them even if it causes harm to others. Mostly they don't have any good reason to lie but they still lie to satisfy their inner self.

- Highly arrogant

High level of pride and arrogance are part of the personalities of psychopaths. They think they are of utmost value and importance and others are nothing. They don't help others even if they can do so easily. Level of grandiosity is higher in psychopaths and they think they must be in power. Psychopaths consider themselves to be capable of doing anything.

4. Everyday Sadists

Everyday sadists share many characteristics with types of dark personalities mentioned earlier. But in everyday sadists enjoy the cruelty of others. They feel pleasure to see others in the pain or being the victim of cruelty. According to Paulhus, the people mostly hired in police or armed forces are everyday sadists where they involve in harming behavior under a legal order.

Earlier work done on "Dark Triad" of personality later became "Dark Tetrad" as Buckles and Colleagues Delroy Paulhus of the University of British Colombia and Daniel Jones of the University of Texas El Paso said that sadism is the different aspect of dark personality, therefore, it should be considered as the aspect of dark personality.

Common actions of Everyday Sadists

Every one of you in your daily life encounters everyday sadists. Many times you are surrounded by everyday sadists without even knowing. Everyday sadists are the one who intentionally or purposefully gives pain to others and feels pleasure in doing so. Everyday sadists can harm others ranging from normal to severe. Following are some of the actions that everyday sadists perform in everyday life:

- *Intentionally tries to harm others in order to please them.*

- *Continuously tries to get someone out of the job.*

- *Unveil the secrets of the people for which they promised to keep private*

- *Providing others with financial, physical and mental harm*

- *Involvement in aggressive behavior. Continuously involves in bullying*

- *Always try to spoil relationships of people with others*

- *Aims at spoiling the public reputation of the person*

- Seeks to harm the people around like classmates, peers, or family members

Everyday sadists just like psychopaths get charming personality which makes them famous within their social group. They are socially very influential and therefore people cannot identify their true intentions. People easily become the victim of their plans. Everyday sadists think that harming others can be beneficial for them in some way. Many times they involve in harming behaviors just to satisfy their feeling of envious, or they may feel threatened, or for them hurting others may be a pleasurable activity.

How to deal with people showing dark personality traits?

Many of you encounter many people around you who are under the influence of dark personality characteristics. It sometimes becomes very difficult to deal with the people possessing dark personality traits. If you are encountering anyone with dark personality traits at your workplace, your house, peer group, or at your school, you can use the following ways to deal with such people.

Dealing with narcissists

If you are having someone with narcissistic personality traits at your place, then it could be very unfavorable for you and your company as well. At first, it can disrupt the team morale and harmony. Morale and harmony are the necessities to work within the group or team. Therefore, you need to make narcissists realize how his behavior is influencing the group members.

Within a group, narcissists often want to take credit of the group work. They don't want group members to get the credit of any task or performance. Narcissists have high egos therefore; they want others to challenge them. To deal with such people, come with solid counter-arguments to meet the claims of the narcissists. Moreover, another way to deal with narcissists is to put him in such a situation where he is dependent on coworkers. This will make the person obey other group members and respect them.

Coping with aggression

The aggressivity of people with dark personality traits could be very dangerous. It is very easy to spot whether the person is in aggression or not. Few symptoms of a person getting aggressive are raised the voice, sweats, face getting red and many others.

When you spot that someone is getting aggressive or you are feeling threatened, then immediately leave that place. Moreover, distance yourself emotionally from that person as well. Furthermore, you can ask various open and close-ended questions from the person.

Active listening is a technique used to deal with people prone to aggression. Active listening is where you listen to each concern of the person and the complete message he wants to communicate. By using these strategies, one can identify the cause of a person being aggressive.

Dealing with manipulators

Within the work setting, there are large numbers of people who manipulate you. But, how it is possible to differentiate between the manipulators and others. It is very simple! If the person who is praising, you have more Machiavellian tendencies then he will surely be a manipulator.

If you spot someone to be the manipulator, then while working with such people always sign a performance agreement. Later on, if the person denies from the performance or work, then show him the agreement he made.

Nonverbal Communication For Dark Psychology

Nonverbal communication involves what you say with your overall body language without the use of words. Our body language is known to send a strong message to others during conversation. Someone may guess the kind of person you are by looking at your appearance and posture. Sometimes you may say something, but if your nonverbal gestures such as facial expression do not reflect it, others may not believe in it. Nonverbal gestures, therefore, are significant in giving feel and touch to our words. Your tone of voice also speaks volumes about what you are saying and how you are saying it. Both verbal and nonverbal communication is vital, and the gestures we express during conversation are equally important and influential, just as the word we use. Nonverbal cues impact how other people will receive what we are attempting to communicate, and their reaction will reflect how we have delivered the message. If you wish to get a particular response from your audience, on your message, then your verbal communication will affect the kind of a response they will give. In fact, accompanying your words with the right gesture will make you sound more real and believable, and add spice to your conversation and speech.

Body Language and Dark Psychology

When we here of dark psychology, then we think of personalities such as narcissists, sociopaths, psychopaths, and Machiavellians. Sometimes we wish that we can deny them the oxygen of nonverbal communication to minimize their charming ways. Unfortunately, they flourish in dark psychology, and they understand the power of nonverbal gestures very well. They know how to use them to manipulate others to their advantage. They take advantage of the power of body language to minimize their target, manipulate their emotion, thought, and behavior to achieve the ends they seek. Some of the nonverbal cues that they capitalize on are:

- The clothes they wear and how they wear them
- Body gestures such as posture and positioning
- A facial expression such as hypnotic gazing
- Maintaining eye conduct or avoiding it
- Voice, where they raise the tone of their voice intentionally
- Proximity where they manipulate the distance between them and their target

Hypnotic Staring and Gazing

Eye conduct is one of nonverbal skill which is very important in communication. It inspires confidence and shows that you are attentive as the other person speaks. Maintaining eye contact has always been preached an excellent way to make others feel like they are really being noticed. But manipulative people know how to take this vital skill a step further. They set their eyes on you with an intense and focused gaze. Such hypnotic gazing is usually done intentionally for the purpose of testing boundaries. The manipulator often does or says something weird after or before the hypnotic gaze. They then stare at you to test and monitor your response.

In an attempt to lie to you, they may stare at you without blinking much. When someone lies, they usually break eye contact and look down or to the sides. But sometimes they go an extra mile to give a steady and cold gaze to intimidate and control you.

Body Touch and Space Invasion

Manipulative people playfully touch you in an attempt to break the rules and boundaries. They usually do this in a very subtle and charming way. They may reach for your shoulder, peck your cheeks, or touch your hand intimately to see whether you will permit it, especially on your first date. They carry you off the ground when you hug intending to pass a particular message, and test whether you accept it depending on your reaction. They will also invade and violate your personal space to create false intimacy. They do this by leaning too close. Even if you step back, they step forward into your bubble to re-adjust. In this process, they also touch your shoulder or arm repeatedly to try to create rapport.

Constant Mirroring of Your Body Language

This is a famous manipulation technique which dark personalities use to influence their target. At the start, they are trying to mirror you so that they can control you. Later you find yourself reflecting them. This creates trust between you and them and helps to establish a connection that they use to exploit you. The technique is usually straightforward and a basic one, because it only involves copying the behavior of a person. The manipulator takes a close look at your body languages such as gestures, facial expressions, and the tone of your voice. If you are standing with your hands crossed, they do the same. If you are speaking quietly without showing any emotions, they do the same. They do it as carefully as possible to make sure that you are talking in the same way. They also make sure that you won't realize or become suspicious of their behavior when they are mimicking you so that you do not become suspicious.

After some time, you will start feeling connected to them. You begin to behave like them, and that is the time that they realize you are ripe for their purpose.

Nice Dress and Haircut

Dark personalities understand well the power of the first impression. They're physical appearance if therefore the first thing that they bank on. They know the best hairstyle that makes them look good. Your entire outfit will be affected by how your hair looks. One of the things that a person you want to influence will notice is your haircut. When you ignore your hairstyle, you won't look good, and they will know it. Be realistic with your hairstyle and if a particular hair cut doesn't make you look good, let it go and look for a better one. Don't rock around with a haircut that looks terrible on you.

Dress well, without going crazy on fashion if you know you can't sustain it. To impress others, you must be well dressed to create a first good impression. If your dress cannot capture the attention of your target, then they will not pay much attention to you. Those who manipulate others know this, and they spice their looks with flashy clothes and makeup.

Raising Their Voice and Displaying Negative Emotions

This is a sign of aggressive manipulation. They raise their voice when you are discussing something, while in the real sense, they are not emotional. They assume that by projecting their voice high enough to show negative emotions, you will give in to their demand and do or give what they want. They accompany their loud voice with strong body language like excited gesture or raising from their sit to stand on their feet.

Self-Comfort Touches and Pointing

Lying comes with discomfort and stress. The liar then begins to make a gesture aimed at achieving some level of self-comfort. These are gestures such as hair-stroking, playing with wedding rings, rocking, and twiddling. Although we all use gesture often, they increase dramatically for someone who begins to fib. This is when they start to feel that their lie will not go through, and you have discovered their hidden motives. In an attempt to get away out, they may begin to use their hand to point to other things happening around to divert your attention from the matter. If you stick to the topic, they will feel embarrassed and never try to lie to you again.

Micro-Gestures

These are little gestures or facial expressions that flash across one's face quickly. They are hard to see, but experts tend to use filmed footage which they slow down to analyze the body language and hence can recognize them at the middle of the lie when the person is performing it. In real life, these may not be spotted, but you can look for other facial expressions that occur after the liar is done speaking.

Either the eyes roll, or the mouth skews as the liar is attempting a quick give-away.

Projected Body Posture

This is when someone stands towering over you. This may happen in the case where the narcissist is physically stronger than you and has a tall and colossal figure. He may lean forward to mask you and inspire fear to diffuse your confidence. He will bring his face closer to yours and look you straight in the face in an attempt to control and manipulate you. He may also stand straight next to you or in front of you, projecting his chest forward to fill up more space and try to minimize you. He may yell at you at the same time to make you yield to his demands and give in to what he is saying or give what he wants.

Avoiding Eye Conduct and Silence

When they are lying to you, and they know that you have realized it, people with dark traits tent to avoid eye conduct. They may begin to look down or blink their eyes quickly or even close their eyes in close succession. Looking to the sides is also another technique used by sycophants to prevent you from getting cues that they are lying to you. They may also remain silent for a while to avoid answering your questions if you have cornered them.

Another time when narcissists avoid eye conduct is when they have silent aggression towards you. If it is in the office, they will get in and avoid looking at your desk to prevent eye conduct with you. They may also greet everyone else in the office and fail to exchange greetings with you. If they exchange greetings, they do so look over your shoulder or looking down to avoid eye conduct. This may be the case when you failed to yield to their demands, or when you have confronted them about their manipulative tendencies which you feel tired of. They may use this silent aggression to see whether you will change your mind and live up to what they want. This may also happen in a relationship.

Fake Smile

A fake smile doesn't reflect the real feeling and emotions. Unlike a genuine smile that involves most of your face, such as the mouth and the eyes, a fake smile only involves the mouth. A smile that doesn't extend to the eyes is fake and may show that you are not reading from the same page with the deceiver. It means that they are telling you something else while their real motives are hidden. A deceiver will often use a fake smile to appear more genuine while trying to convince you to believe in them. By carefully monitoring their smile, you can find out whether it is a real one or a fake one. If you notice a fake smile, be careful, and steer clear of what they are telling you because the chances are high that such a person is not genuine.

Rate and Tone of Speech

Since they aim to control and manipulate you, a person with dark traits will speak quickly and adopt an audible tone, so that they can present so many details to you without giving you time to think. They know that when they allow you time to digest the content, you may detect the exaggeration and the half-truths in the message. Sputtering, without giving you time to respond, makes you get overwhelmed with details. They also know that a tone that is audible enough will make them sound confident and truthful. The aim of all this is to overwhelm you with so much detail before they lay their claim to you. By this time, they know that you are already tired with very little energy to resist. The manipulator then drops the bombshell, and if you are not careful, you may find yourself falling head over heel for the trap. When you confront such a person, and you see their voice beginning to fade and their speech getting intermitted by moments of silence to figure out what to say, then you realize that theirs was a calculated move to achieve a selfish goal at your expense.

The Power Of Persuasion

The power of persuasion means nothing more than using mental abilities to form words and feelings used to convince other people to do things they may or may not want to do. Some people are better able to persuade than other people. And some people are easier to persuade then other people.

The ease of persuading other people is directly tied to their current mental or emotional state. Someone who is lonely or tired is easier to persuade, simply because their defenses are lowered. Someone who is momentarily needy may be easier to persuade than someone who has a strong sense of self-worth. People who are at a low point in their lives are easy prey for others who might try to persuade them to do something they might not usually do.

The first step in persuasion involves the idea of reciprocating. If a person does something nice for someone else, then the receiving person usually feels the need to do something good in return. If someone helps their elderly neighbor carry in groceries from the car, that neighbor might feel obligated to bake homemade cookies for that person. A coworker who helps complete a project is more likely to receive assistance when it is needed. Many people do nice things for others all the time without expecting anything in return. The person who does nice things for people and then mentions some little favor that can be done in return may be someone to watch closely.

Nonprofit organizations use this tactic to gain more contributions to their causes. They will often send some little trinket or gift to prompt people to donate larger sums of money, or even just to donate where they might not have originally. The idea behind this is that the person opening the letter has received a little gift for no reason, so they might feel obligated to give something in return.

Some people are automatically tempted to follow authority. People in positions of authority can command blind respect to their authority simply by acting a certain way or putting on a uniform. The problem with this is that authority figures or those that look like authority figures, can cause some people to do extraordinary things they would not normally do had a person in a position of authority not been the one asking. And it is not simply held to people in uniform. People who carry themselves a certain way or speak a certain way can give the impression that they are something they are not.

For someone or something to be considered a credible authority, it must be familiar and people must have trust in the person or organization. Someone who knows all there is to know about a subject is considered an expert and is more likely to be trusted than someone who has limited knowledge of the subject. But the information must also make sense to the people hearing it. If there is not some semblance of accuracy and intelligence, then the authority figure loses credibility. Even the person who is acknowledged as an expert will lack persuasive abilities if they are seen as not being trustworthy.

The worst part of the power that goes along with persuasion is that things that are scarce or hard to get are seen as much more valuable. People value diamonds because they are expensive and beautiful. If they were merely pretty stones, they would not be as interesting. Inconsistent rewards are a lot more interesting than consistent rewards. If a cookie falls every time a person rings a bell, then they are less likely to spend a lot of time ringing the bell because they know the cookie reward will always appear. If, however, the cookie only appears sometimes, people will spend much more time ringing the bell just in case this is the time the cookie will fall.

There are ways to improve the power of persuasion. Just like any other trait, it can be made stronger by following a few strategies and by regular practice.

Persuasion is a powerful tool in the game of life. Persuasive people know that they have an amazing power, and they know how to use it correctly. They know how to listen and really hear what other people have to say. They are very good at making a connection with other people, and this makes them seem even more honest and friendly.

They make others feel that they are knowledgeable and can offer a certain sense of satisfaction. They also know when to momentarily retreat and regroup. They are not pushy. They are persuasive.

Did you know that your body speaks more eloquently than words? Body language is at work constantly whether you are aware of it or not. When you want to master the art of persuasion, you need not only understand (and read accurately) body language, but also learn to use it to drive your point home.

Body language is a mix of hand and facial gestures, posture and overall appearance. Using these to your advantage you can get people to do what you want without them realizing that you are actually controlling the outcome of the discussion.

Why people are persuasive

What makes a person convincing? Why are they persuasive, and you aren't? This is the answer we're going to pursue in this e-book, but I'm telling you now, there is no single, short answer to that question.

What makes this persuasive influence so difficult to pin down and elusive is precisely this almost mosaic quality it has. It's the result, the perfect merger of several important aspects that you wouldn't normally attribute to such an influence.

These aspects of their being don't only affect them, but affect us, as well. That's the fascination around it. It's all psychological, it's an overwhelming and sometimes unintentional psychological influence on the people around them.

Confidence is the absolute most important aspect when it comes to persuasion. There's no doubt it's been scientifically proven that it's easier to persuade people when you're confident. That's because it's just assumed you're an authority on the topic and they'll listen to you, because they have no knowledge or experience, but you seem to have both.

It's also crucial to understand that humans are doubtful creatures. We're not very confident and we don't really believe in our own abilities or even experience, so when someone comes along and appears to be confident and to know more, we follow them like a herd of dim sheep.

Persuasion is just as much about the impression you leave upon people as it is about your actual skill. Like many other times in life, appearances are more "real" than actual reality, because it's all other people will ever know about you. It doesn't matter if deep inside, you're insecure or you don't really think you know what you're doing. On the outside, you're this dazzling, confident creature that can persuade anyone into anything because you've mastered all the important contributing factors: confidence, eye contact, body language, manner of speaking, tone, facial expressions, as well as your general demeanor.

Confidence

How do you think so many scammers make a living? No, that sketchy guy selling you snake oil isn't really a doctor, but he speaks like he is one, so people believe him and throw money at him, genuinely believing he will solve their problems.

Now, I'm not advocating that you try to trick people, but I am telling you that you need to work on your confidence. You'll notice that every single person you find convincing has some sort of authoritative stance. It's like their presence demands attention and respect.

Eye contact

Eye contact is a classic, natural display of dominance. It's a technique that's even present in the animal kingdom, and if a lion doesn't intimidate you, I don't know who can. It's true that the goal isn't to intimidate? Eye contact can do that very effectively.

Body language

Do you know how often people underestimate body language, or just ignore it outright? I don't know why, because body language is an amazing tool for persuasion. People are always advised to display open body language, like facing your audience, making sure not to keep your arms crossed against your chest, keep your palms open, and all sorts of little tips that we'll discuss at length later.

What you maybe haven't heard is that in order to be effectively persuasive, you also need to take note of and use the body language of the person you're talking to.

Manner of speaking

Your choice of words is overwhelmingly important when attempting to convince someone, because it must be very deliberate. There's a clear strategy behind verbal persuasion, and it relies on appealing to the person's emotions.

The way you speak and what you say are both equally important, because even though your message may be perfect, if the delivery is lacking, it won't do much good. We've already established that speaking with authority is half the battle, but you also have to speak the right words, in order to win it.

Tone

Continuing on the idea that the way you say things is vastly important, let's talk about tone and why it matters. In fact, I lied when I said tone and message are equally important: tone weighs much more on a person's impression.

If someone has a very somber voice, a serious, measured tone, and an equally severe facial expression, it almost doesn't matter what they're saying – you're going to assume it's grave and important; the actual words or what they mean matters less. A joke told with a serious tone isn't funny at all.

Facial expressions

Facial expression goes hand in hand with body language and eye contact and is similarly important to tonality. Creating the impression that you mean what you say involves your face, because it will be the very first to betray you or, on the contrary, help you enforce your message.

What you can obtain through persuasion

Persuasion is a very powerful and very valuable skill that not everyone has, but that everyone should have. It comes in handy throughout your life in virtually any aspect of your existence, from sweet-talking your way into free movie tickets to convincing your boss you deserve a raise.

Your relationship with your spouse

Far from being unfair or manipulative, having the ability to convince your significant other can actually improve your relationship because you have fewer fights about your disagreements and lack of compromise. Now you can use all that extra time and energy implementing your superior decisions.

Your relationship with your kids

Having the persuasion skills and indisputable power and authority to convince your kids to actually do what you tell them to is as close to magic as you can possibly get. If you don't believe me, try it!

Your relationship with your friends

We all have that one friend who always makes terrible life choices and no one can get through to them and steer them towards the right path...except you, that is. If you have influence and persuasion skills, don't keep them for yourself. Use them for good, not evil.

Get paid what you deserve

Negotiating absolutely falls under persuasion, so really, absolutely everyone should have this skill. No matter if you're haggling at the market or discussing a higher salary, you need to have the ability to convince your 'opponent' that you deserve this and you should have it. It's mostly applicable in the workplace, where – let's be real – no boss will ever willingly part with their money and hand it over to you. So it's your job to convince them to do it. You've earned it, you deserve it, and it's rightfully yours. You have to ask for it, but you have to know how, and persuasive skills help with that.

Earn the trust and respect of your boss

You can accomplish that by becoming their go-to person. Offer your bright ideas, come up with solutions to problems the company is facing, persuade them to implement your suggestions and that they're the contribution the company needs right now. In time, you will reap the rewards when your boss comes to consult with your first.

Be a good leader to your colleagues

Obviously, your persuasive abilities will prove to be invaluable to a position like this if you want people to respect you, your work, and your ideas. It should be obvious for everyone that your way is the right way and there will be minimal dissent if you have the necessary influence over them.

Get out of paying tickets

Legally, a ticket is a mandatory consequence of breaking the law in some way, by speeding, failing to wear your seatbelt, talking on your cell while driving, etc. Practically, however…a ticket can be a negotiation, as long as you have the necessary skills.

Get into coveted clubs or restaurants

If you're persuasive enough, you can influence any menial gatekeeper and convince them to just let you through without needing to jump through fiery hoops or grease the well-meaning palms of anyone. Talk about some sweet perks!

Get important information

If you can talk the talk well enough, you can basically convince anyone to tell you anything. Gossip from your friend, preferred customer sales dates from sales attendants, where they keep the extra free peanuts from the flight attendant…you get the idea. Sweet talk yourself into perks and valuable info.

How to Persuade People

The ability to influence someone during a conversation and make a decision is necessary in order to become one of the most important people in the world today. This ability is useful in business negotiations, and in everyday life.

In general, the impact on people is not so obvious. The basic idea is that people's behavior is often guided by their subconscious simple desires. And to achieve your goals, you need to understand the simple desires of people, and then make your interlocutor passionately wish for something.

It should be noted that in order to influence people you should NOT try to impose or force them to make a hasty decision. It may seem incredible, but the person that wants to reach a mutually beneficial cooperation becomes a huge advantage compared to those that are trying to impose something on others. If you are willing to put yourself in the shoes of another person from whom you want to get something and understand his/her thoughts, then you do not have to worry about your relationship with the person.

The secret lies in the ability to help the self-affirmation of the interlocutor. It is necessary to make sure that your companion looks decent in his own eyes. First things first, there are six basic principles that will absolutely affect any of your interlocutors.

To achieve their goals, people often use the influence of psychology, which helps to manipulate man. Even in ancient times it can be seen that priests ruled the people, instilling in them that religion is harsh, and everyone will be punished if they cannot follow the established rules and practices. Psychological influence strongly acts on the subconscious, causing the victim being influenced to be led by a skilled manipulator.

If you want to succeed and learn how to manage people, these words of the great American entrepreneur should be your credo. You will grow your personality only when you are in close cooperation with the community. From childhood we develop the basic patterns of behavior and outlook, produced by the long historical, biological and mental development of humankind.

In order to have influence and control over another person, it is required that you know their personality and behavioral traits. Most importantly, learn how to use this knowledge to master the specific methods and techniques of influence and control the behavior of the other, on the basis of his outlook, character, personality type and other important psychological features.

If you want to learn how to manage people, secret techniques in this article will let you know not only the theoretical aspect of the question but also allow the use of this knowledge in real life.

To help people to look beyond the limits of consciousness, professionals use a variety of methods and techniques. One of the most effective of these is hypnosis. This method of direct influence on the psyche, whose essence consists of the introduction of human narrowed state of consciousness, makes it is easy to control someone else's suggestion and management.

The ability to manage people, primarily, is to combine the knowledge of human psychology and their personal characteristics. They help to change their own behavior so that this change will cause the desired reaction in others. Try to be more observant while communicating; it will help you better understand the individual psychological characteristics of the interlocutor. Based on this knowledge, try using the following methods and techniques that will help you manage people correctly and efficiently.

To learn how to manipulate people, you must know how it feels to be on both sides. After all, you need to understand the feelings and emotions experienced by each side. This section of the learning process will be much more efficient!

Just focus on the moral side of the issue. If you are ashamed to receive from people that are important to you, you do not accept selfish purposes - better close and do not hurt their highly moral consciousness of the information received.

Dark NLP

Neurol-linguistic therapeutic programming or NLP for short, is an epistemological practice which is used to kill damaging behavior models and to change the conduct of the individual, their habits, or behavior.

The technique had begun during the 1970s by creator Richard Bandler and language specialist John Grinder as another approach to deal with psychotherapy, which was implied to help individuals manage a scope of issues, including depression, phobias, bad habits, PTSD, and learning issues. The "neuro" portion of neuro-etymological alludes to the study of nervous system science, while the "linguistic" component alludes to language and "programming" portrays how our biases or thoughts unite with our physical make-up. The objective of NLP will be to accomplish total handle of all our mental and intellectual procedures. This proposes we should begin thinking all the more deliberately and connect just with enabling convictions as opposed to continue sinking into comfortable, diligently harming and strange thought patterns.

Behind the whole concept of NLP there are two basic premises. The first premise is always to comprehend that what you see as reality is destined by our feelings and our philosophy. This shows how we respond to occurrences in life. Realizing that our views and behaviors do not have to limit us, enables us to make strategic life choices that enhance our fast knowledge of fact. The result is that we are more happy and are in charge of what we can influence us. The second principle is the recognition of the total integration of all our structures, including our bodies, minds and feelings, and of the constant search for equilibrium that holds us in our comfort area. However, this comfortable part, called a homeostasis, could not be a whole place for us either mentally, emotionally or physically. NLP may assist us to make the unknown much more convenient. We authorize our characters to extend beyond and beyond our limits to guarantee we master often. We are provided with funds for optimizing our links between mind, body and spirit so that we can more than capture each favorable time we come and reside it.

NLP can cure us by precisely demonstrating where our perception maps are restricted and how a faith in these limits can limit our capacity to see our choices. NLP professionals think that it is essential not to restrict your lives because of poor habits or a mistaken conviction that you have been maintaining for a long time as a effective human being. Can be used to treat phobias and anxiety and be used to encourage personal development.

The different understandings and knowledge of NLP render it difficult to identify it relies on the likelihood that people live within "maps" of the globe where they learn by means of tactile techniques. NLP attempts to recognize and adjust oblivious predispositions, for example, fears or PTSD, that can constrain a person's guide of the world. NLP is not completely based in hypnotherapy (but uses aspects of it).

Rather, it operates by using language consciously to bring about modifications and leads in one's thoughts. For example, a focus element of the NLP is the possibility of a person being prone to a single tactile system known as the preferred representative system or PRS.

Therapists can identify these inclinations using verbal communication. Common sentences like "I see your point" when used, could trigger PRS visually. Or "I hear your point" could trigger PRS auditory, as well. An NLP expert will more often than not distinguish an individual's PRS and focus their MLP treatment work around it. This therapy can include:

- Building rapport

- Gathering information about the patient and the issue

- Setting goals and expectations.

One of the tools of NLP is to work on the removal of negative thinking and feelings of a past event which it is linked to.

NLP definition is broad. NLP experts utilize a wide range of methods for treatment, for example, fears, tension and self-improvement that incorporate the accompanying:

- Anchoring - Turning tactile encounters into triggers for certain enthusiastic states. While in a condition of feeling, if an individual is presented to an exceptional improvement, for example, sight or sound or contact, an association is made between the feeling and the extraordinary boosts. In the event that the remarkable improvement happens once more, the passionate state will at that point be activated. NLP instructs that passionate stays, for example, a specific touch, object, or even a smell related with a memory or state, can be intentionally made and activated to help individuals in getting to valuable or other objective states. Tying down appears to have been acknowledged into NLP from family treatment as segment of the 'model' by Virginia Satir.

- Rapport –The NLP expert works with the person by organizing and arranging their physical practices to improve correspondence and response through compassion.

- Swish design - Change of instances of behavior or thinking to an ideal rather than an unwanted outcome. This includes picturing a 'prompt' which leads into the undesirable conduct, for example, a smoker's hand moving towards the face with a cigarette in it and reconstructing the brain to 'switch' to a representation of the ideal result, for example, a sound looking individual, enthusiastic and fit. Notwithstanding perception, sound-related audio effects are frequently envisioned upgrading the experience. Wash is one of the procedures that includes the control of sub-modalities.

- Visual/sensation separation or VKD for short - attempting to evacuate counter productive musings including emotions related related to a past occasion by re-running (like a film, some of the time backward) a related memory in a separated state. It joins components of

Eriksonian methods, spatial arranging forms from Fritz Perls, reframing and 'evolving history' systems.

- Metaphor - Largely got from the thoughts of Bateson and the strategies of Erikson, 'analogy' in NLP ranges from basic hyperboles to purposeful anecdotes and stories. It will in general be utilized related to the abilities of the Milton model to make a story which works on numerous levels with the expectation of speaking with the oblivious and to discover and challenge essential presumptions.

- State the executives - Sometimes called state control, is a neuro-semantic programming (NLP) strategy including effectively attempting to control the passionate and mental condition of a person. One strategy to effectively accomplish state the executives tying down where an individual partners a specific physical upgrade. It is utilized as both a self improvement strategy and a helpful hypnotherapy method.

- Future pacing - A procedure of requesting that an individual envision accomplishing something later on and checking their responses. It is normally used to watch that a change procedure has been fruitful; (for example by watching non-verbal communication when the individual envisions being in a troublesome circumstance when a mediation). On the off chance that the non-verbal communication is the equivalent, at that point the mediation has not been fruitful. Future pacing can be utilized to "insert" change into the settings of things to come. It gives an individual the experience of managing a circumstance before they get into that circumstance in actuality. This depends on perception where the psyche is expected not to have the option to differentiate between a situation which is genuine and one which has been obviously pictured. The hypothesis is that, having pictured decidedly, when the subject experiences the circumstance again as a general rule the envisioned experience will fill in as a model for how to carry on, despite the fact that this experience was envisioned. The brain can't differentiate between the representation and reality so it acknowledges the perception as the real world and rolls out the improvement.

NLP is utilized as a strategy for self-awareness through advancing aptitudes, for example, self-reflection, certainty, and correspondence. Experts have connected NLP economically to accomplish work-orientated objectives, for example, improved efficiency or employment movement. All the more broadly, it has been connected as a treatment for mental health such as phobias, depression, general anxiety, and post-traumatic stress disorder (PTSD).

"Modeling" in NLP is the way toward embracing the practices, language, techniques and convictions of someone else or model so as to 'fabricate a model of what they do.we realize that our displaying has been beneficial when we can deliberately get a similar social result as the individual we have modeled. The 'model' is then reduced to an example that can be instructed to other people. The organizers, Bandler and Grinder, begun by dissecting in detail and afterward scanning for what made effective psychotherapists not the same as their companions. The examples found were created after some time and adjusted for general correspondence and affecting change. The first models were:

- Milton Erickson (hypnotherapy)

- Virginia Satir (family treatment)

- Fritz Perls (gestalt treatment)

Virginia Satir, likewise a prominent specialist made the Satir Transformational Systemic Therapy or (STST) model. STST, otherwise called the Satir strategy, was intended to improve connections and correspondence inside the family structure by tending to an individual's activities, feelings, and discernments as they identify with that individual's dynamic inside the nuclear family. People looking for treatment may observe STST to be gainful, as specialists prepared in the methodology can regularly enable them to work through past injury and build up a more noteworthy feeling of amicability, unity, and internal harmony.

Lastly Fritz Perls, alongside Laura Perls and Paul Goodman, founded the Gestalt treatment model. The Gestalt treatment model spotlights on mindfulness, by which seeing, feeling, and acting are comprehended to be helpful for translating, clarifying, and conceptualizing (the hermeneutics of experience). This qualification between direct experience versus roundabout or auxiliary understanding is created during the time spent treatment. The customer figures out how to end up mindful of what the individual is doing and that triggers the capacity to hazard a move or change.

NLP displaying strategies are intended to unwittingly absorb the implied information to realize what the individual is doing of which the individual doesn't know. As a way to deal with learning it can include demonstrating remarkable individuals. As Bandler and Grinder express "the capacity of NLP displaying is to touch base at depictions which are valuable". Einspruch and Forman 1985 express that "when displaying someone else, the modeler suspends his or her own convictions and embraces the structure of the physiology, language, procedures, and convictions of the individual being demonstrated".

After the modeler is prepared to do typically replicating the examples (of conduct, correspondence, and social results) of the one being demonstrated, a procedure happens in which the modeler changes and readopts his or her own conviction framework while additionally incorporating the convictions of the person who was displayed. Demonstrating isn't kept to treatment, yet can be, and is, connected to an expansive scope of human learning. Another part of displaying is understanding the examples of one's own practices so as to 'model' the more effective pieces of oneself.

The Milton model is a kind of hypnotherapy subject to some of the studies conducted by Dr. Erickson. It has been depicted as "a strategy for using language to provoke and keep up trance in order to contact the covered resources of our character". It utilizes parts of his Erickson Hypnotherapy model. The Milton model has three essential viewpoints:

- To help with structure and keeping up affinity with the customer. Furthermore,

- To over-burden and occupy the cognizant personality with the goal that unconscious correspondence can be developed.

- To take into account elucidation in the words offered to the customer.

The main perspective, building affinity, or rapport, is improved correspondence and responsiveness. NLP instructs 'reflecting' or coordinating non-verbal communication, act, breathing, predicates and voice tonality. Affinity is a part of 'pacing' or tuning into the customer or student's reality. When pacing is built up, the professional can 'lead' by changing their conduct or observation so the different pursues. O'Connor and Seymour in "Presenting NLP" depict compatibility as an 'agreeable move', an augmentation of characteristic abilities, however caution against mimicry. Vocalist gives instances of the emulate impact of negligible mimicry by certain experts which does not make affinity.

The second part of the Milton model is that it utilizes uncertainty in language and non-verbal correspondence. This may likewise be joined with ambiguity, which emerges when the limits of importance are ill defined. The utilization of equivocalness and unclearness diverts the cognizant personality as it attempts to work out what is implied which offers the oblivious personality the chance to thrive.

The third part of the Milton model is that it is intentionally obscure and metaphoric to get to the oblivious personality. It is utilized to mollify the meta model and make roundabout proposals. An immediate recommendation just states what is needed, for instance, "when you are before the group of spectators you won't feel anxious". Interestingly a circuitous proposal is less legitimate and leaves an open door for elucidation, for instance, "When you are before the group of spectators, you may wind up inclination perpetually certain". This model pursues the roundabout strategy leaving both the particular time and level of fearlessness unknown. It may be made significantly progressively aberrant by saying, "when you go to a choice to talk out in the open, you may think that its engaging how your sentiments have changed." The decision of talking before the crowd, the specific time and the possible reactions to the entire procedure are confined however the uncertain language offers the customer the chance to fill in the better subtleties.

For a few purposes, the decision on NLP's viability is attempted. NLP was not responsible for the same logical care as more established medicines, for instance the therapy for mental behavior, such as the practice and execution of techniques in CBT. The lack of official guidance and the value of the NLP implies that a NLP provider can report or provide instances of adequacy.

NLP providers will be enthusiastic about NLP's achievement with cash, and their evidence is difficult to use. Furthermore, logical NLP study has produced mixed results.

A few tests found benefits in relation to NLP.

For instance, an investigation distributed in the diary Counseling and Psychotherapy Research discovered psychotherapy patients had improved mental side effects and life quality in the wake of having NLP contrasted with a control gathering. In all events, 10 available NLP inquiries were less nice in the British Journal of General Practice. It ended with little evidence that NLP was adequate to treat circumstances linked to well-being, including the problem of discomfort, the importance of managers and substance abuse. This was due to the limited amount and nature of the examination, which was found available, rather than evidence of the NLP's failure to function. In 2014, no clinical evidence of the viability of NLP in treating PTSD, GAD or dropsy was discovered by the Canadian Agency for Drugs and Technology in Health.

In any case, a further research audit distributed in 2015 found NLP treatment to positively affect people with social or mental issues, in spite of the fact that the creators said more examination was required. The hypothesis of NLP is also the result of lack of evidence-based assistance. A 2009 document revealed that the NLP speculations have not yet been trustworthily demonstrated for three centuries, with only episodic evidence of their adequacy. In a 2010 study article, the examination findings that identify the speculations behind the NLP were evaluated. Only 18% of the 33 researchers discovered NLP's concealed speculation to be helpful.

In this way, in spite of over 4 many years of its reality, strong·study has not clearly demonstrated the adequacy of the NLP or the validity of the speculations. It is equally important that research was primarily aimed to restore the NLP's adequacy in company circumstances with little investigation. The way NLP operations work also has some commonsense problems and adds to the lack of lucidity. For example, considering the range of multiple approaches, processes and outcomes, it is difficult to easily view concentrates. While there it very well may be said that there are benefits in the utilization of NLP to take a shot at individual issues, the act of incognito NLP, or utilizing certain NLP instruments and methods without the still, small voice information individual or gathering focused on. While incognito NLP may have negative and vile undertones in its wording, it tends to be utilized in our everyday lives such as:

- Sales personnel are persuading customers to purchase

- Choose performers who seduce you with the excitement of the affair itself.

- Writers and storytellers moving their audience with emotions

• Politicians who persuade you of their cause

Alternatively, convert NLP can also be used to affect someone's sub-conscious in a negative way such as:

- Make significant other whenever they think of anyone else outside the relationship

- Install nightmares into the mind of a bitter rival

- Control the free will of persons

- Make kids fully obedient and always do what parents say.

- Creating suffering for individuals simply by speaking to them

Covert NLP can also be used to affect the sub-conscious in positive ways like:

- Improved charisma which can increase likability within a group or individual

- NLP could make people happier when they are within your company

- Achieve recipocracy within a person or organization and ensure that something more worthy is returned to them.

Today, the business Convert NLP is growing and has many NLP practitioners who will say that their noted techniques can and will improve the lives of their students. There are those practitioners who market and promote certain NLP models for use in manipulation and more infamously, seduction of an intended individual.

Mind Control

Mind control is at its heart the notion that certain psychological methods can alter or regulate the human mind. This practice is said to decrease the capacity of its subject to believe critically or independently, to allow the entry into the mind of the subject of fresh, unwanted thoughts and ideas, and to alter its attitudes, values, and beliefs.

To manipulate, reforming thought, brainwashing, coercive persuasion and control and abuses in group dynamics, are also considered versions of mind control. The fact that so many names exist shows a lack of consensus that makes confusion and distortion possible.

The idea of mental control originally developed in the 1950s, explaining how the Chinese government seemed to create people's behavior with them. Advocates of the concept also discussed Nazi Germany, some criminal instances and the actions of human traffickers. The changes in minds and views of behavior were then implemented to clarify to some new religious movements and other organizations, and critics of these movements came from those in the anti-cult movement Margaret Singer, Philip Zimbardo, and some others in the anti-cult movement. Eileen Barker, James Richardson, and other academics, as well as legal professionals led to a science and legal discussion. They agreed in consensus at least to reject the common knowledge of mind control, as defined by Psychologist Philip Zimbardo:

"a mechanism through which individual or collective freedom of choice and action is threatened by agents or organizations that change or distort perception, motivation, impact, cognition and/or behavioral outcomes."

He also believes that this form of manipulation can be used on everyone.

The Chinese term ("brain wash") can Explain why some US war prisoners cooperated with Chinese captors during the Korean War

(1950-1953), Some of whom were on their side cheated. UK radio operator Robert W. Ford and James Carne, British Army Colonel said that during their war imprisonment the Chinese had subjected them to brainwashing methods.

To undermine POW confessions on war crimes, including biological warfare, the U.S. military and government charged brainwashing. Following the claim by Chinese radios to cite Frank Schwable,, UN Commander General Mark W. Clark, the first Navy air wing personnel chief to admit to germ warfare. Clark stated:

"It is questionable whether these remarks ever passed the lips of these unfortunate men. However, if they did, they are too acquainted with these Communists ' mind-annihilating techniques of extorting whatever words they want The people are not to blame themselves, and they have my deepest compassion for being used in this abominable manner".

American soldiers who were POWs throughout the Korean War, as well as clergy, pupils, and educators which had been imprisoned in China were approached and interviewed by Robert Jay Lifton, Beginning in 1953. 15 relocated Chinese citizens were interviewed by Lifton, along with 25 Americans and Europeans. They spoke of Chinese universities being committed to ideological indoctrination.

. In his book, **Thought Reform and the Psychology of Totalism: A Study of' Brainwashing in China**, Lipton included the research from the interviews he conducted. Through his research, he found when POWs recovered their thinking eventually returned to normal. The Army released a review that delved into the Communist government's methods of interrogation, mind control and the manipulation of prisoner of war, suggesting that:

"ongoing study by several public bodies has failed to show even one irrefutably confirmed case of' brainwashing' an American prisoner of war in Korea."

This was released in 1956 post-Korean War time. Noted journalist and writer Edward Hunter was affected by George Orwell's vision of the sinister use of mind control. The main protagonist in the novel,

Nineteen Eighty-Four by George Orwell is victim to incarceration, seclusion and suffering in forcing him to comply his feelings and thoughts to the demands of the leaders. Although published in 1949, it still represents the common understanding of the notion of command of mind and is still represented in the common knowledge of brainwashing.

The Bamboo Prison, The Rack, The Fearmakers, and Toward the Unknown were among the many American films in the 1950's which had mind control and brainwashing as a subject. Forbidden Area which told of brainwashed Soviet secret agents, where traditional mental conditioning techniques helped protect their identities and their countries involvement. Manchurian Candidate Richard Condon's 1959 book, depicting the Soviet government's plan of taking over the U.S. by using a brainwashed presidential nominee, entitled, The Manchurian candidate. It was released in 1962. The notion of brainwashing became widely linked Russian psychologist Ivan Pavlov the notion of brainwashing became widely linked to his studies. Mostly dogs, not humans, were used as test subjects.

Cordwainer Smith's science fiction stories presented a foreboding vision, where in the future, people use brainwashing as a natural and benign aspect of future medical exercise to remove memories of traumatic occurrences. A significant theme in literature, Mind control is used in Science Fiction. Popular author Terry O'Brian remarked that "Mind control is such a strong picture that if there was no hypnotism, something comparable would have to be invented: the plot device is too helpful for any writer to overlook."

For twenty years beginning in the early 1950s, in an early attempt to establish functional brainwashing methods, Secret studies, such as Project MKUltra was conducted by the United States Central Intelligence Agency (CIA) and the American Defense Department.. Experimentation by the CIA utilizing varying psychoactive drugs along with LSD and Mescaline were obtained from human Nazi concepts.

Constant occurrences in the 20th century incorporated mind control. In 1974, A left-wing militant organization calling themselves the

Symbionese Liberation Army, imprisoned Patty Hearst, a relative of the influential Hearst family. She decided to enter the organization after several weeks of confinement and assisted in their operations. She was caught in 1975 and indicted with charges of robbing a bank and using a loaded weapon to commit a crime. Her attorney, F. Lee Bailey, in her court, expressly indicated that she must not be held responsible for her behavior as the treatment of her captors is equal to Korean War POWs ' presumed indoctrination. Hearst was discovered guilty, but her brainwashing defense has given increasing public attention to the specific subject in the United States like her. Charles Manson's case from 1969 to 1971, who was said to have indoctrinated his worshippers for murder and other crimes.

Along with psychiatrists and psychologists like Louis Jolyon West and Margaret Singer, Bailey built a challenging and difficult case. Both had explored Korean War POWs ' experiences. In 1996, in her bestselling book Cults in Our Midst, Singer presented her theories. In 2003, Lee Boyd Malvo, charged with murder for his part in the D.C sniper case, used a brainwashing defense, but it was mishandled. Some law researchers have asserted that the protection of mind control undermines the basic premise of free will of the law.

Italy had disagreement over the subject of plagio, a crime comprised of a person's supreme behavioral — and subsequently physical — supremacy. It is said that the impact is the annihilation of the liberty and free will of the personality of the individual. In Italy, the plagio crime has rarely been prosecuted and only one individual has ever been sentenced. An Italian court in 1981 discovered the idea to be imprecise, lack coherence, and is responsible for arbitrary implementation. By the twenty-first century, in cases of child custody and child sexual abuse, the concept of brainwashing was applied "with some success." In some circumstances where a parent is accused of manipulation by mind control their offspring into rejecting the other parent. In situations in the sexual abuse of children in which one parent is prosecuted for mind controlling their offspring to accuse the second parental half of sexual abuse, which ultimately leads to or causing alienation by the parents.

> "no reasonable person would question that there are situations where people can be influenced against their best interests, but these arguments are evaluated on the basis of fact, not fake expert testimony."

- Porensic psychologist Dick Anthony, 2003

In 2016, Van Leer Jerusalem Institute member Adam Klin-Oron, who is also an Israeli religion anthropologist said of the "anti-proposed" And ultimately, judges dismissed expert witnesses, including in Israel, who claimed there was "brainwashing." Cults usually execute all or some of these techniques to recruit and gain followers.

Once a follower is gained, these tools are also use to control them. Cults may use these following techniques:

- o   Chanting and singing
- o   *Isolation*
- o   Dependency and fear
- o   Activity and pedagogy
- o   Sleep deprivation and fatigue
- o   Self-criticism and finger pointing
- o   *Love bombing*
- o   Mystical manipulation
- o   Thought termination

The first technique is chanting and singing. Singing mantras is an significant component in many religions, especially Buddhism and Hinduism, as well as other types of mass singing in every organization. As band employees, the phrases are sung or mantras in unison, with all of their voices becoming one, a robust sense of belonging and company distinctiveness builds. When the technique is used, a state of lowered heart rate and relaxation occurs. This occurrence may help cast the worshipping group practice in a constructive light. But the ongoing succession of brief phrasings in a cult is planned to become head-numbing, eradicate rational thought, and establish a state of mood.

Group control using singing and chanting is manipulated by cult leaders to break the individuality, and critical thinking abilities of a person instead of meditative purposes.

Isolation is the second technique. Physical isolation give cults the farther advantage of mind control by moving people away from external influences, such as relatives and loved ones. Public events, such as group meetings and social events with other members can be beneficial and effective for the cult's message to be conveyed. Forced solitary confinement, both as punishment and a conditioning tool is used to strengthen control though isolation. A slower way of building a relationship and persuading to isolate the individual away from outside forces is by establishing a one on one relationship. As long as there are not any dissuading messages are seen or heard, emotional isolation will soon follow physical isolation.

Without the outside influences of friends and families, a cult can use this as proof that the individual is unwanted.

Moving on, dependency and fear is the next technique used in cults. Cults can encourage dependency on them by threatening violence or inflicting punishment. The punishment may sometimes come in forms of beatings, such as what was claimed to have occurred to Most of the time, the punishment is psychological, even metaphysical. This could be in the form of shunning a particular individual by command of the leadership, as what has occurred from within certain fringe Christian groups. This is punishment for those who have a "rebellious spirit". It should be remembered that in a context of induced dependency and mental and emotional marginalization from the former support network of the person, these threats and penalties happen. One example of this form of mind control was the case of Patty Hearst, who was discussed earlier in this chapter.

Hearst was abducted in 1974. during her captivity, she was subjected to abuse, both physical and psychological. Through this conditioning using dependency and fear, she quickly ended up becoming an associate of her captors, who may of taken advantage of her age and reputation (she came from a rather influential family), even participating in an armed back robbery. Her continual refusal of her being brainwashed when asked during her arrest hindered her defense. She was sentenced to prison for seven years, but her sentence was reduced.

Activity and pedagogy are also techniques. Several cults use this, in which they assign or encourage members to perform endless series of activities, such as physical labor or exercise to make the individual tired and exhausted both mentally and physically in order to lower their mental defenses and resolve, which will make them more susceptible. The activities are performed in a group setting, where the individual is never left alone or given any private time. Usually the activity is performed over and over again in repetition. The activity may also be of an academic nature, such as attending a long lecture or study. The leader or a trusted follower may be the "instructor".

What makes physical pedagogy different from regular sports is that the cult will take advantage of the group mentality to showcase certain ideological beliefs, which might be met with skepticism if the prospect were awake and alert.

As an example, Russia hosted mass sporting events for their citizens where they had to participate in physical activity.

In the 1970s, the followers of Jim Jones would work constantly on various duties for the church, It was usually for several days straight. If followers quit or stopped, they would be shamed or threatened.

The next technique is sleep deprivation. Sleep deprivation explains itself. Individuals are not allowed to sleep or rest, which in turn, harms the ability to make good decisions and be more susceptible. Activities such as weekend long events or functions, such as lectures which go on through the night which may include loud music or flashing lights to keep followers awake. Keepings followers on a strict diet containing low protein and other nutrients can also lead members to have low blood sugar, continuing their fatigue. Limiting sleep or rest can contribute to this too.

A former follower of the Aum Shinrikyo described that while campaigning to get their leader elected to parliament, they consumed one meal each day and slept only one to two hours every night.

Self-criticism and shaming is a technique where the group of followers denounce each other, talk about their own faults, leading to feelings of inadequacy and self-doubts, which in turn can lead to a dependency to the cult or group in an effort to "be fixed".

An example of this would be the experience of POWs during the Korean War. The Chinese forced them to participate in sessions where they would talk about their own faults and insecurity about capitalism and the US. These ongoing "discussions" began to work a little and the POWs began to question their own patriotism and their own self-worth. In the end, these sessions were unsuccessful, since only 23 POWs refused repatriotism and the Chinese abandoned their brainwashing program.

Love bombing is an effective technique in which the cult will make them appear welcoming and inviting by using the principle influence of recipocracy by showering potential recruits with affection and attention, since we are more inclined to feel like we must reciprocate the same affection and love. Love bombing is meant to create a sense of debt and obligation. When the generosity is not returned, the individual is supposed to feel guilty and it may reinforce devotion.

Not all attempts at love bombing are negative. Members of the Unification church use this technique as an expression of friendship, interest, concern or interest in a welcoming way. Other churches and organizations such as twelve step programs in which combat addictions practice love bombing as a way to welcome already vulnerable individuals in a genuine and real way as to build a welcoming atmosphere.

Mystical manipulation is a technique where the cult leader controls the information and circumstances in the group as to where it can be conveyed that the leader themselves can get their followers to believe that that they have supernatural or magical powers or divine favor by giving the false impression they give. The leaders claim that their word is indisputable and to question their words is to question the divine.

The final technique is thought terminating clichés. These are the uses and phrases, usually with rhetoric, that when used intensely, can help replace individual thoughts. The words and phrases, noted by Psychologist Robert Jay Lifton, were "all-encompassing jargon". The Soviet Union and China used this technique frequently.

Lifton considered their jargon to be:

"abstract, highly categorical, relentlessly judging"

and was, "the language of non-thought".

An interesting example of this technique was during the trial of Nazi official Adolf Eichman. When questioned, Eichman would constantly reply in stock phrases and clichés which pertained to National Socialism. The Soviet Union and China used this technique frequently. Eichman was so entrenched in the Nazi ideals, that it may have been virtually impossible for him to really understand the magnitude of his crimes, which is what mind control is all about: the complete and utter control of another living being.

Mind control, when used in the ways discussed are still used today. Sex traffickers use some of these techniques to gain a level of trust through feigning affection and generosity before beginning to monitor and control their actions and movements. They can prey on their prospective victims through promises of a great paying jobs, then instill dependency and fear using threats of deportation, involvement of law enforcement and deportation. Some victims may achieve a form of traumatic bonding or "Stockholm syndrome" with their captor or captors through prolonged imprisonment, which could lead to the victim's inability to seek assistance.

Individuals and organizations may use some of these techniques, but may not have conscious knowledge that they are doing so. Many religious sects and denominations chant mantras or sign hymns to promote togetherness or tap into their own individual consciousness to find inner peace.

Mind control techniques, when used in the ways discussed, can be abused to take advance of the vulnerability of the individual to make them more susceptible to the group's/leader/ other individual's needs or gains. Some of us may have wanted or may have been tempted to use these techniques in our daily lives (to make a boyfriend/spouse/ children more compliant, make it so our boss would give us a raise), what mind control takes away is the free will and independence of the person. That individuality at its core builds the character of that person.

Mind Hacking Techniques

I n the recent past, hackers have assumed a lousy reputation in the tech-heavy world. In other words, their activities entail the art of logging into systems without permission and offering illegal commands. The aspect has been detrimental in the sense that organizations have been losing funds, let alone the confidence they have over their customers. However, according to Sir John Hargrave, human beings are all hackers, that is mind hackers. The art is linked to the fact that as human beings can effectively recognize certain situations and control the focus of one`s minds concerning the subject in question. In mind hacking, it is not just about thinking. It involves the art of thinking and rethinking about what one of streamlining off. Thus, Hargrave claims that one can rethink and write the code behinds the thoughts therein. In other words, mind hacking entails the detailed re-cap of what the mind has been thinking. For the accounts to be active, one has to apply some crucial techniques effectively.

Take a look at some of the techniques you can use to enhance practical mind thinking.

Upgrade yourself.

In most cases, when one gets to a training session, one mind may get to wonder and fail to focus on a specific target. However, one needs to refocus and return their attention to the primary goal. It is worth noting that the art of being attentive might be challenging to maintain following many common distractions. It is critical to note that with practice, one can sustain attention and ignore a lot of entertainment that might progressively stay for more extended periods and causing the loss of focus. As a mind hacker, one may log out to what is said to be user mode. It is also possible to log back into what is termed as super-user mode where one can rewire the brains and become more productive and effective.

According to Harvey, the art of logging out of the system is not a problem. However, the major problem is where one logs out of the system without their knowledge. In such situations, training becomes effective where one train on how to remain in the super-user mode for more extended periods and become more productive. In other words, through the art of training, one can keep the mind in the super-user mode, learn more about what they are thinking and become more effective in whatever they are doing.

Think of attention like Money

The art of focusing your attention to the mind is like putting one's money in a bank account with some compound interest. It is worth noting that it requires Money for one to make more money. In the same way, if you want to be attentive, you need to use your attention and remain focused. Scholars have identified that focus is one of the most scarce aspects or commodity in life. Thus, one ought to be careful and work on maintaining this powerful resource that life has offered.

Avoid Attention Fragmentation

There have been studies that have been carried to investigate how active people are as they multitask. However, the results have adequately indicated that the art of multitasking weakens the minds ability to concentrate and remain focused. In other words, people who multitask filter out irrelevancy in most cases. In other words, since their minds aren't focused on what they are doing, their products tend to below, and the results are always sick. The art of multitasking or rather attention fragmentation causes one to explore a lot of things and yet become a master of none. In other words, the one weakens the mind and the ability to focus on the most productive aspects of life is lost; hence, the achievement of poor results. It is worth noting that Excellency requires one to be focused on a particular aspect of life and avoid being swayed by issues. The other demerit about fragmentation is that it steals one ability to recall items. In other words, one unable to manage memories and my end up forgetting the essential things in life.

One is easily distracted and may not be able to recover what they have been doing once they lose their concentration.

In most cases, once they are distracted, they are unable to recover their initial position, and they are forced to restarts gain. For instance, is one was working in a particular experiment, and multitasking, there are chances that if they are distracted, they will probably forget the step they were in and end up restarting again once they recover. The aspect is devastating in the sense that it wastes time and resources as well. However, you need to be focused and stick to one task. The element is critical in the sense that it allows one to channel all their energies to a particular aspect of life and get better results rather than multitasking with the aim of achieving a lot within a short period and end up losing everything when things are messed up. Thus, make a point of deliberating on your attention and remain being focused.

Booking Habits with Rewards and Cues

These are essential habits that are critical in life. Such practices are vital in the sense that they allow one to be more productive and effective in life. For instance, the art of being consistent is very critical in life. If you want to cement a particular habit in your life, you need to be consistent and it times of time and place. Choose a suitable moment, for instance, in the morning when you aren't tired. There are cases where you might have to select a location that will suit you best. For example. You can choose a reminder such as a digital clock that will keep reminding of the habit you want to cement. The approach is critical in the sense that it allows one to remain focused and productive. The other aspect that is crucial in cementing a habit is the use of rewards. You need to reward yourself once you have been able to cement the practice for some time. It is worth noting that most of these aspects are more of a mind-set. Thus, you can effectively hack your mind and cement a particular habit in life that is worth noting.

Tracking your Mind

In most cases, it takes time for the minds to be tuned to a particular aspect of life and remain cemented for a more extended period. In other words, it requires patience and consistency for cementation of a habit. Essential habits require more energy than bad habits. However, the art of starting a bad habit is very firsts; however, leaning them is very challenging. The art developing a specific concept requires one to be consistent in the way they do things.

In most cases, if the habit isn't well acknowledged or embraced, one may easily forget about it. Thus, the best thing that one can do is to establish a chart that will help one follow on the progress. The aspect is critical in the sense that it keeps one focused and attentive on achieving better results.

Writing

Until something is in papers, it is vapor. In other words, once you have practiced new ideas, you need to put them down in an article. The aspect is critical in the sense that it allows one to be sober and keep remembering about the new concepts made. It is worth noting that writing is the gateway behind one`s mind. In other words, the thoughts in most cases become the things as well as the ideas that are brought from the head to the hands. For instance, if you want to lose weight, the best thing is to adopt a particular concept of life and work on via writing. If you decide to utilize the diet as a significant way of reducing your weight, come up with a time table that will help you open up.

Planning is best done via writing. The aspect allows participants to maintain a record of all that is happening. For instance, one may record the way they have been reducing weight over time. The aspect allows one to keep working. In other words, a record of the progress is critical in the sense that it will enable one to check in the improvement achieved as well as the issues that need to be addressed. It is essential to understand that one can appreciate a specific habit of seeing the results. For instance, one may realize having adopted jogging following after seeing that they have improved in terms of their weight as well as their health. The habit will thus be cemented in their minds, and they won`t deviate from it quickly.

Operate it as an Addiction

The art of addiction is considered to be a life-long disease that affects the way a person behaves or think. Thus, professionals promote the utilization of drugs that are causing the brain to re-organize itself and form new neural connections. In most cases, people who are addicted to specific issues of life have their minds tuned to their habits more permanently. For instance, alcohol addicts, at times, fail to be active before they are drunk. However, if the addict rewires their brain and makes deliberate decisions to avoiding their habits, they become more productive and maintain soberness. Thus, most of the things or rather the practices we engage in are wired in the brain. If one wants to achieve a particular aspect of life, repetition is vital. In other words, you may have to plan your time well and enhance repetition within your activities. You may have to plan your entire day and ensure that you establish a habit that will help you achieve what you want. In other words, you need to avoid a negative lope in your life by outlining some of the practices or activities you want to be achieved within a specified period. You need to avoid all the negative minds in your life and work on the things that make you feel good. Record all the achievements and learn to appreciate the simple steps of life you are making.

Sit with Optimistic People

It is worth noting that if you sit around negative people, there are chances that you will give up and start working on other things. However, if you sit around optimistic people, they will encourage what you are doing and help you work out well. Positive people will always try and help you understand the importance of doing certain things in a certain way. For instance, they will help you avoid addiction or rather stay positive. They will help you become the best of you rather than discourage you. Such people are critical in the sense that they will help you set your objectives and help you achieve them. Some will repeatedly encourage you and help you formulate some vital schemes. Most of them have more significant experience, and they know what it takes to be positive and the results of having the right approach. They are the kind of individuals who will outline some of the benefits of achieving a particular aspect of life.

In most cases, they will help you commit your time and resources so as you may achieve a particular aspect. Thus, as you plan to change your mind-set, make a point of associating yourself with people who are relevant in your life. There is no need of having people who are negative in your life, yet you need to achieve the best. There is no need for seeking guidance or rather opinion from people who have been failures. In other words, you need to seek advice from people who are doing great in life and work as per their guidelines. In other words, there is no way you can stop a specific addiction by sitting around with people who are addicted to the same habit. They will easily distract you and corrupt your minds as well. However, if you sit across people who were once addicted and have effectively avoided the addiction, you will be able to achieve more and avoid it easily.

A Constant Reminder

A reminder is anything that will help remember a particular aspect at a specific period. For instance, if you are planning to avoid an absolute addiction, you may have to replace the activity with something else. The aspect will thus force you to have a constant reminder that will always remind you of the things that need to be done. The reminder will help you move from the addict and work on avoiding it. Also, if you are planning on running each morning, there are chances that you may not fully embrace the issue at the beginning. During such moments, a constant reminder is required. You may also need to write something either on your computer or on the wall of the house such that you will always remember that there is something you need to achieve. You need to create reminders that will stick in your minds. For instance, if you want to stop smoking, you can write something like smoking is illegal in this house. The aspect allows one to be active and plan well. Such a reminder will easily stick in one's brain. You may also have to put the reminder in a familiar place such as the washroom, or around your dining area. The aspect is critical in the sense that it allows one to keep posted of the habit or addiction that needs to be avoided. You may also have to formulate formulas or acronyms that will help you remember what you need to do. Also, plan to succeed and fix it in your minds.

Starting Small

There is no way you can achieve something once. For instance, if you are want to lower your body weight through running, there are no ways you can run for the first time and expect a change. However, some of these habits require one to be patient and employ the art of being positive and consistent. In most cases, starting small allows one to learn. If you notice you are getting right, make a point of getting the right things being done as fast as possible. However, for the things that are not immediate, you may have to train your minds and work progressively. In other words, the achievement of certain aspects of life requires the utilization of brains as well as other body systems such as immunity. It is worth noting that such systems can't` be adjusted promptly. However, one requires to be patient and consistent. The aspect is critical in the sense that it opens one to new ideas and achieve them with ease. Such behaviors capture the minds if an individual and there are no ways one may think of otherwise. When the thoughts are effectively captured, they will be easily be manipulated in what Harvey calls mind-hacking. Thus, one can achieve anything in this life so long as their minds are wired to positivity and will power.

Dark Triad

T he dark triad is a psychology term that refers to the behavioral characteristics of a person, which is, in most cases, defined with narcissism, Machiavellianism, and psychopathy. Some people rate it as a mental disorder and some as a disaster that just dawns on someone changing their behavior and how they relate to others. Dark triad generally affects a person's personality, making them take advantage of others. People with these traits tend to be manipulative, deceptive, and egoistic. They attempt to brainwash others to gain success and fame.

Politicians are, on most occasions, the worst group of people affected by this personality disorder. Their lives are full of lies, ego, and manipulation. To gain power, most of them only deceive other people to get public support and seem successful. Many people fall, victims of the dark triad, because they are not well exposed to the point of understanding what it is. They cannot easily tell when this is being used against them.

Persons with dark triad personalities have no empathy for others. They always attempt to have everything for themselves, ignoring other people's importance around them. Narcissists always want to be regarded as the most important people in society. They want to be praised and admired all the time, a kind of behavior that only manipulates others for the benefit of their own personal interests.

You may be tempted to think that these people are insane. From my perspective, to some extent they are. No one in his normal state of mind would want to have everything go their side at the expense of others. To these people that possess a Machiavellianism trait, all they always want is to win and be declared successful. They go as far as deceiving everyone around them to turn out the right person. They easily exploit the "less fortunate" in society to open their ways.

Apart from politicians, bloggers are another group of people that are overwhelmed by these traits. For example, in Kenya, we have Dr. Miguna Miguna, who is all over the social media busy manipulating people—the youth and young politicians being the most affected. He tries to make everyone his psychopath through his blogs, twits, books, and constant drama here and there.

Can we Say Dr. Miguna Miguna is insane? He is all over seeking fame and wants everyone to believe he is always right, and the rest are wrong. He manipulates everyone, and those who follow his steps end up being disappointed at the end. Once he gets what he is looking for, he turns against you and uses your negatives to manipulate others that are not in the same line with him. He comes up with dramas to attract attention and convince everyone to believe whatever he does.

While politicians everywhere are fighting him back, the youth are becoming psychos by his blogs and keep believing that he is right because he is fighting politicians whom he claims to be the narcissists. Not to be personal, I would like to say that if you research deeply into psychology, you will find most bloggers with the same interest showing narcissism, Machiavellianism, and psychopathy traits. They won't feel guilty nor ashamed because they don't even notice that they are too much with this.

Anyone can be a victim of these traits. You may, at one point in your life, find yourself in a relationship with a narcissist, and before you notice it, you will be exploited and used by your partner. Your partner can be that antagonistic person that only feels superior to you and those around you. They will always want to be treated special and can exploit you to serve their own personal interests. They often interact in a way that shows you are less important and not as good as them.

This kind of person usually wants to be listened to. They will prefer seeking attention than empathizing with you or even recognizing your needs. Everything they do is always for their own benefit. They only concentrate on how they can feel better being in the relationship and are never ready to give you a listening year. You have no say in the decisions they make because this makes them feel less important to you and that you don't respect their decisions.

For you to know that you are in a relationship with a narcissist, you will realize that your partner doesn't really care about how you feel. They only expect you to make them happy and superior without considering what you go through for them to be what they want. Failing to meet their interests makes them feel so low and unwanted in the relationship. They make you feel like you are of no good to them and that you don't deserve them.

They can also be antisocial and low self-esteemed. They will always think of their mistakes as the worst ever and that none can be compared to them. Whenever they fail in something, they will feel like they don't fit in society anymore and that they are imperfect people. They feel so drowned and depressed as a result of one mistake. This is always brought about by the fear of being a normal person.

On some occasions, narcissists attempt to praise themselves too much without realizing how grandiose they can be. They never stop talking about their achievements and plans in life. They always talk about how intelligent and successful they are and even exaggerate what they are capable of. They always want people to believe that their success cannot be related to someone else's. Stopping them from doing this only makes them feel stupid, and they can easily hate you for pinpointing their imperfections.

The living standards of these persons are always set high by them, which becoming realistic because they are in a way that has low standards. Their lives are usually filled with a fantasy about success, and they expect everyone around them to respect them because their destinies are thought to be successful. No one can ever change the kind of perception they have in their minds without hurting them and making them feel useless.

At some point, these people are always depressed, and no one will ever understand the reason for their depression. Understanding them becomes difficult, and if you are not a psychologist, you will always be brainwashed to serving their own interests before you notice what you are getting yourself into. You can be advised by other people, but you will not have the time to listen to what they have to say because you will have fallen a victim of narcissism, and the narcissist will, by that time have full control of you.

You are always left torn between thoughts when it reaches a point that you no longer understand a friend or a partner who has a dark personality. Failing to listen to them makes them feel worse than other people while listening to you is useless to them on the other hand. They never have time to listen to you but to seek the audience all the time.

Machiavellian leaders are the most dangerous leaders because they are always cunning and duplicitous. They always manipulate everyone from doing what they want, whether they like it or not, and they never reveal any reason for their actions. They only do that when the favor is on their side. They always make people believe that they are the most intelligent and that no one's intelligence can be compared to theirs. Those who believe in this kind of leaders are never ready to listen to other people's advice unless they are in line with the Machiavellian heads.

Dark triad strikes too much due to a number of reasons that we have discussed above and the following additional reasons.

1. The understanding of dark triad is not everybody's cup of tea

Not everyone has the psychology of understanding dark personality. This leads to many of us falling victims of dark triad without noticing it. We get manipulated easily and exploited to serve the interest of narcissists and Machiavellian leaders without a choice of thinking a second time or even the chance to take an alternative move. We have nothing left if not to follow their steps and support their nature of life.

2. The fear of standing alone

Narcissists always manipulate the big number from being on their side and supporting their ideas. This has left many people stranded between thoughts because they fear being left alone for making an opposing decision. They fear not getting a backup from those around you has led many people to fall, victims of the dark triad, since they are forced to take steps that they were not ready to take.

This usually happens with people who are often close to this kind of person or whose friends are involved with those with dark personalities. These people get convinced easily and fall into the manipulation of Machiavellian persons.

3. I don't want to lose a friend

Many people tend to value friendship more than their own safety. They are too much into their friend's decisions and way of life that they even forget they are also important. Such people are the most common victims of the dark triad. They easily get exploited by their friends into doing what their friends want, what makes them happy.

In this case, when you're are friends with a narcissist, then you have no choice. You will always be a tool for happiness. You will ever be ready to listen to all sorts of boasting and exaggerated stories from your friends. They will always tell you about how intelligent they are and how successful they want to become in life. The sad part of it is that nothing you say or do can ever bring a change. Your words will be meaningless to them because you have always given them room to use you.

4. Investing your trust in the wrong person

In many occasions, we don't always know the right person to trust. Laying your trust in someone without considering their personality opens a gate for you to be used by narcissists. This normally occurs in relationships that are just beginning, and the partners wish to travel miles away together.

Many fall into traps of their partners because they invest too much trust in them that they can never think of the negative side of them. This is what makes the narcissists overjoyed and leave them feeling so highly of themselves. They like the feeling that everyone sees the positive in them all the time and that nothing they do is ever wrong. This gives them a wide room for exploiting their partners and using them to serve their personal interests and needs. They never care about the needs of the other party, and they always want more for themselves.

5. Believing too fast

These narcissists always have their stories told everywhere by them and by those who believe helplessly in them. They always catch the interests of those who believe in all stories they are told because they believe the people telling the story are always right, intelligent, and successful.

The narcissist always catches the attention of others with their striking success that makes others believe in them desperately and follow their steps blindly without a third eye to see into the future and the consequences of following these people. The politicians are easily believed by their supporters, and anything used against them is like an insult to their believers. These people are brainwashed with the politicians to accept and believe in everything they do without posting questions or even having a second thought.

6. Most people don't care

The tendency of assuming everything said by those in authority is final is what makes us victims of manipulation and exploitation. Some of us don't even care about what is going on around them, and having no idea about it for them is even much better. Some say that something you don't know does not hurt. This is the worst mentality we have human beings. We are always there come rain come sunshine.

People with dark personalities easily exploit such people because they know the favor will always be on their side no matter what. No one will stand against them because they don't even care in the first place. What they do is right, and what they say is correct. No one bothers to know the end results of the things that they accepted ignorantly.

7. Psychopathy

Being too possessed with someone is what leads you to become their psychopaths. You will always want to listen to what they say, and at the end of it you will be convinced that they are right and anything said against them is wrong. You will feel pain when they are in pain are depressed when they are depressed because you have become their shadow. Whoever sees you see the person you have invested your personality in.

You are being used to serve someone's interest, and people see you like a curse to the community. Something that you never feel yourself, and you can't be told about it because nothing will ever change what you have believed in. You have invested all your thoughts in one person that you only follow what this person does or say. Every step you take towards supporting them is your best in life. Their striking success keeps you motivated that you are following the right person and that you will soon get where they are and gain as much fame as them.

Being a psycho is the worst mistake people ever make in their lives when they get possessed, not just with the right thing or person. We all need to think about our decisions and personal interests before starting to serve others who at times only need us for fame and prosperity.

Is Raila Odinga a narcissist? Does he exploit and manipulate others? Does he empathize with others or even have a listening ear? Does he ever fulfill his promises to us? This is what keeps us weighing between two people who are running for the same seat. We attempt to look into the achievements of both sides and their successful plans. We get so carried away to look for the one who best fits the seat based on the goals that each has achieved over the other.

Trying to find out what these people have achieved in their lives and starting to compare them to select the one you think can make a good leader makes us believe in the lies that are created by these people and the unseen success. We make ourselves available to be deceived and exploited with these leaders, and we end up serving their own personal needs.

We should give ourselves time to understand others before we lay our trust in them, and don't you ever forget that you are as good as the other person, and you should not be serving their interests at the expense of your own happiness.

Brainwashing

Brainwashing can be defined as the attempt of changing the thoughts and beliefs of others against their will or without their consent. It is a systematic effort to coerce and alter the attitudes and beliefs of an individual in order to change their behavior. Programs of political indoctrination have been known to use brainwashing tactics to get people to change their political beliefs. Brainwashing is also used in certain religious practices especially in cultic ones to manipulate followers. Primarily, brainwashing works by making the victim's beliefs and attitudes obsolete and replacing them with ones that the captor ones and are suitable for the environment. Brainwashing involves total removal of freedom, independence as well as decision-making power from an individual. It is the radical disruption of one's routine, habits, and behavior. It involves complete isolation and destruction from friends, loyalties and associates and calls for absolute obedience to the authority of the captor in every way. Brainwashing in many cases involves physical abuse, threats of injuries, death or life imprisonment. The captive is always presented with new beliefs as the best and acceptable way to an enlightened life.

The techniques used in brainwashing are intended to induce a childlike trust in the victim and dependency on their captor. The captive is encouraged to confess to perceived past crimes where the victim admits to absurd and trivial mistakes and in some cases, implicating others falsely to impress their captors. If there are other captors that have been brainwashed before you, they are likely to be used to reinforce the process by criticizing the victim and showing their support to the captors. Once the brainwashing process has taken hold, the captor starts getting rewards and approvals for their deeds.

How Brainwashing can be part of Dark Psychology

When a person uses brainwashing tactics to manipulate or influence another person against their will, that is dark psychology. Every person has been given the ability of free will. You should be able to make your own decisions, have the freedom of association and whom to be loyal to. When that freedom is taken away from you by force, that becomes part of dark psychology.

People in abusive relationships can also be brainwashed. A husband forbids a wife from interacting with her friends saying they are a bad influence. The wife is mature enough to know what is good or bad for her and she should independently make that choice. There are cases where a spouse would force the partner to stop wearing certain kinds of clothes claiming they are not pleasing among other things. This is a way of taking freedom from your partner so that you may control them.

It is very confusing and draining living with an abusive partner. They blame and manipulate you for things that are not your fault or for things you never did. To keep your abuser happy, you get isolated from your family and friends, change how you dress, change your political beliefs, and the world becomes about you versus them.

An abusive relationship that one partner is using brainwashing tactics to control the other, the abused partner becomes dependent on the other and cannot make simple decisions even on what to cook for dinner. They must consult with everything and they exist for the sole purpose of making their partner happy at the expense of their own happiness. The abuser, in this case, defines what love is and how it should be expressed. The abuser defines everything in the victim's life, what is wrong with them, what they should improve, how they should behave and what is appropriate.

A person can fall into the hands of an abuser in various ways but the most common ways are through emotional, psychological, and physical abuse. Once an abuser has managed to hook their partner, they begin to put them down through belittling remarks and insults.

To keep the brainwashing and abuse ongoing, they periodically have periods where they stop the abuse and start showing kindness towards their victim. This trauma-binds the victim. He or she constantly wants to make their abuser happy, hoping to be treated with warmth and kindness.

Brainwashing becomes part of dark psychology because the victim is imprisoned in their own lives. The controlling partner in a relationship may withhold resources such as a car, money even food. They make the victim be a prisoner in their own home, cause the victim to live in fear and change how they view the world.

The life of a brainwashed victim is overwhelmed with thoughts on how to please their abuser. Even without physical abuse, the victim does not feel free to leave their lives but lives under the shadow if their abuser. They get affected psychologically, develop anxiety disorders and suffer from depression.

The Process of Brainwashing

The process of brainwashing is a systematic one. It is a process aimed at losing self-identity and weakening one's beliefs, attitudes, values, and transformed thought process. The following steps or stages are what manipulators use to brainwash their victims.

Guilt

A manipulator in a relationship will constantly pick arguments to cast the victim as the wrongdoer causing them to feel guilty for the arguments. This behavior is persistent to the point the victim becomes to feel shame for almost everything and begins to think they deserve to be punished. This is the first stage of breaking a person in order to begin brainwashing them.

Self-betrayal

When a person is forced to denounce family and friends, it destroys their sense of self and enhances their guilt feelings. These feelings go to separate them from their past, paving way for the building of a new personality.

Breaking point

When the victim is constantly assaulted, made to feel guilty and have feelings of betraying self, they break down. They may find themselves crying inconsolably, fall into depression and have anxiety attacks. Psychologically, they feel they have lost a sense of themselves and live in fear of annihilation of self.

Leniency

Just when a victim is feeling annihilation of themselves, the oppressor shows them kindness. This is a brief rest from the assault on who they are. During these brief moments of seeing light where there was darkness, they feel deeply grateful to their abusers. This is a calculated move from their abusers before they begin the assault again.

Compulsion to confess

At the point where they are grateful to their abuser for pulling them from their point of breakdown, they are faced with the contrast of further assault against the rescue and leniency. They sometimes feel they owe the abuser and are obliged to repay the kindness extended to them. The abuser may give them the opportunity to assuage themselves from their guilt by encouraging them to confess to perceived mistakes.

Channeling guilt

The feelings of guilt and shame the victim is feeling will be confused by the increased assault to their identity. This causes the person to get confused and lose the sense of what they are guilty of and just believe they are wrong and carry that burden. Because of the guilt, the abuser uses it to redirect it towards anything they please. This is typically done by showing the victim that they have lived a life of wrong decisions and ideologies and they need to open up to new ideas.

Logical Dishonoring

The victim holds to the notion that the cause of their guilt is ideologies that have been imposed externally. They blame their teachers and the ideology instead of seeing the manipulation. The relief of their guilt by making more confessions about everything they did under the "wrong" ideology. They mentally throw away these wrong acts and, in the process, they are completing the act of rejecting the perceived wrong ideology.

Progress and Harmony

With the rejection of the old ideology, a vacuum is created where the new ideology can be introduced. As they become enemies of the old ideology, the person is now in search of a contrasting ideology to replace it. The process is speeded up as the new ideology is shown to be in harmony with them and suited to their needs. At this point, there is a calmness that replaces the pain and punishment of before. The captors all of a sudden are wonderful and kind and the new ideology is embraced as a replacement of the sins of the old ideology.

Final Confession and Rebirth

Faced with the distinct contrast of past pain and the glow of the future presented by the new ideology, the victim completely sheds any remaining allegiance to the old ideology by confessing any remaining secrets. At this point, they took the full mantle of the new ideology.

This is described as a rebirth. Depending on the ideology, it may be accompanied by a rite of passage to completely be cemented in the new order. It may include strong statements the victim is told to confess to in acceptance of the new ideology and swearing allegiance to the new leaders.

The Impact of Brainwashing

Brainwashing as earlier explained is a form of systematically transforming the thought patterns, beliefs and attitudes of a person in order to control their behavior. This is usually done for the benefit of the manipulator and can result in many negative aspects. There are various ways in which brainwashing can impact a person. These ways include:

- Brainwashing negatively impacts the self-esteem of the victim. The victim feels they are not good enough and nothing they do is good. This can lead them to have suicidal thoughts or get depressed.

- Anxiety disorders – a person that is being brainwashed loses a sense of self and gets isolated from their loved ones. They are forced to change from who they are and pick on a new identity. The victim is constantly anxious not to do the wrong thing and may suffer from anxiety disorders that can affect their outward behaviors.

- Depression – most brainwashing victims are isolated from their loved ones and the world. Their world revolves around pleasing their captor and receiving some kindness from them. They have no one else to talk to and their feelings are disregarded. This may cause them to be depressed and not associate well with others.

- Lack of self-confidence – the constant abuse by their captor and criticism makes the victim believe they are good for nothing. They fear to make decisions because they have been made to feel unworthy.

- Living in fear – one of the tactics brainwashers use is creating fear in their victims. They lie to them of impending doom and how the world is unfriendly. They live with the fear that every person is dangerous and if they venture out, they will be in danger. The captor also uses threats of consequences on their victim. The victim lives in constant fear of what may happen if he or she does not do as the captor says.

- Change of beliefs – the intent of the captor is to transform the beliefs of their victims in order to control their behavior. It doesn't matter whether their belief was ethical but as long as it does not agree with the ideologies or beliefs of the captor, then they are not good enough.

Depending on the intent of the captor or aggressor, there are varied effects of brainwashing on the victim. It is important to identify the technique and tricks that an aggressor will use in order to avoid being a victim of brainwashing.

Common Brainwashing Techniques used in Dark Psychology

Where underhand tactics are used by an individual or a group to influence and persuade others against their will to their will is brainwashing. In persuasion, it is possible for honest persuasion to stop an unethical one to begin that can be termed as brainwashing. People face persuasions every day. However, where an individual is being forced to change their belief without their consent is where dark psychology tactics begin. Various tactics are used by different people in an effort to brainwash their victims. These include:

- Isolation – this is usually the first tact in brainwashing. The aggressor ensures that the victim is completely isolated from their family and friends. The manipulator does this so that the victim has no one else to talk to and safeguard their victim from being made aware of the aggressor's manipulation tactics. They do not want their authority over their victim questioned by a third party or for the victim to get information from other parties other than themselves.

- Attack on self-esteem – once the victim is isolated, it becomes easier to break them down and the manipulator can build them up as he desires. To be able to brainwash someone, the victim must be made to feel inferior to the manipulator. The manipulator then starts to attack the victim through ridicule, intimidation, and mocking of the victim. This breaks down the self-esteem of the victim and they completely feel they are at the mercy of the manipulator.

- Mental Abuse – a manipulator will also use mental torture to brainwash their victims. They do this by lying to the victim and them using the truth in the presence of others to embarrass them. They could also constantly badger their victims and deny them any personal space such that they feel imprisoned.

- Physical abuse – there are various physical techniques available to manipulators to brainwash their victims. These may include depriving their victims of sleep, causing bodily harm through violence, denying them food and keeping them cold. A manipulator can also use subtle ways to brainwash their victims. Some of these ways could be by keeping noise levels up, having flickering lights all the time, and in some cases deliberately changing the temperatures in the room.

- Repetitive Music – studies have indicated that playing a repetitive beat can induce a hypnotic state in a person. A manipulator that understands this can use this tact against their victim. The rhythm of the music can alter a victim's consciousness until the manipulator can easily speak suggestions into your subconscious. In doing so, your brain automatically responds to the new suggestions and you begin to change your behavior.

- Contact is only allowed with other brainwashed individuals – the manipulator only allows their victim to get into contact with their other victims. This is because he or she wants the peer pressure from the other victims to influence the victim into submission of the new way of thinking. Because of the isolation also, the victim seeks to adhere to the suggestions of others so that they get accepted and they stop feeling lonely.

- Us Vs Them – when the manipulator indicates there is a Us and Them, he acts like he is giving the victim a choice between the manipulator and the perceived enemies. They do this in an effort to gain complete obedience from the victim. They have been showing the victim the negative side of the others and expect the victim to choose them over the others.

- Love Bombing – with this tact, the manipulator draws the victim into themselves or the group by showing physical affection through touching, trading intimate thoughts, bonding emotionally and showing kindness. This is meant to validate the victim and show them they have made the right choice by completely erasing any affection they may be feeling for others outside the group.

Hardly is brainwashing used for good. Most manipulators use brainwashing tactics in order to gain full and absolute control of their victims. Brainwashing is always harmful to the victim. They lose their sense of self and live to please their captor. Simple things we take for granted like the ability to decide what to wear and when to wear it is taken away from them. They are not allowed to make any decision and are meant to feel unworthy and lucky to be in the good graces of the manipulator.

The first step to avoiding being brainwashed is understanding the tactics manipulators use and their traits. This enables you to identify them before they are used on you or your loved one and call them out. Brainwashing is a common tact in dark psychology where a manipulator uses these tactics to gain control over other people for their own gain disregarding the feelings or well-being of their victims.

Hypnosis

Hypnosis is the next major application of Dark Persuasion that will be discussed. Hypnosis can occur with or without the person's knowledge. If a person knows they are being hypnotized, they may be more aware of what is going on, but they are still susceptive to manipulation.

Hypnosis is used for many different reasons, and it can be used for positive change as well as negative change. Hypnosis has several elements, and they may or may not be present in different iterations of the hypnosis process. It starts with an induction. Remember in cartoons, when they have the illustration of the swirling visual effect, and some head-wrapped mystic is holding a watch with the swirl in front of a person's face? This cartoon depiction is what is known formally as the induction process.

The induction process is when a person is actually trying to change another person's state of consciousness. In order to make the person more suggestible and influence-able, hypnosis uses an actual transformation of the state of consciousness. In order to think about this, you can think about a person who is typical and awake, a person who is paralyzed but otherwise capable, and a person who is in a coma. There are many gradations to the state of consciousness that a person is in. The person who is being hypnotized is not paralyzed, but they are closer to that than normal consciousness. Normal consciousness allows the person to have too much stability and defenses. The state that is induced in hypnosis is one where a person does not have all their defenses in play.

After the induction process has been successfully implemented, then the person can be told what to do or what to think. Since the person who is being hypnotized has their defenses uncovered and weakened, they are able to take instructions without question.

One method that works in NLP as a tool for hypnosis is anchoring. Anchoring is when a hypnotist uses something very familiar to you to bring you to that induction space where you are very suggestible. It might be a nursery rhyme, it might be a name you were called when you were younger, or it might be a song. This works to engage your subconscious, and it tricks you into thinking you are safe and allowed to be engaged in the suggestions.

Another NLP –based method for hypnosis is the NLP Flash. The flash works by switching the reward to punishment, or the punishment to a reward. So, if there is something that you like to do which you are trying to stop doing, like smoking cigarettes, the hypnotist will make you think about a cigarette, and then they will make you experience something very uncomfortable, like an electric shock or some other kind of physical or emotional pain. This is a very dark method and can have very deep implications.

Hypnotism can be a very strong way to persuade someone against their will. It may not be as secretive as the other methods of persuasion, but it can be used without your knowledge.

The next major method of Dark Persuasion is manipulation. Manipulation comes in many forms; what we will talk about here the most is manipulation in interpersonal relationships. Manipulators have many methods, but some of the major ones will be discussed in the following paragraphs.

The first is putting down the other person. The manipulator often will have to be very sneaky about this technique. Obviously, if there is someone who puts you down, you will not like them, and you will start to avoid them. So, the manipulator often starts out as a close friend or a confidant. They build trust in the relationship before diving in. Then, at some point, they will start to disparage the other person in what they do, how they look, or other parts of their personality. The manipulator often knows exactly how much they can push buttons, and they know how far they can go before being recognized as a manipulator. Along with their technique also comes the making the other person feel guilty. The manipulator makes the other person feel like they have wronged them, rather than the truth, which is that they are being tricked. The manipulator will make the person feel like they have some sort of debt to the other so that they enter into a sort of pact where there is inequality. Ultimately, what happens is that the manipulator puts the person down, which makes them feel bad about themselves, and it makes them feel like they don't deserve to stand up for themselves.

Another technique of manipulation is lying. Lying may be one of the more straightforward techniques of the manipulator. They will use excuses and complete fabrications to get other people to behave the way they want to. Lying is something that can start small and morph into a larger problem. The manipulator knows how to keep a person stuck in their web of illusions. Overall, they create a larger illusion of what the "truth" is. They try to create something that appears true to the manipulated person. The lies might have to do with any number of subjects. If the manipulator wants money, they might lie about how poor they are, and make themselves seem broke and desperate. If they want loyalty, they might make up lies about how important the other person is to them. If they want a job, they might lie about their experience in that field and make it sound like they are very successful. If they want sex, they might lie about a whole host of subjects.

Deception

Deception is the last major method of Dark Persuasion that we'll talk about. Deception is similar to lying, but it has some different components. One of them is equivocation. Equivocation is when someone makes vague or ambiguous statements. The point is to make things unclear so that you are not able to point out the mistake in their logic. Deception is making things seem a certain way when they are not that way. Deception is when a person uses any tactics to help make a situation seem different than it is. Lying by omission is one example of this. Lying by omission is when a person leaves out important information for the sake of changing others' perception of reality. Deception is done without a person's knowledge, and it is something that changes their perception of the situation without actually lying. Camouflage is another example of this deception technique. This happens when someone is trying to hide the truth in a way that another person won't realize that they are missing some of the necessary parts of the story. This will be used when someone is employing half-truths. Camouflage will happen when somebody is trying to hide their real name or what they do for work. Camouflaging can be conceptualized as a way to hide in plain sight in metaphoric terms. A person who is skilled in employing camouflage will be able to change their entire persona, including body language, when necessary.

One unique, more specific strategy which is often used in Dark Persuasion is the "give and take." The give and take technique works by fitting you into a dialogue about whatever the subject matter at hand is. The "give and take" technique works because a tricks people into thinking that they are actually in an equal relationship when they are not. People tend to trust those who they engage in a back-and-forth with. They start to think that, because there is a feedback loop, they are in a relationship that is fair. This is often not the case. One way to do this is to ask for someone to do a small favor for you. Once they have done the small favor, you then require that they do something else for you. Once both of these are completed, you pay them back. This might be by doing a small favor for them. It might be by offering some kind of material response, like money. Money is one of the biggest motivators for humans living in our time. Now, by establishing this loop of the give and take, you have established a relationship.

The number-one way to do this concretely every day and learn about you is journaling. You can journal every day and never write the same thing twice. Journaling doesn't have to be your homework. It can be fun, it can be creative, and it can be a way to release yourself from the shackles of what binds you.

When you write about yourself, you are looking at yourself through the lens of another person, or at least not through your own. By writing about yourself, you are also able to tell your story. Let's talk about both of these aspects of writing.

When you write about yourself, you get to look at yourself through your own eyes, but in a more objective way. Or at least, that's the hope. When you open up the journal and start writing about yourself, and it is all negative stuff, then you should be able to tell yourself that you have a problem there. When you are writing about yourself, try to be as subjective as possible. When you find that you are not able to do this, it might mean that you are too much up in your head.

You see, we start to develop ideas and concepts about ourselves that may or may not be true. Even if they are true, they might not be so good to dwell on. Many people have problems with invasive thoughts or automatic negative thoughts. If you are one of these people, just take your writing and see if you notice these thoughts in writing, and see if you can stop yourself and try to write out thoughts that are kinder and more accurate.

By talking about writing about ourselves in a more objective way, we can get more in touch with ourselves in terms of our real desires, goals, and ways of living. When we are in our heads, we don't get a really good idea of our perceptions vs. the world's perceptions around us. When we are all up in our heads about how we are, the world seems like a movie that we are starring in. When we write about our lives, it is a movie that you are writing. An objective perspective will let you talk about yourself as a friend rather than yourself. You can start to think of this guy or girl as a person who is closer to the world than to your own experience, and when you do that, you reduce the number of feelings and thoughts that might get mixed up with the perspective. When you take out the emotions and thoughts and just go with the facts, you'll find that you can be fairer and more realistic about yourself. Some people will find that they have self-esteem issues that they need to deal with. Others will be more on the side of narcissism, and they will need to learn about how to reduce their selfishness and start to think more about others.

The Internet And Dark Psychology

I t is an established fact that psychology is the scientific study that encompasses the study of human thoughts behavior emotions mind and so on. The beautiful thing is when one gets a deeper understanding of how psychology operates, it can be of great benefit not only to oneself but also in our everyday interactions with others. Man is a social being, therefore must process social behaviors which psychology seeks to understand, most time explains and sometimes predict.

Despite having many branches a large part of psychology is aimed at the diagnosis and treatment of mentally derailed individuals who possess a threat to the general public but depending on the perspective, Psychologists are versatile and cuts across many other areas. Also, note that psychology is all around you, your everyday activity, your interaction with others, that TV commercial you saw recently, the print ads, the website you are most frequent on and so on. All of these and more are either trying to persuade or convince you to bulge to whatever they are trying to offer.

Interestingly, there is psychology for any human problem no matter the age or gender which is why psychologist is bent on making life better and improving human behavior. As constructive, educative and informative as psychology maybe, there is a dark side to it. This aspect focuses on human consciousness as it relates to the nature of people prey on or victimizing others.

Dark psychology aims to understand the various thoughts, reasoning, perception or feelings that often lead to human predatory behavior because it entails the inhumane and brutal victimization of others without any reasonable human comprehension. Predators commit theft, abuse, and violence upon their victims and they appear in any form of personality. They are most times less compassionate and suspicious-looking.

Trolls generally can be annoying and irritating and can also be an agent of destruction/destruction. An internet troll starts quarrel and offends people on the internet. According to psychology, such people sometimes might have dark personality traits to them. They live such a life that is based on their sadistic nature and others must suffer the same fate and they naturally make you feel bad. Most times, there is a psychological disorder that is triggered by past experience or an ongoing occurrence, the best thing to do when you encounter one is to completely ignore them as they feed on your suffering which gives them great pleasure.

These internet trolls can be called a predator according to Michael Nuccitelli of predator.co. These people are first-class cyberbullies, stalkers, criminals, sexual predators, and the likes. These set of people use the power of the internet to gather useful information about their victims or targets.

A predator can be a group of people or persons that one way or the other, directly or indirectly enjoy stalking, exploring and victimizing unsuspecting individuals by using the power of information communication technology(ICT). They are most times consumed with their desire for power, imaginable fantasies or just suffering from loneliness and searching for acceptance. Age or gender is not a barrier as a predator can be of any age, gender or economic status. Initially, all we had was the human predator but with the rise of the technology age, things are now even more complicated as predators harness the power of ICT and use it to their advantage create profiles and stay almost untraceable.

Dark Traits And Online Activities

The internet is a world on its own, it is a chain of network communicating with other billion networks out there as long as you are connected and the other party also, no matter where you are, you would definitely be connected. With the internet a whole lot can be done, you have access to almost anything you can think of. Information is just a click away once you stay connected and it has also made communication way easier. Despite having wonderful advantages, the disadvantages are life-threatening. One of the common disadvantages is that people work online 24/7 and spend a lot of time sitting while working in front of a computer often get ill. They get weaker, develop eye issues, back pain, and the likes. Some people get addicted, some fall into depression and isolation and others, serious health issues while many ends up with serious social issues or psychological disorder.

The internet often encourages the use of different behaviors and activities that have done offline to be practicalized online. Imagine someone addicted to sex, games or shopping, when such a person gets online, it becomes unlimited which later turns to a habit. If as a normal being, the internet has such an effect, imagine what it would pose in the hands of a predator. The Narcissism is proud and lacks empathy, the Machiavellianism is manipulative and lacks moral while the psychopathy is selfish and remorseless. Above all traits according to research has some things in common such as the lack of empathy.

Categorically, dark personality triad is a big influence in the behaviors of predators that trolls online. The online behavior of a Psychopathy can be a remorseless behavior while a Machiavellianism manipulates and Narcissism preoccupied with getting attention because of their self-behavior. All of these traits, one can easily use it to pinpoint an internet troll that possesses a dark personality. From several researchers, it was discovered that the personality triad behaviors are mostly found on social media platforms like Facebook and most trolls have a psychopathic tendency, unlike the Narcissist who promotes themselves or social status by the same social media platform.

The online activity of a Narcissist since he has pride would be a display of superiority by uploading images that shouts expensive, they can be materialistic and display a sense of superiority; they can be domineering and a thirst for power and Status. Machiavellianism on the other hand even though can have self-interest but theirs is to manipulate and deceive unknowing victims to achieve their own goals. The Psychopath in their own way is destructive of all the 3 personalities.

The Psychopath has no conscience, is violent in nature and very aggressive. The psychopathy is attracted to people that catch their attention either by social life or social status and so on. Hypothetically speaking, Psychopathic is most likely associated which trolling and are more attracted to popular people on Facebook. Narcissism, on the other hand, might not be a troll but see themselves as being superior to everyone. They look down on people and they believe that they are special. Above all, Psychopathic traits can be sadistic and may find pleasure in harming others for fun's sake because they derive pleasure from it. So it is acceptable to say that abnormal online behavior is mostly Psychopathic traits.

How The Internet Promotes Different Vices And Negative Traits

The majority don't know that the internet is like an onion bulb consisting of different layers; we have the surface which is the aspect accessible to everyone, like your Google or Yahoo where we can buy things online or access our social media handles and the likes. Surprisingly, this surface web does not even make up for 10% of the internet we use, the remaining 90% is the real deal. They are what we call Deep Web and Darknet respectively. The deep web is only accessible to authorized persons as this is where private data such as legal documentation belonging to the government are stored. Also, medicals and academic information and not left out. The Deep Web is overseen by authorized and special services.

Moving deeper is the Darknet which is the most dangerous of them all, it uses the Onion Router (TOR). To have access, one would have to download the app. With just a click, one can end up in dangerous sites like the uncensored hidden wiki and many more. A site such as these provides information on drugs, weapons, pornography and so on. Various transactions can take place on the Darknet using our everyday services such as FedEx. An important thing to note is that users of the Darknet can be anonymous, every personal data can be concealed, secure and untraceable.

In regards to psychology, Psychologists have come to an understanding that there is a big relationship between the Dark personality traits which is the dark side of the human mind and the dark side of the internet. Some researchers even claimed that the amount of time spent online can increase or lead people to develop dark traits.

The question now is "is it the various online activities that attract individuals who already exhibit a good percentage of dark personality traits? Or can we say it is a long period spent on the internet that has increased these traits in individuals? There is a probability that both assumptions might be correct either way, the internet has over time become a sort for humans to explore their dark side. The internet has bred addicts because some negative traits seem to have been nurtured and encouraged by the internet which now possesses negative consequences when offline. The internet negative effect on personality is a functional part of online Psychology. With the help of the internet-related digital lifestyle, its effect on gambling or shopping is clear evidence of impulse control disorder.

Another negative trait is the rise of suicidal persons; it is no news that the suicide rate has risen over the years. One cannot commit suicide online but the increase of suicide definitely can be linked to an internet effect. The internet has also promoted online shaming, cyberbullying, name-calling and so on which is regarded as a violent online discourse which can lead to a less cohesive offline society. What about violent online games? Research has shown that offline aggressive traits can trigger exposure to violent games online.

The internet generally has psychological effects that once portrayed online, can remain relevant and be manifested offline even after one has logged off and these technologies are advancing as the day goes by. I asked how the internet has promoted or influenced the lives of people, the response definitely would differ as we have individual differences. The way of life nowadays can't be compared to the way people lived 20 years ago. These days we have fewer physical encounters and more of online interactions which in return creates a huge gap in humanity. Let us consider some disadvantages of the internet using social media as a case study;

- Reduction in emotional connection. In the days of old,if offended or you are the offender, you can easily talk it out with the other party, cry if you want to or perhaps punch some sense into one another and seal it off with a hug, case settled. in today's world with the rise of the internet or technology generally, if such should occur, one could send an 'I'm sorry' text and you wouldn't even know if the person is sorry or not. Using social media as a means of communication has killed our emotional connection one way or another. This is what some dark traits feed on you would never know what the other person is up to, all you see is an exchange of words until it gets too late.

- Avenue to hurt others. Remember the internet troll? They are the expert in this. They find pleasure in hurting others through hurtful words. It's a free world on the internet, you can say anything and get away with it. They forget that at the other end is a real person who has feelings and emotions but they can crush all that in just a line or two sentences. That is why some people end up timid or even commit suicide in extreme cases because of cyberbullying.

- Face-to-face interaction has gone. The way Mr. A would respond to you or communicate with you face-to-face can't be compared to how Mr will do the same if he is dependent on the keyboard. People now prefer to talk over a chart other than the old-fashioned meetup. No wonder a whole lot of Psychopaths are on the loose.

- Dead expression. You can be as angry as an erupting volcano but still, type LOL as a reply to a message. In the actual life, you are boiling with anger but laughing out loud via chat, who are we fooling? Laughter is an expression of a pleasant emotion and cannot be done otherwise but the internet has made it so.

- Lack of understanding. Because everyone is busy online, people tend not to understand other's feelings or emotions. Someone might be crying out for help but no one will be listening to why lack of understanding or perhaps thoughtfulness.

- Awkward interactions. Gaps have been created in so many relationships these days, friends and family now live as strangers; you are hanging out with friends or family and a single decent conversation could not be made because everyone is busy with his or her phone - someone is gaming online, another keeping up with the latest blog post or fashion trend or Sports update to mention but a few. There is a disconnection thus affecting relationships and creating this awkward feeling even when it's your loved ones.

- False self-image. This is the driving force of Narcissism, the average human lives a fake life on social media. We all tend to amplify our personalities to look cool and acceptable, your post must be perfect and flawless. You live in a world of imagination which you play online for others to see and admire. Sometimes, these displays cause others to feel bad about themselves only if they knew. Nobody wants to stay true to who they are and their identity, they cannot be blamed the Internet caused it.

- No family Bond. It's a family movie night, a time for the family to bond but Facebook, Twitter, texting or Instagram and the whole lot would not permit that to happen. We pretend to be watching the movie but in fact, we are not.

- Lack of attention. Findings have it that some accidents these days are caused by phone users, either the ones behind the steering or the ones walking by the roadside, why? Distractions here and there. The Internet can make one popular over time especially when you have a whole lot of friends and followers on social media platforms, you need to keep up with the trend so you spend most of your time online. This way you wouldn't take cognizance of things going on around you. Everything would suffer because of your lack of attention; your schoolwork, your businesses, friends and even families.

It is important to know that some people cannot imagine their lives without the internet and if you are among such people, then you might as well be a victim of the negative impact of the internet.

- Depression and anxiety because it promote poor mental health which is a result of spending long hours online.

- Anxiety, the fear of missing out which is also a result of your frequent online activities; so you get anxious when you are not online because you feel a whole lot is happening and you are not a part of it.

- Body shame for someone who has no self-esteem such that would be thrown off balance by social media. If you don't value or love your shape, size, height or complexion, when you come on the internet you will encounter people who are better than you, the celebrities, wealthy people and the likes. These might have a negative effect on your body Image, never believe all you see some might just be a narcissist.

- Insomnia, it is no news that spending too much time online can create an unhealthy sleep pattern. It can make one lose quality sleep which in returns, effects general productivity.

Conclusively, the internet is more addictive than alcohol and the likes. Can you boast of a day you went without the internet or checking up on your social media handles? If Facebook decides to go off the radar today, would you be emotionally okay to bear it? We all are addicted one way or the other but the degree varies and it's on this note that the emergence of dark personality traits came to be.

Harmful avenues of Dark Personality

Apart from the internet having disadvantages, it has also provided an avenue for people to lay their hands on harmful information about dark psychology thereby using it intentionally against one another. They should be searching for information as to identifying a manipulator or how not to fall victim instead people are after ways of hurting others or getting back at someone. They want to learn the art of dark personality traits and how they operate. Some of these harmful information is aimed at seeking to get an edge or more power in their everyday life. In the world of dark personality there are many faces to it, let us take a look at some of them;

1)You can manipulate another person's thoughts without the person's knowledge, this simple trick is called Covert Emotional Manipulation (CEM). With this act, you can hide your true nature and intention and the victim might have no idea until the dying minute which is always late the hour. In CEM, you can choose to focus on the aspect of emotions you want to manipulate which makes the process easier in some way. In a situation whereby the victim has a stronghold on his/her emotions, then the mission might be impossible.

Conclusion

T hank you for making it all the way through to the end of *Dark Psychology Secrets*! It was not an easy read and required a college-graduate level of reading comprehension. Congratulations! We sincerely hope it was informative and as much fun to read as it was to write. Be careful when using the tools provided within, and we hope that you use them to make your life better and to achieve your goals—whatever they may be.

After reading this book, if you find that you are in an abusive relationship with someone using dark psychological secrets and techniques on you, seek out professional help. There are many resources available to you, and all it takes is a quick search on the internet. You no longer need to accept being the victim of manipulation.

If you are interested in learning more about this subject matter, there is a wealth of information for you to research online. Good luck in your journey, and we hope Dark Psychological Secrets has helped you to see the bigger picture of the world you live in, as well as how the techniques described in this book affect our everyday lives.

Manipulation Techniques

Learn Advanced Techniques of NLP, Improve Your Empathy Skills, Dark Psychology and Mind Control to Influence and Persuade Others

ADAM JOHNSON

Introduction

We recognize that sometimes the words out of our mouths are not the best, and we feel guilty right after we say them. However, there are those people in the world who are emotionally controlling and manipulative. They will use passive-aggressive behaviors to get their way, and they will keep using these behaviors to prevent you from saying or doing anything that they do not like. Many times, you may not even realize that the other person is using this kind of behavior because they are very good at deceiving you and keeping the information hidden. This often results in the victim leaving the situation a little bit confused on what happened.

On the other hand, there are some emotional manipulators who use more force and are more overt in their tactics. They will use tactics that will leave you shamed, in fear, or they utilize guilt trips, and often the victim will be left feeling immobilized and stunned. This is exactly what the manipulator wants them to feel. If the victim is stunned and not able to respond to them, they can walk away as the winner, and in their eyes, that is enough.

Either way, emotional manipulation can mess with the mind of the victim. The longer the victim is exposed to this, the more confidence and power the manipulator will gain, and the better they become at manipulating. This kind of manipulation can easily destroy a relationship because all the respect, intimacy, and trust will crumble. This is true whether this kind of manipulation is occurring in an intimate relationship, a professional relationship, or other kinds of relationships.

Mental Manipulation is perhaps one of the most common forms of manipulation people will try to use on you. As a result of how often it occurs, it can be somewhat challenging to know when a behavior should be considered mental manipulation or not.

Simply put, think of mental manipulation as mind games, mind games that people will try and play with you. Some people will try to play these games at any chance they have no matter who you are and no matter the consequences they may face because of their behavior, especially in the workforce we all know someone who will try and kiss up to the boss or put you down to make themselves look more appealing.

People will be better able to take advantage of you and use these tricks if you are not aware of what you should look for. That is why it is important that you pay attention to the subtleties of mental manipulation and what to look for these little stages people put themselves on when they are trying to get what they want. Your number one defense against all of these manipulation subtypes is knowing what to look for in individuals who use them, more important understanding mental manipulation and all the techniques that encompass it.

Manipulators follow a Pattern

The good news is that most of these tactics all follow a similar pattern in how they work and as a result, once a few are understood it becomes much easier to understand them all as a group. This will be the primary focus of this chapter, what kind of forms mental manipulation can take on, how it hides and what to do when you encounter it.

With each form of manipulation mentioned building on the next and so on. That last step of knowing what to do when you encounter manipulation is perhaps the hardest because.

The reason for its difficulty comes from the fact that an in-depth understanding is the most necessary component of defusing it, and that can be difficult to have. But once you gain this knowledge you can even perhaps use it for yourself income certain situations to others try and gain something difficult peacefully or to make money. Take the real estate industry, for example, most of what will drive someone to buy a house is not usually always if it has the latest and greatest build materials but the things that "matter" to them these things that matter are based on simple primitive emotions and realtors know this.

Chapter 1: Manipulation Techniques

K nowing how to use some of these mind manipulation techniques make it much easier to make money if you work in the corporate world. With the knowledge, you will learn from this chapter you are now equipped with armor to use against anyone or any institution who would intend to manipulate you for their nefarious purposes, and you are able to do the same should the time or opportunity necessitates it.

Lying, is perhaps the simplest tactic mental manipulators like to use on their prey. The simple reason is that lying is fairly easy to accomplish and does not require much skill. Truthfully their real reason for lying tends to be to hide information that would damage them or become a barrier to their goals. Because if they did something bad. Well, they're not going to want you to know about it. As while manipulators love to be charming. The thing they love above all else is maintaining appearances. So, if they can keep the appearance that they are a good person through deceit then they most certainly will. We encounter liars every day in our life but, often, fail to realize they are telling us falsehoods. Detecting a liar can be difficult, as some people have mastered the craft of spewing falsehoods, so you're not going to be looking for overt signs like nervousness, scratching their nose, etc.

You want to look for patterns of untruthful behavior that you can notice and from there, you're able to slowly build up this pattern as a log in your mind, use that to your advantage. Sadly, the truth is that you have a very high likelihood of detecting a liar in a romantic relationship than you do say the nine to five workplaces.

This is because during a romantic relationship emotion is high, therefore this places the emotional stakes higher. This, in turn, means that someone who would do something that crosses these emotional stakes is willing to do whatever required to not get caught. A liar in a relationship will probably take the form of a partner who is never home but always has some elaborate excuse for why they're absent. Also, they may try to quickly divert the conversation from the matter at hand when asked where or what they're doing. Defusing a liar through thought is easy enough, but you must be persistent and firm in your belief of the truth.

Do not falter the manipulator will try and get you to become convinced that it is, in fact, you who is wrong and not them, that your version of the truth is the real lie. Remember though if someone is innocent, they will not protest their innocence and will trust you. Simply put, think of the old saying that if you have nothing to hide, then you have nothing to fear.

Tying well into lying as a manipulation tactic, some people will spin the truth to make themselves look like the victim or to allow blame to be placed on you. This kind of manipulation tends to just be called playing the victim and spin.

Most of us commonly associate the idea of spinning the truth with news and politics. But the truth is cover manipulators will do that whenever they can. Take the example I used earlier of the partner who is always absent and always seems to have a convenient explanation for them not being present. At times when confronted with this information, they will try and pin it on you by claiming you must be insecure in the relationship and how it has to be you who is jealous since you're so suspicious of them. This covert manipulation tactic works by preying on our own emotions and getting us to question them. Getting us to look at our feelings and actions with distrust allows the manipulator to convince us that we must be the crazy ones, we must be the manipulators. In simple terms spinning the truth works by trying to downplay whatever someone is being accused of in hopes that you will believe and trust them.

Flattery will Get You Everywhere

Moving on from lying and deceit I would like to discuss one of the more effective methods of manipulation and that is flattery. Flattery is an idea we think of when the thought of relationships come to mind. The husband and wife out to dinner joyfully juking and jiving with each other. Or someone at a bar trying to pick up a girl. On the surface that is technically flattery as in its simplest terms, flattery just defines a behavior where someone goes out of their way to give platitudes to you regardless if their truthful or not. Because of how flattery can make us feel good about ourselves, it can be challenging to view it as something manipulative or bad. And the strange truth is that flattery or outright being a kiss-up is not always a bad thing if you want to get ahead in something. As mentioned, prior this is especially true if you are trying to woo a girl.

To be honest flattery in its milder form is one of the integral parts of our whole courting process as humans. Flattery used well in the workforce, for example, can be extremely advantageous for the person doing it. As it allows them to try and endear themselves to their boss or other co-workers. In doing this they will gain those individuals' trust allowing them more upward movement within the company.

The issue with flattery is that it can be used to create relationships on false pretenses, i.e. it lures someone into a false sense of security about how someone views them. Trust like this that is easily generated is always something you should be cautious about. For example, you start dating a man and he is overly flirtatious and goes seemingly too far to make you feel good then perhaps consider that maybe his intentions are not quite pure. The line between flattery and genuine true compliments lies first in you knowing yourself and your self-worth. If you are a strong confident person than you will know if someone is trying to compliment you in a way that seems to both try too hard and also be untrue.

So, remember generally flattery is not always a bad thing but it can be a segue for someone into getting you to give them a false sense of trust which is not always the best. Remembering this and what kind of behavior to look for will help you avoid being a victim of a manipulator in the future. As the line between simple flattery to be friendly and flattery for malice has a fine line, just as anything does.

Remember – Manipulation isn't Necessarily Bad

As I mentioned earlier, not all manipulation has to be used for bad purposes. Some forms of manipulation we encounter regularly such as advertising and mass media. It can be used for good, so much so that they can make someone a profit. Or they can be used in the corporate world to climb up the ladder of hierarchy. In simple terms at times, it can be required that you grease some palms and perhaps act a certain way to get ahead.

Using manipulation techniques such as bending the truth or flattery may be required here to give you an advantage over the competition. In this case, it could be argued that it can be morally permitted due to the honest fact that if you don't try to push your way into these positions someone else will. At this point you are only playing the game everyone else is playing so by going out of your way to being friendly to your boss or bending the truth in how you present your accomplishments. Yes, you are using manipulation by giving your boss the impression an assignment you just completed may be better than it really might be.

Is that form of manipulation so bad? All you are doing is simply leveling the playing field. This type of behavior is less manipulation and more in line with the idea of being persuasive or charismatic.

The difference here is you are using charm and ingratiation to convince someone further toward your line of thinking regardless of what that may be. It is still them making the decision in the end, all your doing is guiding and influencing them. This is far different from coercion where you are using subtle threats and fear to get what you want. An example of this type of coercion would be lying to your boss about the performance of another coworker to put them down and allow you to get a position that they currently hold.

Now that you understand manipulation from a moral aspect let me explain how you can use it yourself. I am sure we have all been at home watching the television when a flashy add with cool music comes on and it catches our attention. But did you ever stop to realize that those ads are designed purposely like that to draw and suck you in? Pay attention next time you walk down the supermarket at how so many different items have such colorful and unique packaging, it's all done on purpose to draw you in and make the item you may or may not purchase all the more enticing.

Marketing and Manipulation

For simplicity sake, think of the mass marketing campaign for popular consumer electronics like the I phone. Apple the company that produces the I-phone will release a new one every year that is not all that different from the one they released a year prior. The way they do this is first by hosting these big insider conferences and then allowing in only a few select journalists.

On the surface, this may just seem like perfectly normal industry practice done to perhaps protect job secrets. But the opposite is, in fact, true, by making access to this new product seem exclusive and hidden they are then able to get people interested in it simply because people will always gravitate to what is mysterious and new.

Speaking of new the main tactic most companies like to rely on for sales is a psychological phenomenon called the "fear of missing out" simply put all this means is that, you a potential customer are more likely to purchase a product because it is new. In your mind, if you do not purchase the new fancy phone you have somehow fallen behind the social curve and are now missing out on something exclusive that all the cool people own.

This form of manipulation relies heavily on spinning the truth by the fact, that while, yes, the new product they are selling is slightly more advanced than the prior it really is not all that new, and the accompanying excitement around it is somewhat synthetic and not perhaps a natural occurrence.

So how can you use this tactic for yourself, well the best place this kind of covert manipulation works is the business world. Especially if you are in a sales-driven business. When trying to sell a service or good people tend to only focus on what said service or good offers, not so much ring home how much it can benefit a potential customer.

This may sound like common sense but in plain terms play up and ingratiate yourself to your customer base, let them know how lucky they are for looking into your product and how if they purchase the product they will be amongst some exclusive group. In these kinds of instances, you are not really harming the customer as you are persuading them to your side of the aisle. By making them feel good about this potential purchase they, in turn, leave feeling validating and like they have perhaps earned something useful in their life.

While you the salesperson has just sold a said product to the customer, therefore, increasing your profit and meeting your requirements. Moving away from the idea of selling something, you can use this type of manipulation in your personal life to meet new and interesting people. Put on an air that you are someone unique, cool or special when you are acting with someone. They will pick up on this and it will translate into the appearance of confidence, in short sell yourself, why should they be friends with you, what do you bring to the table.

These are all the things you can covertly show by how you make yourself appear to them. By using flattery and charm while also being integral you make both you and the people your meeting feel good something that is rarely a bad thing. Some people will call this charm the truth is that this a form of manipulation.

Now that you are aware of these kinds of sales tricks you are now armed to defend against them. But how do you defeat something that prays on basic instinct?

Manipulation and Basic Instinct

Well, the answer lies in your basic instinct. As I said earlier confidence brings with it the appearance of charm by putting on a confident mask you can get a potential manipulator into thinking that you are a hard target to hit. Think of the common image of the used car salesperson an individual who will try to sweet talk an individual into an overpriced purchase even though they know the person can't afford it.

They prey on people they can tell are not going to call them out on their behavior. This stereotype exists for a reason, it is because it is somewhat true if you present yourself as weak and powerless people will pick up on that. Recognizing that confidence is needed is only one step in the battle against manipulation.

The second is using a bit of common sense and taking a step back and thinking. If something someone is telling you seems too good to be true, then do not just take it at face value. Start by considering the context of the situation and what could motivate someone to be untruthful or manipulative in a situation. What if someone is cheating in a relationship? They may be willing to lie and be dishonest to keep that relationship going. Or, if someone is trying to sell you something then they have the incentive to lie in that context because their livelihood most likely depends on how many of a good or service, they can sell someone. Knowing this context allows you to look at what your being told as a piece of a much larger picture instead of just an isolated occurrence.

Manipulators Try to Wear You Down

Moving ahead a little bit and diverging from lying. I would like to bring up one of the most common tricks that manipulators like to try and use on you. That trick would be wearing you down. We have all probably other seen in person or on the internet videos of children throwing temper tantrums when they don't get their way. And the parents after a long period of their child screaming and yelling finally giving in to their kids' demands.

Well, the same fact goes for covert manipulators they love to waste time and try and get you to wear the hell down. Take an example of a friend trying to get you to give them a ride and you say no I am busy right now at work and as a result, cannot come and pick you up. Well then, this friend may begin, and excuse my language here "bitching and moaning." In short, they will begin to complain about how you are being unfair to them and they are your friend and would do the same for you.

Manipulators Want You to Feel Sorry for Them

This act of trying to say they would do the same for you is another common form of manipulation that manipulators like to use on you. They try and get you to feel sorry for them, even if the situation they are currently in is one of their makings. This constant badgering is done in the hope that you will forget the boundaries you have set, between you and them. Finally ending with you giving in and giving them what they want. To protect against these types of manipulators your only real course of action is to simply walk away and ignore them.

At the point in which someone has begun to constantly badger you with annoying claims and emotion, their already too far gone to help. At this point, there's nothing you can say that is going to get them to shut up they are just going to continue with what they are saying until they either get what they want, or you leave.

I am sure we have noticed how sometimes when we are at the store or talking to a salesperson about buying a specific product that they may try and tell us to buy now due to us missing out on some special sale of some sort.

The fact is these goods will always be marked as on sale and are usually not any cheaper or pricier than they normally would it is just a trick to suck you in. You can use this tactic in your own life by trying to make things seem more exclusive than they are, for example, if you're having some big get together and want people to attend it but don't think they will. Use the idea of something exclusive being there to draw them in getting them to consider what may be in it for them, as opposed to what's in it for you.

Remember that for manipulation to be used successfully in relationships or business, driving home what is in it for the other person is the most important thing, they need to feel rather true or not that they are being valued and getting something of value. This may sound like something cruel, but it is not, as long as you don't start using these kinds of tactics to harm people i.e. misplacing their trust and spreading rumors are just outright ripping someone off. The use of the tricks in the sales world, for example, is what can set apart a mediocre salesman from an exemplary one. Being confident in trying to utilize these covert tactics is almost more important than it is in trying to defend against them.

You would probably buy something from someone if they did not seem confident in what they were selling and the kind of service their offering. The same should go for you, give off a sense of pride in what you are doing makes your goal seem like the customer's goal. When using these things in interpersonal relationships always remember to use flattery as an entrance point, as mentioned earlier, it is a good way to get someone to trust you.

Trust and Manipulation

Without trust, nothing can be gained either in business or in personal affairs. You can gain this trust in a variety of ways, but you first want to begin by presenting yourself as trustworthy, because if you were not then why would someone want to pay attention to you.

Knowing now how commonplace manipulation is, and how it can occur from your house down to the sales floor. It allows you to defend yourself against manipulation which could harm you and stop you from accomplishing your goals. While also allowing you to use some of the tricks lightly to attain your own.

Simply put using your enemies' weapons against them is your best approach to defeating them, there's nothing wrong with trying to be overly friendly and flattering to someone. It makes them feel good about themselves and gives you companionship. This same moral attitude can be taken with business.

Think of it this way, if you can get the customer convinced that what they are about to purchase will benefit their lives in some way or the other then you have fulfilled a need of theirs. They will always go to someone searching to fill that need regardless of what it may be, so why shouldn't it be you who fills that need? Finally, you then gain something from a job well done, because you understood these tactics. By fulfilling two needs through one act you could argue that using these manipulation tactics for good could be better than using normal behavior to accomplish a goal. On the other hand, you may sometimes find yourself in situations that require you to use manipulation for survival or to even just get a meal.

Concluding this chapter, I will always remember the context of the situation you are in before you do anything regarding manipulation. By knowing how to navigate using these techniques effectively you can go far with them. As opposed to being in a situation you are unsure of and trying to apply manipulation tactics.

One of the most important components of manipulation is of course confidence. If you are not confident in what you are doing, then why should anyone else have confidence in what you are saying?

It may seem difficult to try and be confident when you know you are being somewhat deceitful.

To try and avoid this think of it as an actor would. In short look at what you are about to do and engage in as a performance of sorts. Convince yourself first of what you are saying. Now, this does not mean that you have to wholeheartedly believe every word coming out of your mouth.

But what it does mean is that you need to create the appearance that you believe what you are saying. This is the same tactic that politicians like to use when trying to get elected, they try and seem personable, and like an everyday joe. Remember this when you are trying to use manipulation tactics to your benefit. Because if you do you will be amazed at how well it goes and how much you can convince someone of.

Chapter 2: How to manipulate the mind through the NLP

Neuro-linguistic programming is a method to self-improvement and personal development that depends on the concept that successful characteristics can be brought through structuring and the underlying thought patterns and interpersonal communications.

How does it work

NLP isn't hypnotherapy. But it works through the conscious application of language to create change in thoughts and behavior.

For instance, a major feature of NLP is the concept that an individual prefers one system.

Therapists can realize this preference via language.

An NLP expert will search for a person's PRS and use their therapeutic framework. This framework may require building rapport, setting goals, and information-gathering.

Effective mind control techniques tip in NLP

The methods used to control the mind of others is an amazing type of destructing power that exists in society. The mind is more responsive in paying attention to activities in the external world.

Some are recognized, and the rest are just skipped. However, these pieces of information are mainly processed by the brain. We get 100s of information in a second using our five senses — both our conscious and subconscious mind filters this data.

This filtering relies on specific conditions. And this made it weaker to these powers where it is an important tool to regulate the thoughts of a person.

The mind control methods can affect one's proceeding actions because these measures are the outcome of the thoughts in your mind initially regulated. These methods depend on Neuro-Linguistic Programming that can regulate the mind of people using effective patterns.

Regulating thoughts

The activities of the mind can be reviewed using EEG, and this reveals the state of one's consciousness, alertness, and the intensity of the thought.

The baseline is the beta state using higher frequencies of the mind with the constant collision of thought waves. Mental frequencies are also said to be greater than the beta state.

After the beta state, there is the alpha state with a lower rate where the mind becomes calm with decreased thought waves. This condition is one of the most critical states of the mind in psychology,

The classical hypnosis relied on the process of subjecting the individuals in the alpha state so that their mind becomes more suggestive to the commands and can be enhanced. But the NLP techniques can induce the thoughts in the target's unconscious mind.

The persuasive spirit is high in neuro-linguistic programming, and this approach is applied in the politics, business, and socializing.

While the state of mental frequencies of the alpha or theta state of meditation is similar, they differ in their characteristics. Alpha is the first phase of meditation, and it will be upgraded to an advanced level with a modified state of consciousness.

A 30-minute meditation can generate the effect of six hours sleep by activating the chemicals linked to sleep, but a sleep of six hours does not generate the benefits of a 30-minute meditation.

The perception of the mind

The perception of the surrounding reveals an unconscious influence on one's thoughts to a specific degree. About 99 percent of our cognitive activity can be nonconscious.

This means it is possible to deceive a person's mind by putting an object or anything in the vicinity of the subject that overcomes the conscious mind which is acquired by the subconscious mind.

Several tactics of the mentalist employ this principle as they may put on a red tie that will be ignored by the conscious mind, and directed to the subconscious mind of the observer applying specific methods.

These thoughts are induced in the observer in an organized way that is applied by expert NLP professionals. The point is that the subtler the suggestions are, the more subconscious the mind gets affected.

The restrictions of mind go past our perception. It can be made to perform amazing stuff.

Mind control methods

Here are some of the best mind control techniques applied by NLP experts to control others mind.

Being attentive to the person

The experts pay attention to the cues of a person such as a pupil dilation, body language, eye movements, and breathing. They can interpret the state of mind of an individual because the immediate emotion of an individual is the link of such cues. These eye movements can be identified to analyze how an individual perceive and process information. For example, if one subject was requested about the color of his car, and he responded with his eyes moving to the right, it will be a visual recall of the color of the car.

Speaking with a suggestive human mind frequency

Speaking words close to the beats of the human heart. For example, 45-72 beats per minute, that is enough to activate the higher state of suggestibility to the mind.

Secretly establishing the rapport easily

The expert NLP professionals employ vicious language to improve suggestibility. The connection with you will be developed closely by examining you, and subtly pretending your body language, making you weaker to their recommendations.

Overcoming the conscious mind using Voice roll

This approach is the process of the voice roll. An approach which overcomes the conscious mind to the subconscious mind of the person. This is achieved by stressing the required phrase in a monotonous patterned approach.

Anchoring and sublimely programming the mind

This is the process of establishing an anchor in you so that it becomes easy to subject someone into a given state by sublimely programming the mind.

The proper way of applying hot words

The NLP professionals apply a certain sequence of words that appear normal but are more agreeable and suggestive. These words are linked with the senses. The words like hear this, eventually, see that, could immediately trigger a certain state of mind like feeling, imagining, and experiencing the desired perception in mind. They also apply certain vague terms to regulate thoughts.

Simple interpersonal subconscious mind programming

This implies that you dictate a person to plant a different thing in the subconscious mind of the subject.

This covert hypnosis approaches can affect the mind of people to a bigger extent but not to oblige them to do things that they are opposed to, which may demand a lot of mind programming.

4 NLP Tips to reconnect your brain

Change is difficult. So many of us struggle to shift from intention to action.

For instance, assume you want to quit smoking. You speak to yourself: It's such a bad thing, I need to stop. But wait, you have your birthday in a few weeks. You should wait. You know it will be tempting. I don't have any time to make any developments between now and then.

Can you see what happened there? In a few seconds, your thoughts go out of control. As you begin to think about a goal you wanted to accomplish, you went far ahead. Since you felt depressed, you procrastinated. You chose not to take action.

From a scientific point of view, procrastination is the means through which the brain controls stress. It is meant to protect us; our brains prevent us from achieving specific things that might be dangerous — things we consider as a big threat.

To make changes, we need to change how we think. With neurolinguistics programming, we can reconnect our thoughts and behavior.

One of the major tasks of an NLP practitioner is to highlight a person's favorite representational system. A person may prefer one sensory system to another. This can be established through language. For instance, if you like to say statements such as "I hear what you are saying," then that might show that you have a more auditory PRS instead of a visual PRS.

The five representational systems comprise:

Auditory

Visual

Kinesthetic

Olfactory

Gustatory

The language we apply reflect our subconscious perception of ourselves and the environment around us. In case our perception is incorrect, this generates a false internal belief system. Since our thoughts directly impact the way we think and behave, positive, permanent change begins with rewiring your brain.

The main aspect about beliefs is that it resembles a program that continues to run, where you continue to verify things whether it matches your beliefs or not.

So when your belief says that things are possible, and things will make you feel well, then what is going to take place is going to change your physiological differently than if you believe it is impossible. When you believe that things are difficult, you don't try, and you probably don't try with every fiber in your soul and every cell in your body.

Your beliefs are more powerful than what you always know. When your beliefs are strong, you can change your biochemistry. If you believe that medical treatment is going to heal you and it works, then you open yourself to every possibility.

If you want to close the gap between where you are and where you want to be, then here are some NLP tips that you can try today.

Do some affirmations

Why affirmations are great is because they work at every goal-setting stage.

You need to learn to say affirmations in the present tense because your subconscious mind will change the positive intention into reality, thus rewiring your brain faster.

Affirmations raise your self-awareness. By applying repetition, the new thoughts replace the old ones, making it ingrained in your mind. With sufficient practice, you can change your belief structure. This method is useful in addiction. When it comes to change, your brain requires to get on board first, and then over time, your body will follow.

Visualization

Are you aware that your brain cannot tell the difference between something imagined and something real? This means, your imagination is clear enough, you can convince your mind into experiencing positive emotions that match with a positive memory or mental picture. Determine the type of images that match with your goals.

Visualizations generate clarity to your dreams. The more positive visualizations you have, the more positive thoughts you experience, which will lead to positive behavior.

Content reframing

Try to recall a time when you felt angry or sad. For example, assume you ended a relationship. When you consider this, you are likely to experience negative emotions. To change your negative emotions to positive, you need to change the situation.

For instance, you are now open to a better relationship. The choice is yours to explore new options, and you have emerged from this challenge as a stronger and better person.

It is normal to panic when you lose a job, but this only builds emotional turmoil. By changing your concentration and changing your perspective, you will feel at peace.

In a certain study, researchers analyzed a group of nursing and midwifery students who were divided into two groups. The NLP training was administered in five 2-hour sessions, and the groups were studied.

Both nursing and midwifery group revealed differences in the scores of mental health, social function, and depression. It was concluded that NLP strategies are important in the enhancement of general health and different dimensions.

Anchoring

In this technique, you link a positive emotion to a certain phrase. This makes your brain to relate positive feeling with the gesture.

First, consider the emotion you want to feel. Decide whether you want to become confident, calmer, or happier?

Next, remember the last time you experienced that emotion.

Then, select an anchoring phrase like "I am happy. I am confident. I am calm."

Repeat this phrase daily until you can say the anchoring phrase and your mood changes to happy, confident, or calm.

Repetition is the key. The more you practice this method, the more it sticks in your mind. When you feel, think, visualize, and act by your intention, you will break the chain of negative habits.

The most important of all is to remember that these approaches are just tools. You have to work hard to experience positive effects continuously. For you to change, you have to decide to change.

Chapter 3: Identifying Hidden Manipulation

There are different types of manipulation that you will encounter during your life. When we are talking about covert manipulation, we are talking about a kind that occurs under the level of your conscious awareness. If you are a target of this type of manipulation, you probably will not be aware of what is going on, which makes it the most difficult type of manipulation to spot and deal with.

Some of the most skilled manipulators will be able to make you doubt your emotional well-being and self-worth, which makes it easier for them to be able to control you. When you fall into this trap, the manipulator is then able to take away your identity and a lot of your self-esteem. This does take a lot of time to accomplish, but then they have time to get you to do what they want.

Most experts will refer to these skilled manipulators as covert-aggressive people. They will have a tool belt of tactics that they can use to get their target to do their bidding. And, they are usually so skilled at what they do that the target will fall prey without ever noticing. Some of the tactics that a covert manipulator will use includes:

- The ability to hide their aggressive intentions,

- Make you afraid, make you doubt yourself, and more, until you are willing to concede or give in to them.

Dangerous manipulators

Good emotional manipulators can use almost any type of behavior to accomplish their goals. They are even more dangerous when they can read behavioral patterns and the actions of their target. When they can read their target, they will soon know their target inside and out, such as their level of conscientiousness, weaknesses, fears, insecurities, and beliefs. And in the hands of a manipulator, knowledge is power that they can use against their target.

In some cases, the manipulator can even become known as a psychopath. There are many manipulators who do not fall into this category, but still, manipulators are really hard to have real relationships with. They will take a lot of time to study people, and then they will never think twice when they use that information against their target. They are more concerned about being able to get what they want in every situation that they will not stop to consider their target's feelings or how they should be acting in a real relationship.

One factor that you need to keep in mind is that manipulators have a need to be in control. They are power hungry, and they will do whatever they need to achieve that goal. They will often hurt people in the process, and it will not bother them at all. If you ever feel that you are less superior, less intelligent, less strong, or less confident in your life, especially if you are around a specific person, then this person may be manipulating you.

Think about the relationship that you are in right now. Are you able to remember back when you first met them? Was it something magical, something that swept you off your feet? You will find that most manipulators are sweet talkers. They are experts at being able to hide their real personalities and real plans from their target. They already have plans to trick you to get what they want, and they will start from the first moment that they meet you.

In the beginning, this person will make you believe that they are willing to do anything for you, and they will keep up with this act until you are hooked deeply, and until you show them your vulnerability. Once you have done this, they will start to bring out the manipulation, and sometimes the extreme abuse will start if you let it.

Over time, usually pretty slowly, so it is hard to pinpoint when it actually started, you will be able to notice that your ideal relationship has changed. It has become more confusing, exploitative, and demeaning. You will notice that the self-esteem that you had in the beginning (whether it was strong or not) will start to turn into doubt, and it is likely that you will start to blame yourself for this issue.

At this time, the manipulator will have full control. It will not be long until you are fine with just getting crumbs out of all the interactions in the relationship. You will be blamed for everything that goes wrong, even if you had nothing to do with it. You will have to take care of all their needs and care about them all the time, while they will no longer care about you or your fears, needs, and emotions. These manipulators do not really care about any of these things; they only pretended to care in the beginning to get you hooked on them.

It is amazing how quickly things can change. Once a target is under the control of their manipulator, even those with very high self-esteem will turn it around. They will start to blame themselves for anything and everything that goes wrong in their relationship. They will start to over analyze things that happen in their lives, and usually, they will do this until they are so confused that they do not know what is going on in their lives. Every part of their day can start to suffer because of this confusion and the tactics of the manipulator such as their mental health, physical health, social relationships, and career.

The sad part about all of this is that the manipulator will be able to do all of this without you seeing where it started. It is not something that happens one day, and then you can see it and leave. It starts out slowly, usually with a few little remarks or tactics that are used. Then one day, the manipulator will have taken over all the control, and you don't know how to handle the issue at all or to understand what is going on.

Chapter 4: The power of persuasion

T here are many times when the human mind is pretty easy to influence, but it does take a certain set of skills to get people to stop and listen to you. Not everyone is good with influence and persuasion, though. They can talk all day and would not be able to convince others to do what they want. On the other hand, there are those who could persuade anyone to do what they want, even if they had just met this person for the first time. Knowing how to work with these skills will make it easier for you to recognize a manipulator and be better prepared to avoid them if needed.

The first thing that we need to look at is what persuasion is. Persuasion is simply the process or action taken by a person or a group of people when they want to cause something to change. This could be in relation to another human being and something that changes in their inner mental systems or their external behavior patterns.

The act of persuasion, when it is done in the proper way, can sometimes create something new within the person, or it can just modify something that is already present in their minds. There are actually three different parts that come with the process of persuasion including:

- The communicator or other source of the persuasion

- The persuasive nature of the appeal

- The audience or the target person of the appeal

It is important that all three elements are taken into consideration before you try to do any form of persuasion on your own. You can just look around at the people who are in your life, and you will probably be able to see some types of persuasion happening all over the place.

Experts say that people who are good leaders and who have good persuasion powers will utilize the following techniques to help them be successful:

- Exchanging

- Stating

- Legitimizing

- Logical persuasion

- Appealing to value

- Modeling

- Alliance building

- Consulting

- Socializing

- Appealing to a relationship

The above options are all positive ways that you can use persuasion to your advantage. Most people will be amenable to these happening. But on the other side, there are four negative tactics of persuasion that you can do as well. These would include options like manipulating, avoiding, intimidating, and threatening. These negative tactics will be easier for the target to recognize, which is why most manipulators will avoid using them if possible.

Now, you can use some of the tactics above, but according to psychologist Robert Cialdini, there are six major principles of persuasion that can help you to get the results that you want without the target being able to notice what is going on. Let us take a look at these six weapons and how they can be effective.

The six weapons of influence

Reciprocity

The first principle of persuasion that you can use is known as reciprocity. This is based on the idea that when you offer something to someone, they will feel a bit indebted to you and will want to reciprocate it back. Humans are wired to be this way to survive. For the manipulator to use this option, they will make sure that they are doing some kind of favor for their target. Whether that is paying them some compliments, giving them a ride to work, helping out with a big project or getting them out of trouble. Once the favor is done, the target will feel like they owe a debt to the manipulator. The manipulator will then be able to ask for something, and it will be really hard for the target to say no.

- Commitment and consistency

It is in the nature of humans to settle for what is already tried and tested in the mind. Most of us have a mental image of who we are and how things should be. And most people are not going to be willing to experiment, so they will keep on acting the way that they did in the past. So, to get them to work with this principle and do what you want, you first need to get them to commit to something. The steps that you would need to follow to get your target to do what you want through commitment and consistency include:

- Start out with something small. You can ask the target to do something small, something that is easier to manage the change, before they start to integrate it more into their personality and get hooked on the habit.
- You can get the target to accept something publicly so that they will feel more obligated to see it through.
- Reward the target when they can stick to the course. Rewards will be able to help strengthen the interest of the target in the course of action that you want them to do.

- Social proof

This is another one that will rely on the human tendency, and it relies on the fact that people place a lot of value and trust in other people and in their opinions on things that we have not tried yet. This can be truer if the information comes from a close friend or a person who is perceived as the expert. It is impossible to try out everything in life, and having to rely on others can put us at a disadvantage. This means that we need to find a reliable source to help us get started. A manipulator may be able to get someone to do something by acting as a close friend or an expert. They are able to get the target to try out a course of action because they have positioned themselves as the one who knows the most about the situation or the action.

Likeability

We all know that it is easy to feel attracted to a certain set of people. This can extend to friends and family members as well. So, if you would like to get others to like you and be open to persuasion from you, you first need to figure out how to go from an acquaintance to a friend. This will work similarly to the reciprocity that we talked about earlier, but some of the basic steps that you will need to follow to make this work include:

- The attraction phase: You need to make sure that there is something about you that instantly draws the other person to you.

- Make yourself relatable: People are more likely to be drawn to you if you are relatable to them in some way. It is also easier to influence another person if they consider you their friend.

- Communicate like a friend: Even if the two of you are not quite friends yet, you will be able to make use of the right communication skills so that the target will associate you as a friend.

- Make it look like you are both in the same groups and that you are fighting for the same causes: This can make it easier to establish a rapport with them.

Authority

If you want to make sure that you can influence another person, then you need to dress and act the part. This means that you should wear clothes, as well as accessories, that will help you look like you are the one in command. Some of the ways that you can do this include:

- Wear clothes that are befitting to what people will perceive an authoritative figure would wear.
- When you communicate with the target, you need to do so in a commanding fashion.
- Make sure that you can use the lexicon and the language of experts in that field.

When you can position yourself as the authority figure, people will look to you for the answers that they need. It does not matter how well they know you or not. You will have a great opportunity to influence them the way that you want them to behave.

Scarcity

The last weapon that you can use for persuasion is known as scarcity. Humans like the idea of being exclusive and are drawn to anything that they are not necessarily able to find anywhere else. When you make something exclusive, you have a chance of making it appear more valuable. People are also going to become fearful when something they desire starts to disappear. This whole idea is part of the supply and demand principle. If you have something that is abundant, then it will be perceived as having a lower value and cheap. But if it is rare, then it must have a higher value and be more expensive.

This can work for human beings and for products in the same way. Some things that you should keep in mind when you want to use the scarcity principle with persuasion include:

- Always imply that the thing you are offering is not going to be available to the target anywhere else.
- If you can, it is a good idea to implement a countdown timer on what you are offering. This gives a physical indicator to the target that what you are offering is truly going to disappear.
- You should never go back on the stipulations that you said in the beginning. You need to make sure that the target knows that what you offered is scarce, or this method is not going to work very well.

All of these principles can be effective ways for you to be able to use persuasion to manipulate your target. It is important to learn how to use them all and to do so in a covert way so that your target is not able to realize what you are doing.

When you are successful with bringing all of this together, you are sure to get the results that you want each time.

Chapter 5: Reading of the mind

A s I mentioned before, there is no such thing as "real" mind-reading. This opinion has been proven through the overwhelming plethora of academic studies, research, sting operations, and in so many other attempts at validating or debunking the "psychic arts," in no unspecific terms.

Consider the impact of that statement. It means that there is no one who is born with the ability to perform this art, and that it's an open field for anyone who wishes to indulge in it. As long as you have the patience and dedication to study and apply it to every aspect of your life with as much perseverance as you would, say, pursue survival in a jungle with a 500-pound tiger on your tail. While there will be some people whose natural inclinations and environment make them more attuned to the areas of observation that make up most of "mind-reading" techniques, it's a question of degree. Nonetheless, success isn't dependent on any esoteric information or talents which can't be learned.

This particular fact has been accepted so readily by practitioners and academics of psychology that it has led to the development of an entirely new stream in psychology known as Neuro-Linguistic Programming or NLP, the basic idea of which is that there exist speech patterns that are more likely to elicit positive or negative associations in the minds of listeners. Furthermore, NLP allows practitioners to exert small measures of control over willing listeners (or at times, even unwilling listeners) by nudging their behavior along positive or negative paths of action – but none that didn't exist within the minds of listeners to begin with.

If "mind-reading" techniques allow practitioners to understand and establish trust and credibility with their listeners, NLP enhances that bond and allows the practitioners small measures of actionable leverage on the behavior of listeners. However, the science of NLP is intricate and immensely complex, and therefore I will be providing only the need-to-know components of it in this book.

Without further ado, let's go ahead and delve into the art of "mind-reading," and discuss the various pillars that support and are responsible for the success of these techniques. Although they are only mentioned rather succinctly in this chapter, their application to the practice will be discussed in greater detail as we move along.

- While everyone is unique in some way, no one is truly unique.

- The reason why mind-reading works well is because everyone wishes and believes they're truly unique. Yet, refer to rule A.

- Even people who don't seem great at making connections want to make a connection, but are either afraid of rejection, have trust issues, or tend to hold themselves back by repeating to themselves that no one out there can truly understand them.

- People are always willing to share more about themselves than they realize, and only refrain from doing so because no one has used the proper approach to get them to open up yet.

- As long as you're confident and hold your own, a significant number of people will deeply believe the version of themselves that you paint them out to be, since they themselves want to believe that that's who they truly are.

- No one wants to believe as deeply as a skeptic, yet no one is as much on their guard as a skeptic either.

- Perception almost always trumps truth or reality.

- A mob is far easier to predict than an individual. However, two to three people are far harder to convince than an individual, unless one individual in that group is significantly higher in the power dynamic than the other two. In that case, if you target and convince that individual, the rest of the group usually follows along.

- When starting off, always go from vague to specific. Mind-reading works as a pyramid, where you move towards specifics as you reach higher.

Try to remember these basic pillars as we move on to the more practical parts of mind-reading, which we will explore in sequence in the subsequent chapters.

Chapter 6: What to Do If You Get Caught?

Any people fear that if they are using some of the techniques that come with manipulation that something bad is going to happen if the other person or their target figures out what they are doing. After all, the public opinion about manipulation is that the process is generally frowned upon, and most people are under the idea that manipulation is only going to be done when the manipulator is ill-intentioned. The idea of getting caught while performing these acts can sometimes be enough to convince some people not to use it.

Of course, your goal is not to get caught when you are using these techniques—it is a possibility at some points. This can happen at any time, whether you are brand new to using these techniques or if you have used them for some time. A simple slip up could be enough to get the other person to catch on to it—and if someone is already well-versed in how to spot manipulation, it is going to be even easier for them to figure out what is going on early in the game.

The good news is that getting un-caught in what you are doing is really simple. It is a good idea though to learn how to do this and to get the right skills to get un-caught before you ever need it. Hence, this chapter is going to take a bit to explore some of the things that you can do and some of the steps that you can take if you do end up getting caught by your target.

What Not to Do

The first thing that we need to understand is the things that you should not do when you get caught. If you are new to this game, you may find that it is easy to say and do the wrong things, which is going to make the situation so much worse. It is instinctive to go on the defense when someone catches on to what you are doing, and you may say something like:

What are you talking about? I'd never do that.

Are you kidding me, that's what you think?

I can't believe you would think that of me.

These are all unhealthy types of manipulation that are meant to place some guilt and blame on the other person, and they are a sign of immaturity in this process. They are found in some processes of manipulation that are intended to take advantage or exploit the other person, rather than to bypass them simply, and it is best to find some other methods to help you get un-caught, rather than resorting to these.

When you get caught, this can sometimes be your first reaction. Even if you are only going to use manipulation in order to encourage an honest and thought out answer rather than the predetermined no, you may still find that you are outraged and a little upset that anyone would think in a negative way towards you.

The point to remember here is that despite your initial reaction, you need to be able to find ways to override it.

Do not, under any circumstances, try to displace the blame, create any feelings of guilt in the target, or even deny what the other person is accusing you of. The first reason for this is that you would be lying if you did. If you were unable to reverse the situation completely, then this turns you into a liar and a manipulator—and the second thing, extreme defensiveness, is a bit sign that you are guilty. Even if you don't realize it, you are pretty much admitting that you are guilty of whatever the other person accuses you of, and this can make it impossible to defend yourself down the line.

So, even if it may seem like the right thing to do at the time, don't get defensive, and don't try to shift the blame over to the other person. This is just going to make things more difficult in the long run, will make it so that the other person starts to assume that you are guilty of what they accuse you of, and so much worse.

What to Do Instead

Now that we have talked about what you need to avoid if you don't want to arouse the suspicion of the other person, you may be wondering what you should do instead to get them off your trail. Instead of trying to blame the other person or trying to defend yourself, there are two things that you can do right after someone starts to accuse you of being a manipulator. These are simple, and they are going to offer you the best hope of getting things back on track, and getting the accusations to stop.

The first thing to do is stop every effort of manipulation that you were participating in before. Stop using persuasion, stop making requests, and stop doing anything else that you have been utilizing in order to manipulate the other person. If you are accused of using these tactics and then you continue to use them, no matter the level, then you are just giving the accuser further evidence to justify their belief that you are manipulating them.

The thing that you want to strive for here is to make sure that there is no evidence for the target to link the manipulation back to you. Instead, you want to make it appear that the thoughts about manipulation were just in their head, and they were overreacting to the situation. If you keep using your manipulation tactics, then the target will see that you are actually trying to manipulate them, and they will stop being near you or paying attention to you.

You want to make sure that you are creating the illusion that the manipulation was just in the mind of your target. You may want to say something like "I can definitely see how you think that. I am so sorry. That was not my intention at all." You want to apologize, but keep that apology short and sincere. Do not admit that you were manipulating them, but let them know that you understand where their concern and thoughts are coming from.

With this method, you do not agree with them that they were being manipulated. Instead, you are showing that you understand them. Your target is not going to expect you to apologize or agree for the behavior that you did, and they will decide that it was all in their mind, or that they were overreacting to things.

When you completely stop doing everything manipulative that you did before, and you make sure to apologize for what they believed to be manipulation, you are going to get the target to doubt what they accused you have, and sometimes, there is going to be a level of guilt for even accusing you in the first place. In some cases, they are going to feel bad enough about the accusations, especially since you have now given them reasons to doubt what they had said, that they will want to find some way to make it up to you—and once this happens, you have the target right back where you want them.

So, to help you clarify this point, you want to go against your instincts when someone accuses you of being a manipulator. You don't want to get defensive, and you don't want to try and hide your trail. Instead, you want to make sure that you get them off your trail. You want to make them start to doubt that you ever tried to manipulate them in the past. Once you are able to do that, with the tips that we discussed above, you will find that you will be successful with manipulating any target that you want.

How to Get Back on Track

Once the target is at the point of doubting their accusations towards you, and they may even feel a little bit guilty because they pointed some fingers at you, it is time to slowly and intentionally get back on track with the whole process of manipulating them.

Remember that you have to take your team here. The other person is already on the lookout for anything that seems odd. They may be doubting themselves, but this doesn't mean that they have let you off the hook quite yet. This means that you don't want to jump right back in with full force. If you do that, the target is going to catch on to what you are doing, and they will walk away for good. Instead, you must take your time and work your way back up to manipulating them.

The good news is that you can just start back up with the three main steps that are needed to make manipulation successful in the first place. First, you will need to take some time to analyze the other person. Notice how your conversation is going, what the other person is saying to you, how they are responding to the things that you say, and what their tone is like. If the target has already pointed fingers at you and made some accusations, then you need to slow down and wait to rebuild some of that trust with them again before you get started with the manipulation again. The amount of time that this is going to depend on the individual you are working with; some are going to be easier than others.

Once you notice that the target looks a bit more relaxed, and like they have started to open up to you again, then it is time to restart the manipulation. You want to make sure that the target has some time to trust you while being in a pressure-free zone that has no attempts at manipulation before you dive right back in again.

If you jump past this part too much, and you miss out on giving the other person enough time, then the other person, who is already on the defensive, is going to catch on to what you are doing and will put their defensive up again. If you have already been caught, it is important that you take your time. Being caught a second time means that you are going to lose out on that target, and who knows what other damage could occur to that relationship and to other prospective relationships that you may have in the future. Taking your time can help you get back on track once you are caught and will ensure that the other person isn't going to run off and make it impossible to manipulate them again.

Once you have been able to work on your analysis, and you are certain that the other person has had time to get comfortable with you again, and you notice that the conversation has begun to flow freely again, then you can start to introduce the manipulation back into the conversation. Take your time, just like with before, and try to be as subtle as possible with this.

Your goal here is not to tip the target off that you are working to win them over again, so tread with caution here. Go slowly and then build your way up to where you were in the past, and where you would like to be in the future. This part of the game is not all about speed or a race of some sort to get back to the top. If you do this, you will end up losing the other person—and your goal of manipulation will be all gone.

Take your time and be patient. Try out a few of the techniques of manipulation, and see how they go. This can build up over a longer period of time, depending on how well you know the other person, and how often you get to see them. If you take it slow and steady, you will get yourself back at the top you just need to be willing to take your time, watch the cues that the other person is sending over to you, and learn when it is time to press forward and try a few more of the techniques that you know, and when it is time just to wait a bit longer. Once you have been able to manipulate the target again, and you are back to using all of the different techniques that we have been discussing in this guidebook, you will find that the target is going to be more likely to agree with you. This can help you to build up your confidence again, and then you can bring out the full blown manipulation requests once again.

One thing to remember here is that you need to make sure that your manipulation request is different from what you were using when you got caught—and choose a request that is going to be subtle, one that is hard for others to recognize and catch on to. This can make it harder for the target to realize what is going on and can keep you as the leader in this game for as long as possible.

If you utilize the manipulation techniques that we have talked about in this guidebook, there is a very low chance that you are going to get caught by your intended target, but it is something that can happen. Once it does, you can follow the steps above in order to help you get yourself back on track. These techniques are going to be the best way to ensure that you get yourself uncaught and that you will be able to resume manipulating the other person at some point, just as if nothing happened.

If you want to be really good at manipulating and getting others to do what you want, it is important that you know the proper way of displacing the blame and how to execute it, and then you must be able to cover yourself back up again. Approaching it in any other way is going to make it easier for the target to have evidence against you and they will be able to prove that you are manipulating them—and once this happens, it is hard to regain the trust and control that you once had.

Chapter 7: Watching Your Body Language During Manipulation

He next topic that we need to take a look at is the idea of body language and how it can work to help influence the other person. We spent a bit of time talking about the body language of the other person, your target, and how you can use this to your advantage—but you also need to pay some attention to the body language that you are showing to that target.

If you are able to showcase a strong and secure person—someone with a lot of confidence, which is easy to get along with and actually interested in what the other person is saying—you will find that it is easy to manipulate any target that you would like. Some of the things that you can concentrate on to make this happen include:

Make Yourself Look Nice

One of the first things that you need to focus on when it comes to your body language is that you need to look nice. If you try to manipulate a target when you are in your pajamas, looking like a slob, and without good hygiene, then they aren't going to take you seriously, and they are likely just to walk away and not want to listen to you at all.

There is something about likeability that can make it easier for you to really get the results that you want. If the other person likes you or is attracted to you, they are more likely to say yes—but if you are not desirable to them, then they will find that it is easier than ever to say no. So, how do you make sure that you are likable and that your body language and appearance will get the other person to like you?

First, you need to work with basic hygiene. You will find that most people have an evolutionary attraction towards people who are clean because these people were the ones who were considered the safest to be around in the past. We still have some of these traits, and this draws us to those who smell good and are clean. Plus, how are you supposed to get close enough to someone to manipulate them if you stink?

The good news is that good hygiene doesn't have to be difficult to achieve. You can make sure that you shower on a regular basis, wear deodorant, brush your teeth each day, and use some nice perfume or cologne that isn't too strong, and you will be ready to impress anyone you come across.

Next is to make sure that you have a nice haircut or style that suits you and make you look good. You will find that how good your hair does look is going to affect the entire outfit directly. When you are talking to someone you would like to influence, your haircut is definitely something that they are going to notice.

There are a lot of people who choose to ignore their hairstyles, but they still want to have a nice appearance to others. You also need to have some realistic expectations about things. If the haircut doesn't suit you, then it is time to let it go. You may have to experiment a bit to figure out which hairstyle is the right one for you.

And finally, make sure that you dress crazy. Find a style or fashion that works well for you. You need to be able to impress the person you would like to manipulate, and going crazy with style, especially if it doesn't fit with you, is going to backfire on you.

You may find that you can't go wrong when you are working with a simple and classic look. There is nothing wrong with having some fun with your style, but only if you really know what you are doing, and you don't try out something that looks horrible on you. If a person doesn't like the way that you dress and feels that your style is a mess, it's very unlikely that they are going to take you seriously—and in this kind of situation, it can be hard to influence the other person at all.

Look Directly at the Other Person

Your full attention needs to be on the other person when you are having a discussion on them. Eye contact can be a great way to form a connection with this target—but mastering the right kind of eye contact can be really hard to learn. You want to make sure that you are giving enough eye contact that the target knows that you are paying attention to them and that you are actually interested in what they have to say—but if your eye contact gets too intense, then it can make the other person feel very uncomfortable in the process.

Put on That Nice Smile

There is nothing better than a smile. A smile can show that you are open and receptive to what others are telling you. A smile can open a lot of doors. A smile can make the other person, your target, feel comfortable on another level with you—and people who smile are seen as more likable than others. What could be better than that?

One of the most important things that you can work on when it comes to your body language during manipulation is to make sure that you put on that smile. You don't want to go with a big fake smile though. Your target is going to be able to spot a fake smile from a mile away, and this can make them feel uncomfortable, or at least make them feel like something is wrong, and they are going to walk away from you as fast as they can.

Learning how to have a genuine smile, even if it is a fake one, can be so important when trying to put the other person at ease—and if you are successful with it, this smile can help others to like you. It is a proven fact that your target is more likely to say yes to you if they like you—and since a smile is one of the easiest ways for you to do that, it is worth your time to learn how to do a great smile for your target.

Pay Attention to the Way That Your Body Is Pointing

One thing that you should pay attention to when talking to your target is the direction that your body is facing. Most of us don't realize it, but with a lot of the conversations that we have, it is common to point the body away from the other person. We don't usually mean to do this of course, unless we are trying to get away from that person and they just won't quit talking, but it can send off the wrong message to the target.

When you point your body away, it can lead to some negative connotations. This body stance is going to really show a level of unfamiliarity between the two parties, and when your goal is to be familiar and comfortable with the target, this is not the message that you want to send out. It can also make the target think, at least subconsciously, that you are trying to get away from them or that you aren't all that interested in the conversation at hand.

A better way to stand is to make sure that the whole body is facing towards the target. You want your front, your feet, and your face to be pointing right at the target. This brings in a level of familiarity with the target and can make it easier for you to start up some rapport with them and get the results that you would like. It is a slight shift, only a few degrees in one direction or another, but it can make a world of difference in how far you get manipulating your target.

Don't Let Anything Distract You

When you are trying to manipulate the other person, your full attention needs to be on them. If you are constantly looking around at other people, your phone, and any other distractions that are out there, you will find that it is a big turnoff to your target. They will assume that they are not that important to you and that you find a lot of other things more interesting than them, and you will lose their attention in no time.

When you are manipulating your target, your full attention needs to be on them. Ideally, you will be in a location where it can just be the two of you—or at least a location that is a bit quieter so that you can focus on just them. Of course, this isn't always going to happen. If you do end up in a location that is loud and has a lot of people, then you still need to keep your full focus on that target, at least for the duration of that conversation. If you struggle with this, then add it to the list of things that you need to practice.

It is so important to get rid of all the distractions possible when you are dealing with your target. Turn off the phone, make sure that the social media and the internet are turned off if you are dealing with them near a computer. Don't pay attention to the other conversations that are going on around you, and don't let the television or anything else distract you from the cause you are working on right here and now.

Your target is definitely going to feel more at ease when you are able to give them your full attention. In a world where we have a million things grabbing for our attention, and we are asked to look in a million directions at once, it can be nice when someone is willing to put their full attention on just you. This is exactly how you want the target to feel as well.

Try Mirroring the Other Person

Another method that can work really well when you are trying to manipulate another person is the idea of mirroring them. This is when you try to copy what they are doing with their gestures and their body language because it helps them to feel more comfortable around you subconsciously. If you do this in the right manner, they will find that they are drawn to you more, without even knowing why.

There are a lot of little things that you can do to make this happen. First, you can look at how they are standing. Do they use a lot of gestures when they talk or do they like to keep their arms folded? You can mirror this. Are they standing still or tapping their foot, tapping their fingers or making some other small movements that you can notice?

You can pay attention to the way that they are talking about. Are there certain articulations that they are making when they talk to you, ones that you could use in your own speech as well? You don't want to make this so obvious that they feel you are teasing them—but making some minor adjustments in your own way of talking can help you to match up with them a bit more and can encourage the target to feel a bit more comfortable with you.

Now, you don't want to make these gestures too obvious. If you are blatantly copying them and making it look like you are mimicking them, it is going to come off as you making fun of them. The other person is going to get defensive and offended at what you are doing, and they will just walk away and not talk with you any longer. This is why there needs to be a good balance with what you are doing. You want to be able to impress them and make them feel comfortable, without them really catching on to what you are doing.

This is something that can take some time to perfect. It is hard to get other people to feel comfortable with you—and while mirroring can be a great way to make that happen, it is a technique that takes some time and talent to accomplish. The best way to get better is to do a lot of practicing until you can perfect the technique.

Stand a Little Bit Closer

You don't want to be so close to the other person that you have invaded their personal space, but standing across the room isn't a good alternative either. There is a certain level of familiarity and comfort when two people stand relatively close together. This means that you can convince the other person that you are someone to trust and someone they should be near—just by moving yourself a tiny bit closer than you normally would.

Think of it this way: how are you likely to stand near a stranger compared to near a close friend or family member? When you are working on manipulation, you want to aim for the latter, even if you don't know the person all that well. This makes it easier to talk with that person, allows you to hear them better and respond to what they are saying and can instantly help them to feel at ease around you and like there is some kind of bond between you.

Always pay attention to how the other person is reacting though. Most people won't mind if you stand just slightly closer to them—but others are going to have a wider personal bubble, and it is important to respect that as much as possible. If you get too close to these kinds of people, you are going to put them on the defensive, and they will not want to spend time listening to what you have to say, and your tactics of manipulation will be hopeless.

While it is important to pay attention to the body language of the target you want to manipulate, you also need to make sure that you are paying attention to the body language of your own first. If you get too agitated, don't look nice, and seem sweaty and nervous in the process, you are going to find that the other person just won't be drawn to you, and they won't be interested in listening to what you have to say.

It is your job here to come off as likable as possible. You want the other person to look at you and feel like you are friends. You want them to trust you—and the best way to make these things happen is to be likable. It may seem a little bit shallow, but people respond better and are more likely to say yes to, those who they see as likable. If you are able to follow the tips above, you will find that it is easier to become likable and to get people to say yes to you.

Chapter 8: How to Say No

Why are people so mean? Why are they so selfish? Why can some people not be trusted? Why?

Most people who find it hard to say no have one thing in common: they find the world hostile and they would like to be able to live quietly without being continually forced to be on the defensive.

It is regrettable that the world is filled with crooks, egotists, and manipulators of all kinds. We can regret that we can no longer trust anyone, but these recriminations do not change the case. There is no point in playing the ostrich while regretting that the world is bad or difficult. To moan about the harshness of life (or to dream of a better world) prevents one from seeing reality and, therefore, from acting effectively. As we dream of an impossible world, the one we live in becomes hostile and we feel less and less able to change anything.

To dare to say no, one must first accept to see the world as it is. There are selfish people, others who are thirsty for power, there are manipulators, and there are also cheaters, liars... There will be a long list. It is useless to groan or lament, this is how the world is made. Let's open our eyes and accept the facts!

How to Say No to a Charming Manipulator

The Finding

Whether a man a woman or a child, the charming manipulator draws us and lulls us in an illusion because we found the manipulator attractive, fun, touching, friendly, etc. He seems so full of attractions that we would like, in return, if not please him at least to not displease him.

His art of seduction paralyzes us and prevents us from saying no to him. We are afraid of disappointing him, we are afraid of appearing ridiculous; we do not want to be seen as "stingy," jaded or selfish. As long as we believe in the image presented to us by the charming manipulator, we do not dare to resist him, and so we find it difficult to say no to him.

To Resist

Facing a charming manipulator, the first thing to do is to break through the illusions. To achieve this, one can ask oneself the following questions: what do these smiles and beautiful manners hide, what is his real purpose, and what does he really want from me? Beyond what he shows me where does his interest lie? Why is he doing all this? In this story, who will be the real winner? Where is the trap?

Then, to put an end to small manipulations, the simplest is still to say no with the firm intention not to go further in the discussion. This no must be clear, clean, and unscrupulous and must not engender any sense of guilt. Do not be afraid to oppose the manipulator! There is really no danger in saying no to a charming manipulator who asks you for a service or tries to sell you something.

Remember that you cannot hurt a manipulator. We can only hurt honest people. If a manipulator told you that you hurt him, do not believe him and especially do not enter his game. It is still an attempt to manipulate to make you give way to his request.

The real goal of the manipulative charmer is not to please you, but to take advantage of your credulity, one way or another. Also, do not give him time to develop his arguments and convince you. Time (the length of discussion) always plays in his favor. Each additional second spent listening to it makes you fall a little deeper into his trap.

Remember that you are in the presence of a Type II manipulator who thinks only of his interests (even if he says he only thinks of yours). Abbreviate! Tell him no, simply and as quickly as possible.

To say no is both to affirm one's refusal and one's willingness to put an end to communication. By saying, no thank you, or no it does not interest me, the intention must be clear, concise, and straightforward. No ulterior motives or scruples! Above all, no guilt! The more perceptible your confidence and assertiveness, the more effective your refusal and the more the manipulator's maneuvers will be quickly stopped.

Sometimes we cannot just say no in a simple way. Either we waited too long or we know the person too well. In these circumstances, it is better to know how to formulate your refusal correctly.

When we do not want or when we cannot meet the expectations of a charming manipulator, we must know how to say no in these forms.

A friend asks you to take her somewhere when you have to go to an appointment: "It would be really nice of you if you could drive me to a place."

Rather than giving in and missing your appointment, you tell her no, as follows:

"Look, I gladly would have accompanied you, but it is at the other end of town and I have this appointment that I absolutely cannot push back. Maybe you could take a taxi or ask someone else to take you? Now forgive me, but I must go."

Let's take a closer look at this kind of answer as it contains all the necessary ingredients to say no to a charming manipulator.

You first show him that you understood his request, and that you are not against it but you absolutely cannot do her this service: "Look, I would have gladly accompanied you, but it is up to the other end of the city and I have this appointment that I absolutely cannot push back. . ."

You then offer her an alternative without giving her time to breathe. "You could maybe take a taxi or ask someone else to take you."

Finally, on your way, you cleanly break from the interaction under a valid excuse and you leave the scene: "Now forgive me, but I must go."

To say no in this manner:

• Describe the situation by repeating the words of the manipulator to show unambiguously that you understand the nature of the request.

• Calmly express your point of view or expose your constraints without justifying or losing yourself in useless details: I cannot or I do not want to do it for this or that reason.

• Search for and propose one or more solutions: Maybe you could... Have you thought to ask...?

• Put an end to the conversation with a short sentence to signify to the person you are talking to, that for you, the communication is over: Well, I hope you will find a solution. Good luck and goodbye!

"Do you want to buy into the lottery with me? It will cost us less and we will share the winnings."

"Thank you for thinking about me, but you know I do not like gambling. If you win, I prefer that you keep everything. I do not say "good luck" since it seems that it brings bad luck."

The sense of repartee or appropriateness is not invented. It is a form of ease that is born with an understanding of things and grows with self-confidence.

A person who is sure of herself is not afraid to express her point of view firmly and calmly. She defends her rights while respecting those of others. She is able to assert her personality and needs without provoking hostility. She does not let herself be walked on and knows how to say no without feeling guilty.

Remember

To overcome a charming manipulator, you must first realize that behind the charmer hides a manipulator. Discovering one's hidden purpose is one of the best ways to break the spell. In order to put an end to the simplest manipulation is to dare to assert your refusal quietly and without excess complexity. Depending on the context and the quality of the relationship, the expression of no will be more or less realized in the ways we discussed above.

How to Say No to a Guilty Manipulator

As far as most type II manipulations are concerned, you have to know how to say no to get rid of them. Unfortunately, some manipulators still manage to extort what they want by playing on our feelings of guilt. In this case, saying no is not enough.

The Observation

Here is a non-exhaustive series of guilt phrases used by a manipulator:

- Listen, I am your friend, you cannot refuse me that!

- After all, I've done for you, is how you reward me?

- I never denied you anything and you had the nerve to say no to me...

- You only think about yourself, and I had cared about you completely!

- How dare you do such a thing?

- It's always the same thing, as soon as I ask for something, I'm refused ...thing

The essential thing is to understand that the guilt-maker tries to play with our conscience and make us feel bad. In this way, he strives to make us regret our refusal and thus intends to change our minds. See how some beggars know how to play in this register to get the passer-by to open his wallet more easily.

Find one or two situations in which the manipulator was able to make you feel guilty when he countered your refusal, or simply to better get you to give him what he wanted.

Guilt is an honorable feeling that is related to our education. Our parents, school, friends, and life in a society taught us what was good and what was not. In the same way, we learned, often at our expense, what it cost to break an established code.

Guilt is also a natural feeling in the normal man. Only the great perverts, war criminals, terrorists, serial killers, pedophiles, and other sick people feel absolutely no remorse. When they are called to trial, they are completely insensitive to the evocation of their crimes. It is this indifference and lack of compassion that disturbs the victims and their families (as they testify in front of the cameras at the end of the courtroom).

Guilt is a normal and easily accessible emotion. The skill of the guilty manipulator is to know how to activate it wrongly in his victim. It is not the guilt itself that is in question, but its justification. As long as we do not carefully study this feeling to question it, eventually, the manipulator manages to make us submit. In fact, he wins as long as we believe we should be guilty.

To Resist

To resist a guilty manipulator the question to ask is: Am I really guilty of what I am accused of? The answer is not easy and it is not a question of disguising yourself as a justice of the peace to determine who is wrong and who is right. What counts is to know how to evaluate, even approximately, the reality of guilt. For that, it is enough to ask: Is there a balance between what he asks me and what he says he gave me?

A friend requires you to come and help him move and you absolutely cannot do it:

"Say, I'm counting on you to help me move next Thursday."

"You know I cannot, I'm already taken."

"I thank you! When you needed me, you were happy to find me. Now that I need you, you drop me like an old sock."

You actually remember that you had invited this friend to help you restore your country house. In fact, he got up at 11 o'clock and did not participate in any work, even housework. From time to time, he came to see if we needed him and went back to take a nap or go for a walk. Now, thanks to this quick review, you can answer him calmly. "Yes, I was very happy to have friends to help me when I needed it. It was a good holiday for everyone. Besides, you have benefited well. But when it comes to your move, I really cannot help you, I'm already taken elsewhere. Ask someone else or call a company."

When we find ourselves in the presence of a guilty manipulator and we realize that there was no reason to feel guilty, we can then oppose him calmly and tell him no without needing to justify.

In spite of what he tells you, you owe him nothing. Do not embark on endless explanations either. Abbreviate the conversation without complexity, avoiding aggression, devaluation, and irony.

Guilt and Legitimacy

The desire and the will of others are legitimate, but that is not a reason for them to impose their will on us by making us feel guilty. We also have needs and aspirations just as legitimate. To regain our legitimacy, in the face of this feeling of guilt, it is essential to take a little time to reflect on our present and future rights.

To help you feel confident when faced with guilt, study and complete the list below.

I have the right: to think differently from you; to rest; to do what I want; to not make myself do it; to not always agree; to work at my pace; to think about me; not to love; to refuse; to not give any explanation...

The Right to the Difference

To widen this reflection on the legitimacy of your rights, remember situations where someone has prevented you from asserting your own taste or expressing your preferences, your opinions, your feelings, and your reactions.

Take the time to see how you could have asserted yourself more with what you know now. Do it for each of your rights. This is not lost time, quite the opposite!

The Right to Imperfection

Know that you are not a superman or a wonder woman. You have the right to have weaknesses and to display your limits and your misunderstandings. There is no objective reason to be guilty of these "inadequacies."

These are not flaws but are simply proof of our humanity. In this case, too, see how you could have reacted differently by claiming these rights without making it complicated instead of hiding them.

Remember

The guilt or the threat of rejection is ways that the guilty manipulator uses to enslave us. By becoming aware of our stagnation (which submits us to blackmail), we free ourselves from both guilt and manipulation. We are then able to assert ourselves for what we are and become able to say no to manipulation.

How to Say No to a Respectable Manipulator

The difficulty with respectable manipulators is that one does not even think of telling them no simply because one does not realize that one is being manipulated.

The Observation

When a doctor, a journalist or someone with a higher social status than ours speaks, we tend to listen to him and believe him without question. Respectability fascinates. It is enough for information to be signed by a researcher or announced by a known journalist to become credible. If it's written in the newspaper or seen on TV, it's a seal of validity that makes us accept the message without further ado.

In 1986, when we were told that the radioactive cloud of Chernobyl had stopped at the borders of France, few people thought to question the words of the ministers and those of the journalists who reported the case. It took years for public opinion to become aware of the manipulation and its consequences. In the same way, the tainted blood scandal was based on the respectability of those who knew but manipulated the public by saying the opposite.

Around us, there are many respectable people who are worthy of being respected, but there are also those who disappoint us or who betray us. Regarding the latter, we only realize it when it is too late. Indeed, hypnotized by the knowledge, fame, social status, or ascendancy of someone, one does not think to put his word in doubt.

Manipulation through respectability is, for example, a friend who was thought to be loyal but who repeats what she was told to keep quiet. It is the partner, the banker, or the notary (professions oh so respectable), in whom one had placed all his confidence and that ruin us by starting suddenly with the cashier. It is the husband who cheats on his wife when she believes him to be faithful, the politician who lies to us to be reelected, or the honorable journalist who distorts or "falsifies" the information to be the first to share a story.

When we experience manipulation done by someone respectable, we feel a deep sense of injustice related to the feeling of betrayal. The disappointment is commensurate with the trust or respect one had for that person. Whose fault is it? Does it always affect the person who is accused of having betrayed us, or are we partly responsible for being too naive? The problem posed by the maneuvers of a respectable manipulator is complex because the responsibility is shared between the manipulator and the manipulated. Although it may seem strange (at first glance), a tale of ANDERSEN, "The Emperor's Clothes," will allow us to bring to light this subtle mechanism.

Illustration

Once upon a time, a long time ago, in a country very different from ours, an emperor was passionate about new clothes. In order to please his people, he changed his costume at every opportunity and had one for each hour of each day of the year.

One day, two crooks who called themselves weavers, came to see him and told him that they were able to make the most beautiful fabric. Not only would the colors and designs be exceptional, but this fabric would also have the incredible property of being invisible to incompetents and fools.

Subjugated by the words of these eminent specialists, the Emperor exclaimed: "What a marvel! I want and I demand that you wear a suit made from this stuff. I will be able to discover who serves me competently and distinguish intelligent people from imbeciles.

It will be much easier for me to govern because I will know how to behave."

To close the deal, he agreed to a significant advance and helped them set up by exempting them from taxes. The two accomplices established their looms in a chic neighborhood of the city and obtained large quantities of bristles (the finest), gold and silver threads, and countless precious stones, as many treasures as they could. To give credence to the illusion, they pretended to work on their machines which were actually running empty and stayed late at night in their workshop closed to the public.

Sometime later, the excited and impatient emperor wanted to know where the work was. He, therefore, sent his best minister, whom he trusted, to report to him on the work of the weavers. When he arrived there, the minister was very surprised to find that the two weavers were working on empty crafts. His experience in diplomacy made it clear that he should not give himself away, and although he was troubled, he made no comment.

As he approached, the two weavers described to him their work: "Is not it wonderful, look at these colors, admire these lovely designs that we created especially for the emperor. What do you say, is not it absolutely sumptuous?"

The poor minister's eyes widened as he saw nothing that the two crooks described with passion. He thought, "Shall I be a fool or an incompetent? It is unthinkable! No one must know, much less suspect, that I do not see this stuff." He answered aloud, "Oh! It is absolutely delightful, these colors, I do not know how to express my admiration. I will speak of them to the Emperor who will be absolutely delighted. You can believe me because I am his most faithful servant."

"That encourages us," said the two weavers, smiling. Then they handed to the Emperor's minister an elegant confidential file to fill in his information, and the clerk went to the door with all the deference due to his rank.

Concerned about the situation, and before going to see the Emperor, the Minister nevertheless took the precaution of sending one of his advisers to make a second visit to the two weavers.

The latter went to visit the workshop and carefully inspected the looms on which the crooks wove, very diligently, and of course, always without the slightest touch. "Is this stuff not beautiful?" They asked, showing him and explaining to him their invisible work. "Your minister admired it a great deal during his last visit."

"I am however not a fool," said the adviser before continuing, "My diplomas prove that I am not incompetent. All this is very strange, but I must leave nothing to it." He then praised what he did not see and warmly congratulated them on their work. Returning to the ministry, he prepared his report by skillfully using the arguments and words that the two weavers had used to convince him.

Comforted by this testimony, the minister then went to the Emperor to tell him all the good he thought about the work of the two weavers. On leaving the Emperor's office, the minister was interviewed by a large number of journalists. The rumor about the beauty of the stuff was huge and everybody was talking about it. One said he knew about the origin of the drawings, another knew someone from Europe who had seen the fabric. People even placed bets to see when the clothes would be finished.

At last the big moment arrived. The two crooks, who had been working all night to put the finishing touches on their work, entered the great audience hall of the Emperor. In the presence of all the dignitaries, they undressed the Emperor and then pretended to give him his new clothes. They exclaimed: "Feel how light these clothes are, so much that you will think you do not have them on your body. Your majesty is of an unheard-of elegance. We've never seen anything like it!"

While the emperor was tossing and turning in front of the large mirror, admiring courtiers commented loudly the beauty of the costume, "God you're beautiful, as these colors go together so well! We have never seen such a beautiful suit, as well worn. These drawings are splendid! It is both classic and revolutionary. Believe me, it's really art, we'll continue to talk about it for a long time, and it's an expert who tells you that."

Nobody had the words to proclaim their admiration. There were even some women who faked a faint before the king. Each one, anxious to prove that he was neither stupid nor incompetent, endeavored to show that he saw the clothes.

The enthusiasm was such that the emperor decided to immediately show this splendor to the people. The announcement was made and the parade was organized in the blink of an eye. The two crooks approached the monarch and carefully hooked on a huge trail of the same fabric, and then humbly recoiled under the applause and cheers of the audience. Nobody wanted to show that he saw nothing, the procession moved and went through the city. A large crowd came to admire the event. Everyone applauded. Here and there we heard a few laughs, but they were quickly covered by a "hush!"

However, a little child's voice came through the crowd: "He is naked, gentleman. Why does he not wear a coat?" His father, who carried him on his shoulders, exclaimed "Listen to the voice of innocence. Listen to what this child says to you!"

Hearing these words the emperor realized what was happening but he did nothing to show his realization. Enough about the small wind that swept the city, he said to himself: "This child must be right, but I must keep up the show until the end of the procession." The imperial cortege thus continued its course, and the ministers continued to carry a trail which did not exist while some fanatics sang: "The Emperor is naked, the Emperor is naked."

Fortunately, the police watched and everything quickly returned to normal. The costume was placed in a safe as a national treasure and the two weavers were awarded the highest honors from the country. Later, their name was even given to an imperial weaving school.

Let's draw together the teachings of this tale.

Exercise

Take a few moments to try to determine the real culprits of this manipulation. Are they the weavers or one of the victims of the manipulation?

First Lesson

The first lesson to be learned from this story is that the one who needs recognition is placed under the authority of the person whom he wishes to draw attention to. The emperor seeks the admiration of his subjects to keep his power as long as possible. Ministers and courtiers copy the emperor to be noticed and to obtain the best positions in the government. Finally, the subjects themselves want to show that they are not inferior to the great ones of this world by behaving like them.

The thirst for recognition and the need for identification create a dependency that opens the door to manipulation. Thus, adolescents who want to exist on their own are at the same time very sensitive to the behavior of their idols. They copy their ways of dressing, styling, or behaving. This mimicry is a way for them to appear different from adults and to oppose what they know of the world they are discovering. But if this challenge to the established order can be a source of renewal, it also places these young people under the manipulative dependence of opinion makers, gurus, sects, and other unscrupulous people who know how to exploit their enthusiasm and their nobility.

Later, when teenagers have become adults, they still do the same thing. For the sake of compliance or fear of being rejected by their community, they continue to duplicate the most characteristic behaviors. They obey the "politically correct" of their generation, their social category, or their professional environment. To be accepted and recognized by those whom they consider respectable, they speak, think, and consume as they do. They follow their advice and submit to their laws. But for lack of hindsight, they quickly become slaves to the taste of others and are, one might say, "manipulated without the knowledge of their own free will."

To avoid being and acting like the emperor's courtiers, one of these questions may arise: Who should I please, and what is my opinion? Why do I want to think like others? Am I being me? What would happen if I did not think like the others? Why do I want to be admired? What will happen if they reject me? Are there other possible points of view?

After re-reading the tale, try to imagine how each manipulated person might not have fallen into the trap of the weavers by asking one or the other of the questions above.

Second Lesson

The second lesson of the tale was that respectability is in the imagination of the one who bows to the people he thinks, rightly or wrongly, to be estimable. Respect must not be demanded, it must be deserved.

The real question is: How can you recognize someone really respectable? Really respectable people are easy and enjoyable. They make you feel smart and you can easily understand what they are saying. Listening to them makes you feel bigger, smarter, and more confident. Someone truly respectable listens to what is said to him. He seeks to help those who approach him grow and if he believes that someone is superior to him, he seeks to understand and feed on his knowledge.

Conversely, the respectable manipulator degrades those who surpass him and pushes those who are inferior to him. For fear of ridicule, we dare not question his word. If you do, he is surprised at your ignorance. For him, it is always very simple and obvious, but his explanations explain nothing. He gives references without worrying about whether others understand or know what they are about.

Whether he is a politician, a journalist, a doctor, a lawyer, or a guru, he must first appear eminently respectable before he can be taken seriously. He, therefore, relies on his appearance to impress or defraud his victims and uses others to enhance himself.

The respectable manipulator is also based on the idea that we should not doubt people whose job is to know about something. It works with people who are afraid to appear uneducated, rough, or ignorant. Fashion and snobbery are also based on fear of not being like others or of culturally or politically incorrect behavior.

Take a break and find several situations in which a manipulator has manipulated you by using so-called respectability. Then answer the following question: What impressed you the most about him?

Chapter 9: Identifying Manipulator Types

Have you ever felt a sudden lack of self-confidence or, worse, this curious and agonizing impression of not knowing how to communicate? Have you ever been deafened by doubt about your skills or qualities? Have you ever been inhabited by that feeling of inferiority that paralyzes you, chills your blood and prevents you from reacting normally? If you have ever experienced this kind of situation, it is because you have been the victim of type III manipulation and placed in the line of sight of a manipulator.

We remember that the second type of manipulator is a selfish or egocentric person who thinks only of his interests, without worrying about the consequences. But the type III manipulator, which is also called the manipulator, has a very different characteristic intention. His only goal is to destroy. Everything he undertakes is meant to kill you, to ruin what you do, or to destroy an aspect of your personality that does not suit him.

The manipulator is characterized both by his will to harm and by a formidable ability to conceal. This is why many people do not trust him or take him for another.

The manipulator does not display distinctive signs and his perversity does not necessarily read on his face. He is a true chameleon that hides behind deceptive appearances to better destroy. He can take the appearance of a parent who is "overprotective" and who, out of selfishness, prevents his child from becoming independent. The manipulator could be a nice grandmother who, secretly, gives money to her little girl who is in rehab to, supposedly, "help her hold on." It can also be a mistress, a lover, a boss, a neighbor, a teacher, or a long-time friend. In the cozy atmosphere of the offices, it is the collaborator willing to do anything to take your place or that colleague who seeks to devalue you because your expertise is shady.

His intention is to destroy. Sometimes it may bring him something, but in this case, it's a secondary benefit because what he's essentially aiming for is the destruction of who you are, what you do, or the other of your behaviors.

Illustration

It is through these situations and testimonies that we will examine the harmful activity of a type III manipulator.

A man wanted his son, Jean, to succeed him by also becoming a doctor at all costs. When Jean announced his desire to leave school to become a musician, his father did everything to break that dream and bring his son back to what he thought was the right path. He tried to persuade his son that he was right in seeking to destroy this vocation. "I did it for your sake, you'll thank me later," he told him then. But what he put his son through was a terrible ordeal that almost drove Jean to suicide, as he felt rejected, devalued, ridiculed, humiliated, and disavowed deep within himself.

A husband insidiously belittles his wife, Christelle, so that she stays at home. He has nothing against her. He simply does not want her to become independent because it's not how things are done in his family and he earns enough to make her happy. As she does not agree, he will do everything to prove (by demeaning and humiliating her) that she is unable to do without him. From his point of view, he thinks he is acting justly and in the interest of his wife. But one can easily imagine that Christelle does not see things in the same way.

A department head, who confronts and belittles a better-performing collaborator than himself, does not necessarily feel particular hatred toward this person. He is simply trying to break the person because he feels they are a danger to him and the only way he can defend his own mediocrity is to belittle them, to diminish them, or to put him in his place so that he does not do not encroach on the department head's work. He destroys what seems to him to be a threat that could prevent him from continuing to dominate the situation. In return, the employee can talk about bullying.

The type III manipulator is a weak man who, when he feels he is in danger, tries to diminish others. He advances masked. Where a normal person tries to surpass himself to become stronger (than whatever threatens him), the manipulator has no other resource than to weaken or treacherously destroy everything that worries him.

He destroys for the sake of destruction. He is mean and does not allow others to exist on their own. He wants to control everything. We cannot impress him. It makes you feel that you are small, weak, and shabby; it turns you into a "mop," it tramples you and makes you incapable of any development.

He destroys you by giving you the impression that it is for your good, but we feel very bad in his presence. We cannot win. We are not recognized for what we would like to be. He does not listen to you and his criticism is never constructive. When he says something it's always negative. With him, one feels humiliated, discouraged, and degraded. He is a "mental assassin" and life with him is like slavery.

This test separates the appearance and truth of the situation and highlights the perverse maneuvers that the manipulator uses against us.

Harassment and Concealed Manipulation

Type III manipulation often goes unnoticed by those who experience it. This is called harassment or hidden manipulation. A large number of victims are thus abused and destroyed without their knowledge by the deceit and duplicity of a manipulator. After two pregnancies, Chloe cannot seem to get back to the weight she was as a young girl. She explains her fight against the pounds:

"When I discover a new diet, I hasten to try it. I am sure this time it will be the right one. I do what it takes, and I feel good. I have a clear mind, I am dynamic. Sometimes I even go back to playing sports. I do everything I can without effort and I start losing weight. And then, brutally, without my understanding why, I fall back into the fog. I have no courage, I ruminate on the same black thoughts, I do not do anything, I am exhausted, and I spend my time sleeping. Then, seeing all the tasks accumulating around the apartment, I feel guilty and without realizing it, I start eating again. I call myself names while looking at my belly and my thighs in the mirror of the bathroom. Every day, I decided that, the next day, I will put myself firmly on the diet and that this time I will get there. Today, I am completely desperate because despite all my attempts, every time I get on the scale, I can see that I still gained weight."

While a hidden manipulation is hardly perceptible from the inside, this is not the case when we observe it from the outside. This is what a friend of Chloe tells us about her weight problems:

"I have known Chloe for many years. She was always a little concerned about her weight, but it almost became an obsession from the moment she met Guillaume, her future husband. He is a charming boy, but he attaches great importance to appearances. Since Chloe gained a little weight, having had her children, he frequently comments on it. He always comments nicely, in the tone of the joke, but I think it comes a little too often. I also see that Chloe is touched, even if she pretends to laugh with the others about her 'little bulges' as she says. But I can see that deep down she is hurt when he makes fun of her in public. Moreover, in the days that follow, she regularly buys clothes that are too small, claiming that she is going to lose weight. The other night, I was at home and he did not stop criticizing a common friend who had grown enormously. He told multiple bad jokes about his plumpness and talked about the contempt he had for people who do not know how to control their weight. When Chloe came out of the room with tears in her eyes, he suddenly changed the subject of conversation.

Everyone was embarrassed, but he did not seem to notice. The worst part was that he seemed satisfied with what he had just done as if it were a good joke. I thought about Chloe and it was really awful to see how happy he looked."

A manipulator can be extremely pleasant and user-friendly. By appearing charming, playing on someone's guild, or using a respectable or simply authoritarian position, he creates a mirage that deceives his victims and prevents them from seeing that behind his disguise of the moment, hides a purpose that is invariably destructive and harmful. Moreover, it is very difficult to blame him for the behavior because he always has an excuse to justify himself: "I am only following the instructions. I do not have the right to disobey. I only did my duty. I acted believing it was the right thing to do. It was a joke."

To be sure, we can examine (below) the two sets of symptoms that signify the presence of a manipulator. The first contains the essentials of what one feels when one is a direct victim of a manipulator and the second enumerates what one perceives as a mere observer of a hidden manipulation.

Internal Symptoms of Concealed Manipulation

These are the main internal signals that can be seen when one is a victim of type III manipulation. These symptoms are far more indicative of the presence of a manipulator than the analysis of his words or deeds:

- I alternate moments of enthusiasm and discouragement. I often feel a sense of guilt or doubt.

- I find it difficult to defend myself or counterattack. I feel a sudden loss of confidence in myself.

- I sometimes feel that I am "drained" of my energy. I feel physical or mental discomfort in the presence of someone.

- That person belittles me one way or another. It is impossible to impress or affect her.

- There is always a form of ambiguity between what she does and what she says. I am not well in my head or in my body when I am around that person.

If you have at least three symptoms there is a good chance that you have been the victim of such manipulation. When all five symptoms are reached, manipulation is certain and you should focus on finding out for sure who the manipulator is and how he proceeds.

Do not hesitate to ask for advice or help!

Generally, someone with an outside perspective can find out much more easily because they will often notice things that one who is a victim and who lives things from within misses.

External Symptoms

The following are the main symptoms that can occur when hidden manipulation is observed from an outside perspective:

- Irrational behavior

- Bad recurring atmosphere

- Discord between people

- People are often sick

- General or chronic discouragement

- Mental and physical exhaustion

Behaviors Are Irrational

This means that people behave strangely. They do things that a sensible person would not do. Due to the active and harmful presence of a manipulator, the victim embarks on utopian projects that are unrealistic or far beyond his/her abilities or skills.

Sometimes, some people succeed in what they do. But for more than 99 percent, it is a failure that awaits them. Many teenagers thus adopt irrational behaviors to show their independence and oppose the guardianship of their parents. This does not mean that parents are true malicious manipulators, but it is a sign that teenagers see them as such.

The Bad Mood

If high fever is symptomatic of the flu, a bad state of mind or a heavy atmosphere also may indicate a type III manipulation. Unconsciously, we feel that something is wrong. Relationships are tense and we deplore the situation.

In the presence of such manipulation, we are often mistaken as guilty and wrongly accused that the manipulator is us. He is a real expert at confusing simple things and disturbing people's judgment. That's why it's so important to know the anatomy and physiology of type III manipulation before you can begin to resist it effectively.

Illness

In the workplace, when one observes that employees frequently take sick leaves, there are many accidents at work, or there are many requests for transfer or departure, one can be certain that there is a type III manipulator. It's his way of getting rid of those who bother him. In the presence of a heavy and deleterious atmosphere, it is normal that the bodies of the people concerned eventually crack. To contract a disease and to be the victim of an accident are unfortunately the most common reactions of those who undergo too much a concealed manipulation without being able to defend against it.

It is the same in the family environment when, coincidentally, we find that all members of the same family are chronically ill. In such cases, the disease is, again, the direct result of manipulation.

Another remarkable signal is that the manipulator is the only one who is not sick. But this is not infallible because the manipulator sometimes invokes a so-called disease to better enslave or destroy those around him. In the latter case, this kind of "Aunt Danièle" will be unmasked because of a surprising resistance and a great ability to survive (against all odds).

Discouragement

The manipulator is surrounded by unlucky people who are as enthusiastic as they are discouraged. When manipulation is rife in the world of work, we notice that the best are leaving or looking to leave.

Concealed manipulation is fertile ground for fiascos and repeated failures. When he has the means, the manipulator sabotages the activity of those around him by giving imprecise orders, contradictory instructions, or simply by not giving them the means to succeed.

In private life, his relatives are depressed, sick or un-ambitious. Generally, they miss everything they undertake. The hidden manipulator likes to devalue others or diminish the value of their efforts. Whatever you do, you will never be up to it. If you ever are, he will come to disturb you by pretending to help you or he will discreetly put sticks in the wheels.

This kind of manipulator will never tell you that you are doing something right. He does not know how to congratulate and we must not wait for any acknowledgment from him. On the other hand, he knows how to find any little detail that ruins your efforts or proves that he is superior to you and knows better than you. In short, it makes you think that you could succeed in what you want to do.

By discouraging his entourage, the manipulator keeps them helpless or mediocre, which allows him to feel stronger and to more securely establish his power, control, and supremacy.

Exhaustion

The mere presence of a manipulator can be enough to drain you of your energy. It is normal to experience moments of despondency or discouragement, this happens to everyone. When this exhaustion becomes chronic or occurs for no apparent reason, it is a very strong sign that may reveal the existence of hidden manipulation.

If you regularly feel "gutted," find out who is always present in those moments. There is a good chance that you will discover a manipulator that you might never have suspected otherwise. But before you say anything, submit the person to the confidence test.

Depression can also come from a succession of failures. At more than 38 years old, Claudine has been suffering since childhood from her mother's lack of consideration. Her mother has always considered her a bit simple because she had trouble attending school. To receive a little of this love that is so lacking and also to show that she is someone worthwhile, Claudine is doing everything she can to please her mother. She goes to see her every day. She does her housework and accompanies her to shop at least once a week. Her mother finds this normal and does not feel the need to thank her with a word, a gesture, or a gift. On the other hand, she phones her for hours to complain about her health or her problems with her neighbors. Patiently, Claudine listens to her and tries to comfort her. Obviously, the mother does everything to come and live with her daughter, but Claudine turns a deaf ear. She is torn between her need for recognition that would push her to take her mother home, and her need to live an independent life with her husband and children.

Blind to this manipulation and unable to say no to her manipulative mother, Claudine is exhausted in responding to the ever-growing demands of a mother who is becoming more and more of a burden and who complains to anyone who wants to hear that her daughter "abandoned" her. However, she continues to serve as a servant because she is still unconsciously waiting for a sign of recognition from her mother. Unfortunately for Claudine, this liberating signal will never come.

Feeling more and more helpless, useless, and worthless, Claudine finally sinks into a deep depression. This will allow her mother to shamelessly assert that her daughter is definitely worthless and cannot be counted on under any circumstances.

This example shows us that when exhaustion, discouragement, and sickness affect the same person, it is clear evidence that hidden manipulation is occurring.

The manipulator always thinks he is right. He never questions himself or changes his mind. It is the others who are wrong, never him. It's impossible! Whoever ignores this incapacity can only be exhausted in wanting to change someone who absolutely does not want to.

The Essentials of This Book:

When one realizes that a manipulator is a weak person and a coward who abuses the power that one lends him to belittle and enslave, us and when one discovers that the thirst for being oneself is stronger than his threats, his weapons, or his blackmail, then the anxiety disappears.

By going beyond one's own fear, one goes beyond one's intimidation and one discovers that in reality, one does not risk much in opposing a manipulator. Awakening from the nightmare that he makes us live in, we understand that he is afraid of others and draws his power from our ignorance of his true weakness. One can then begin to react, to defend oneself and regain the power to say no to him.

Contrary to appearances, the manipulator knows himself incapable of overcoming others if he is uncovered. That's why his weapons are lies, cunning, and slander. We cannot impress him. He will never acknowledge his wrongdoing and he will refuse to be helped or changed.

He paralyzes us. Even when we suffer his blows, we do not dare to fight back for fear of hypothetical reprisals or for fear of hurting him, especially when we know him well. The biggest mistake is to believe that time will fix everything, or that the manipulator will eventually change, understand, or get bored. But that hardly ever happens.

The weaknesses of the Type III manipulator are within his strengths. As long as we believe in the blackmail of his threats, we complain but we do not dare to react. The reality is that it dominates us only as long as we fear it.

When one discovers that he draws his power from ignorance of his true weakness, paralyzing fear disappears. We know that he is helpless against direct opposition and counter-attacks and that he can only run away from those who dare to challenge him. In these conditions, one is ready to say no to him.

It is time to organize our defense and to counter-attack. In addition to the tools used against Type II manipulation, there are special techniques to stand up and defeat the Type III manipulator.

Observing and understanding what is happening brings a release. To perceive the manipulator as they give you the courage to dare to attack.

Dare to challenge him! Show him that you do not fear him. Do not be afraid to ridicule him but never humiliate him. Avoid devaluing him or using guilt because then he will advantageously position himself as a victim. If you are persuasive enough and insistent, his cowardice will do the rest and he will leave you alone.

If you have to attack him, do it, but make sure you have enough ammo! Find out exactly what he's doing and expose his misdeeds in the presence of the witnesses concerned. Accumulate concrete evidence against him, then clearly point out what's wrong. Prevent him from spreading rumors and, if you can, institute very strict rules to control him and neutralize his harmful actions. Do not stop before he bends or breaks. In some cases, it is also necessary to know how to ask for help because the fight is often very hard and nothing is ever gained in advance.

Break off the relationship! Sometimes you have to know how to completely cut communication with the manipulator. The price of independence can be heavy to pay. But it is up to everyone to determine what they are willing to sacrifice to live in peace, free and serene.

Chapter 10: Practical Ways to identify and Resist Manipulators

It should be noted that manipulation does not work for the manipulators alone and no one, either the victim of manipulation or the manipulator, gets any real profits. Whether you manipulate or get manipulated, the end result is a loss. Before getting to know how to identify and resist manipulators, you need to know how manipulation negatively affects the manipulator and the victim.

Powerlessness – It is due to the helplessness feeling that manipulators opt for manipulation. It is due to impotence that a victim gives in to manipulator's trickery.

Inadequacy – Manipulators feel that they lack some qualities possessed by other people and in the pursuit of such characteristics, they manipulate those they believe possess these qualities. Once manipulated, a victim feels stupid and regrets if only they had acted smarter to outwit the manipulator.

Victimization – Manipulators believe that life has victimized them by not being fair to them or giving them what they deserve. A manipulation victim also feels victimized when they fail to do what the manipulator demands.

Anger and Frustration – Manipulators are always frustrated when their targets turn down their demands or requests. The victims also feel bad when doing what the manipulator asks them to do, especially if it is forced manipulation.

If you allow yourself to be manipulated, you sacrifice your rights to self-determination, self-esteem, finances, energy, and even your principles. If you manage others as well, you surrender your self-respect and self-reliance when you try to use others to benefit yourself.

Either successful or not after manipulating others, there is the emotionally immature feeling that always haunt a manipulator.

How then should you resist a manipulator, persuader or a cult leader?

Resisting a manipulator

Unless you have obligated yourself to refuse with a clear conscience when you want to do, it is not your obligation, and if it is not a genuine requirement. You do not have to have any guilty feeling if you refuse to do anything you are requested to do. When a manipulator requires anything, you have to say 'NO,' without backing it up with excuses or explanations. The more you reply to the manipulators with such responses, the more proficient you become. This means that you should never do anything you do not like just to please another person.

Important concepts to consider when resisting and avoiding manipulation, mind control, and persuasion.

• Your time and energy are as important as anyone else's.

• Your 'not wanting to do' is equal to the manipulators 'wanting me to do.'

• You are never required to support your decision with explanations or excuses.

• Insisting you should do something means manipulation.

• Your silence might mean a 'Yes' if you fail to respond with a 'No.'

• It is challenging to get manipulated if you cooperate.

• Your happiness, needs, and desires also matter just like anyone else's.

• Being a manipulator yourself is an added advantage to avoid manipulation.

• It is always your right to say 'No' to anything that does not please you.

- Failing to do another person's request does not mean you are stubborn.

When you put these points into consideration, it will be difficult to be manipulated since it will be easier to spot and resist manipulators. It is easier to identify a manipulator since they all have the same characteristics.

- All types of manipulators, persuaders, and cult leaders who mostly use mind control can tell your weakest points.

- When they know your weakness, they start using it against you.

- They start convincing you to give into their interests.

- When they succeed in manipulating you for the first time, they are likely to continue controlling you more and more.

The following tips have been tested and proved to be the best in handling manipulators and resisting being manipulated. Firstly, being aware of your rights helps you to realize when you are being manipulated. Defending your rights is very crucial provided you are not harming anyone. You should know that it is your right to be treated respectfully. It is your right to explain yourself, how you feel, what you want, and your opinion over any topic.

You should never be guilty after saying 'No' to anything that you feel is uninteresting to you. Having divergent views with others is normal, and you should never be worried about it. Whenever you protect yourself from any kind of threats, it is never wrong, but right for your own benefit. You have all the reasons to prioritize your happiness over anyone else's. If you maintain these rights, everyone will know their limits, and it will be your beginning of a manipulation-free life. Anyone who tries depriving you of your rights is a manipulator, and you should resist them and be in control of your own life.

Secondly, identifying a manipulator is as easy as mastering their actions and faces when to dissimilar people in different places. Most of the manipulators are either polite to some people or rude to others; they never have one side. At times, a manipulator can be aggressive and other times polite. When you note these kinds of behaviors, distance yourself from such people. They can fake their character to you as well. It is never your role or responsibility to change this kind of people as it might be a deep case of long-lasting mental manipulation.

Thirdly, you should be aware that a manipulator's big agenda is exploiting and taking advantage of your weakness. In case they blame you for not satisfying their demands, feel okay, the last thing you can do is blaming yourself or feeling guilty of your actions. That is the weakest point the manipulator take advantage of; outwitting your power and strength. If a manipulator insists on one demand severally, feel free to ask and answer yourself these questions: are my rights respected? Are the requirements and requests that this person is asking me to do credible? Is there anything good that can make me keep this relationship with this person, or should I end it? If you find answers for these questions, then you will know where or who the problem lays with; you or the manipulator.

Fourthly, once a person tries to manipulate you, you should not always focus on how you are going to help them out. You can opt on asking them a few questions. These questions help you to know whether the manipulator is aware of the inequalities created by their demands. You can ask the manipulator: Does whatever you are requesting sound credible on your side? Is it fair for me to grant your demands? Are your orders a question or a statement? How am I going to benefit out of this? Are your expectations that I should give in to your wish without questioning? These questions act like a mirror whereby, the manipulator views themselves and the kind of demands they are asking for. If the manipulator is aware enough, the request or claim will be withdrawn immediately.

Fifthly, every manipulator wants an immediate response to their demands. This is their tool in maximizing their control over their target. To resist this, you should never reply immediately to any of their conditions. You should instead use the time to your benefit. Keep a distance over any force that wants you to respond promptly. Take your time and tell them, "let me think about this." This loosens their expectations, and the manipulator or persuader is less likely to come back to you with the same demand. They will fear to get back to you since they have read your first reactions.

Sixthly, you should be aware that a manipulator or persuader can also turn to be a bully once their requests have not been granted or once other people hurt them. You should resist by making yourself strong and avoid being passive. The manipulators will back down and stop their tactics the moment they realize you are aware of your rights and are not easy to manipulate. Many of the bullies and manipulators are desperately seeking attention, love, and peace since they have been victims of violence in most cases. Once manipulated by a bully, resist by standing tall, and by having some people around you to help in case it turns to be physical or abusive manipulation.

Seventhly, some manipulators would not take a 'No' for their prerequisites and this requires you to set some consequences. Once you give outcomes to any manipulator, their tactic will be pushed, and if they were violent, they would shift to a more respectful mode immediately.

With these practical tactics, be rest assured that no manipulator will ever succeed in manipulating you. It may not be a direct manipulation, but even if you see your friends being manipulated, you can apply these tactics to try and help them avoid or resist the manipulators.

Conclusion

You've met your goal and will surely take the next step to activate your powers of observation. Now, you will naturally find yourself working from these indicators and communicating with others in a more effective and persuasive way.

Can you imagine standing in front of your colleagues, able to eloquently deliver your amazing plan? You need not imagine any longer. Finally, everyone will see that you with authority and will naturally want to follow your lead and make you happy.

Others will be drawn to you as a person they can trust. Those around you will feel they really connect with you even though it may only be the first time meeting you. As you gain experience and confidence with this new information, you will find ways to utilize it in your everyday situations, and extraordinary ones, to get what you want and help others. It's amazing to think if you've already come this far and where you're going next.

You've been provided with all of the tools you need to achieve your goals whatever they may be. The world is your playground. If you put your imagination to it, there is an opportunity in every single interaction you have, if you look for it.

There are many different personality types in the world, and you now have a better understanding of what those various personality components, how they work together, and how you can identify them through straightforward interactions and analysis. You understand how cold reading works, and you are anything but gullible when it comes to people trying to convince you that they know more about you than you think. You will be able to pick up on this immediately and have learned how people plant the seeds in others' minds to convince them that they have knowledge above and beyond what they actually possess.

A lot more is going on when two people meet for the first time than most people pick up on. Many people are so preoccupied with themselves and other thoughts that they would never notice the subtle cues that people are continually giving off, broadcasting their feelings and thoughts. When you know the tricks of the trade when it comes to picking up nonverbal communication and body language, you will be able to read a great deal about people before they even open their mouths to introduce themselves. When you can read the room and size people up, you already have an advantage over anyone else who might be trying to vie for that person's affection, political support, or sales transaction. It's all about taking the time it takes to learn and practice in the real world once you've decided to undertake the art of dark psychology. It's impossible to become comfortable with these techniques without observation and practice. You will find that the more confident you are with your strategies, the more comfortable and more natural they will happen, leaving your targets entirely in the dark about what's going on under the surface.

Finally, you were introduced to the 16 different personality types, which are part of the Myers-Briggs personality analysis. Perhaps you were convinced to go ahead and take the test yourself to get a better idea of which personality traits you most exhibit. Now that you know more, you can continue your research into how these traits interact and what your inherent strengths and vulnerabilities might be. Many people remain blind to the weaknesses that they seek to ignore for as long as possible. Knowing yourself is the best way to begin constructing how you will operate in terms of getting what you want out of any situation.

If there is one thing you've taken away from this book more than anything else, it is my hope that you've become much more confident in your own ability to recognize and fend off those who might wish to harm you in some way through the practice of manipulative techniques and other tools of dark psychology. As has been stated many times throughout this book, I hope you value the fact that you've become much more knowledgeable and capable of identifying when someone is trying to use you or hurt you for their own gain. You should now feel that you can recognize the sociopath, narcissist, or even the psychopath in the room should there be one, and you consequently know to stay as far away as possible.

CPSIA information can be obtained
at www.ICGtesting.com
Printed in the USA
BVHW042050291020
592143BV00008B/290